Pay WAY Less Tax!

250+ Deductions, Credits & Tips from a Leading Tax Lawyer
Proven Methods Guaranteed to Reduce Taxes.

By Dale Barrett

First edition 2021.
Barrett, Dale 1974-

Save Your Tax Dollars: 199 Tax Deductions, Credits and Strategies to save tax.

ISBN: 978-0-9867559-9-6
Issued also in e-book format ISBN: 978-1-7775331-0-6

DEDICATION

I dedicate this book to my three beautiful children Chloé, Claire and Joshua and my amazing wife Nicole, who have been patient with me even though I promised them that I wouldn't write a third book this year.

I would also like to acknowledge the assistance of Simone Barrett, Darryl Getz, Jamie Elliot, and Simon Townsend all of whom made invaluable contributions to this work.

FORWARD

Dear Reader,

This book is designed to help you pay as little tax as possible (legally). Hopefully this book saves you many more times its cover price. And if you borrowed this book from a library or a friend, you have gotten a great value (good for you, bad for me and the Canada Revenue Agency).

But what I truly wish for is that you take this book, which is an anthology of tax tips, advice, and helpful tidbits gathered over the last 12+ years of the practice of tax law and use it to its maximum potential to save yourself tremendous amounts of tax and avoid tremendous amounts of pain.

With all that said, we'll start the rest of the book with the first tip, that being: Canadian tax law changes regularly. CRA processes and procedures change. The most important thing that you can do to be able to pay as little tax as possible while staying on the right side of the law is to make sure that you re-examine your tax plan and the way you do things from time to time.

- **Dale Barrett**

LEGAL DISCLAIMER

As you read though this book please remember that its purpose is to provide you with information only. I have taken great care to ensure that the information is current at the date of writing, however things change, and mistakes do happen – typographicallll and otherwise. So, the information presented herein should not independently be relied upon for any purpose and if you choose to use the tips herein they should be independently validated.

Also, please do not consider the information in this book to be legal advice, regardless of having been written by a lawyer. It is not legal advice and reading this book does not constitute a lawyer client relationship between you and the author. If you think that you require legal advice, please do consult a tax lawyer, including the author.

TABLE OF CONTENTS

01 INITIAL CONCEPTS

Future Value of Money

The analysis of money and time is paramount in financial decision making. Time value of money concepts such as present value of money vs. future value of money are used to calculate and to compare the values of sums of money at different points in time.

The "time value of money" refers to the fact that a dollar today is worth more than a dollar in the future (due to inflation). We all know this intuitively. What you can buy for one dollar today will cost you much more than a dollar in the distant future. Similarly, what you can buy for a dollar today would have cost much less than a dollar in the past.

Consider the following example: Assume somebody owes you $100. You would rather get the $100 now than in 5 years' time. This is intuitive to us all. On one hand, the $100 bill is worth $100 both now and in 5 years' time. But because of inflation the $100 bill will buy you less in 5 years than you could buy now. Similarly, if you invest the $100 bill now, it will be worth more than $100 in 5 years' time.

The future value of a dollar is simply what the dollar, or any amount of money, will be worth if it earns interest for a specific time. So, if you got the $100 now rather than in 5 years, the future value of that $100 in 5 years will be more than $100.

Tax Deferral (And Why It is a Good Thing)

Tax deferral is a common tool used in tax planning. It refers to delaying paying tax into the future. Instead of paying the tax now, but paying the tax in the future, you can hold onto your money now, invest it and allow it to grow. Plus, you can pay the tax debt in the future with money which is worth less than today. As discussed earlier, due to inflation a $100 bill in the future is worth less (and has less buying power) than $100 now. So, if one has a tax debt of $100 – it is better to pay it with $100 future dollars rather than $100 today dollars. In other words, it is better to defer the payment of the tax until the future. And if you can hold onto the $100 for a while and invest it until you have to pay it to the CRA, that is even better.

With investment vehicles such as the Registered Education Savings Plan (RESP) and the Registered Retirement Savings Plan (RRSP), rather than paying tax now with today dollars, taxpayers can choose to pay tax on income in the future at a time when they are subject to a lower marginal tax rate.

The RESP and RRSP are the most common vehicles for the average Canadian to benefit from tax deferral. With an RESP, a subscriber contributes income and in turn interest, dividends, and capital gains are earned within the RESP. When the money is finally withdrawn, it is taxed at the low marginal tax rate of a student enrolled in an eligible higher education program such as a university, college or trade school. An added benefit of an RESP is that the Canadian Government will include up to $7,200 as a no-strings-attached grant in an RESP. Up to $500 a year can be received as a grant depending on what the subscriber contributes into the account annually.

An RRSP is another popular vehicle for Canadians to benefit from tax deferral. With an RRSP, taxpayers can deduct the amount that they invest from their tax returns. This means that no income tax is paid on the amounts invested. In turn, the investment can grow tax deferred inside the RRSP. Similar to an RESP and a Tax-Free Savings Account, there are massive financial benefits to tax sheltered compounding. Although tax is paid upon withdrawal from an RRSP, the taxpayer has control over when it is withdrawn. If a taxpayer retires at 65, and only has pension income (which places them in a lower marginal tax bracket than where they were pre-retirement), then they could save anywhere from 4-30% on each dollar withdrawn from the RRSP. This is notwithstanding that they have also benefited from earning tax sheltered income on a pre-tax investment.

In a nutshell, an RRSP helps reduce taxes in several ways.

EXAMPLE

If a taxpayer is in a 50% tax bracket, they would pay $5,000 tax on $10,000 of income.

But if they put that $10,000 into an RRSP, they will not pay the tax on that income right now.

Instead, when they are retired and are in a 20% tax bracket (for example), they can withdraw this $10,000 and only pay $2,000 tax. Plus, they are paying $2,000 future dollars rather than $5,000 today dollars. Plus, they would have had the benefit of having the entire $10,000 invested inside the RRSP to earn income over the years – giving them much more that they can withdraw in the future.

Buying with Pre-Tax Dollars

Using pre-tax dollars for investment or purchases leads to increased buying power. This is a very basic concept. Consider a taxpayer in a 50% tax bracket. If they earn $10,000, it turns into $5,000 after tax. So, while they earned $10,000, after tax the taxpayer can only afford to buy something worth $5,000. But if they could purchase something with pre-tax dollars, that $10,000 earned could buy them something worth $10,000. This is the difference between buying with pre-tax vs. post-tax dollars.

There are ways to make purchases with pre-tax dollars vs. post-tax dollars. For example, if a taxpayer purchases an investment in a vehicle such as an RRSP that allows one to use pre-tax dollars, then the amount invested can grow without being taxed until it is withdrawn.

Other contexts of using pre-tax dollars are when employers pay for specific benefits.

Most benefits one receives from an employer are taxable and considered to be "taxable benefits." A taxable benefit is a good or service one receives, from their employer such as a free use of a property. Other examples of taxable benefits are allowances or reimbursements of an employee's personal expenses. And because they are taxable, being allowed to use the company car is treated by the CRA in the same way as if an employee were receiving the cash equivalent of a car lease.

However, exceptions exist, and some benefits are non-taxable. These include non-cash gifts in a year with a total value of $500; trivial gifts such as coffee or tea; educational allowances if schools in the area do not meet educational needs of a child, and the parents have to live in a specific location for that work; discounts on merchandise of the employer; disability-related employment benefits, such as transportation costs; a work cell phone; certain child care expenses; private health services plans (such as medical or dental plans); professional membership dues under certain circumstances; and so on. So, it is possible for an employer to use their pre-tax dollars to give things to their employees in a way which does not cause the employee to have to pay additional tax.

EXAMPLE

If an employer pays $2,000 into a dental plan for an employee every year, and the employee uses that plan instead of paying for dental costs out of after-tax dollars, then their buying power has increased.

Consider that if an employee needs $2000 dental work, and if that employee is in a 50% tax bracket, they would have needed $4,000 of pre-tax income in order to afford the $2,000 of dental work. But when the company provides the $2,000 dental plan which is not taxed in the hands of the employee, the employee is in essence able to buy that dental work with pre-tax dollars and increase their buying power.

Tax Credits vs. Deductions

Tax credits are amounts that directly offset tax payable, while tax deductions are amounts which are used to offset and reduce a taxpayer's income.

To understand how deductions and tax credits interact with the value of money coming out of your pocket, it is helpful to consider the full process of recognizing income and paying tax, from start to finish.

The calculation begins with one's income, which is made up of income from sources listed in the Income Tax Act. For Canadians this includes all one's worldwide income from sources.

In turn the taxpayer deducts expenses incurred to earn income. This will cause the taxpayer to arrive at their taxable income. Taxable income is then multiplied by the taxpayer's relevant tax rate to arrive at their tax payable.

Once a taxpayer has arrived at their tax payable, they may then deduct the applicable tax credits. Once this deduction is made, a taxpayer arrives at their full tax liability for a given year.

EXAMPLE

A taxpayer earns $50,000. This is their total worldwide income from all sources.

This taxpayer has $10,000 of tax deductions, which leaves them with $40,000 of Taxable Income (the tax deductions offset the income).

If the taxpayer is in a 25% tax bracket, they will have to pay $10,000 of tax.

In turn, if the taxpayer has $2,000 of tax credits, they will have to pay $8,000 of tax since the $2,000 of tax credits are used to offset the $10,000 of tax which would otherwise have to be paid.

Tax Deductions

Considering deductions in more detail, their basis is s. 9(1) of the Income Tax Act, with exclusions provided elsewhere in the Act. Section 9(1) defines profit which courts have assessed as a net concept. Given that the term profit includes deductibility, whether an amount is deductible is first considered from the standpoint of commercial and accounting practices.

If it is deductible from that standpoint, then s. 18(1) is used to determine whether a deduction is otherwise excluded by the Act. In a nutshell, no deduction should be made in computing a taxpayer's income from a business or property, except "...to the extent that it was made or incurred by the taxpayer for the purpose of gaining or producing income from the business or property." The test to determine whether a deduction is disallowed according to s. 18(1)(a), is whether it was incurred outside the process of earning income from a business or property. As such, valid deductions must generally be tied to the operations of an income-earning undertaking.

And while the deduction of personal or living expenses is broadly rejected by s. 18(1)(h) and inferentially by s. 18(1)(a), taxpayers are empowered by the Act to deduct certain childcare expenses. Certain expenses are also deductible by employees, such as home office supplies, and travel, if the employer does not reimburse the employee. However, these expenses must generally be contemplated in the employment contract to be deductible.

Tax Credits

The Income Tax Act provides for various tax credits. These include: a basic personal credit, a dependant spouses credit, an equivalent to spouse credit, a dependant minor credit, a family tax cut, and charitable tax credits. With regard to charitable tax credits, they are calculated by multiplying the first $200 donated to a registered charity by the lowest federal marginal tax rate, and an amount over $200 by the highest federal marginal tax rate. These amounts are added together, and the same process is completed by applying provincial rates. The total of this gives the taxpayer an amount they can offset against their tax payable.

If a tax credit exceeds the taxpayer's payable tax, the government makes a payment to the taxpayer equal to the difference - only if the credit is "refundable." If the credit is non-refundable and this occurs, then the Government does not make a payment.

Source Concept of Tax

In order to be taxable, the Canadian income tax system requires income to be allocated to a "source" either contained in the Income Tax Act or recognized by the courts.

Section 3 of the Income Tax Act provides the starting point from which Canadians calculate their personal income tax. It requires a taxpayer to determine all sources of income that they have inside and outside of Canada. This includes income from each office, employment, business, and property.

Section 56 of the Act supplements s. 3 and provides other sources of income to be included in finding tax payable. That is, pension benefits, employment insurance benefits, amounts received out of a registered retirement savings plans, retirement allowances, as well as scholarships and nurseries.

Capital property involves a unique calculation in terms of assessing your income. A taxpayer only includes half of their proceeds when they sell property, other than personal property, in their total income. However, they include all of their income which comes from using that property. So, if you own a truck for the purpose of making deliveries, then you include all of your income from the contracts for those deliveries. This can be characterized as income from a business source. If you turn around and sell the truck, you only recognize half of that gain for tax purposes. This is the distinction between capital property and income generated from capital property.

Section 4 of the Act completes the process of determining a Canadian's tax payable. Once the taxpayer's sources of income have been established, the Act provides that one can deduct permitted amounts from each office, employment, business, and property. In other words, all of the losses from each source for a year are subtracted from all of the gains of that source.

For instance, your truck in the previous example needed repairs that cost $5,000 and therefore before adding the $50,000 of income from contracts for delivery to your larger pool of income (or losses), you are permitted to subtract $5,000 from $50,000. After this process unfolds for each source of income, the sources are then combined which lands a taxpayer on their total income, or tax payable. Tax payable for a given year is then remitted to the Canadian Government.

An important aspect of this regime is that if a source of income or a deduction is not recognized by the Act, then it need not be added to your income or cannot be deducted. A deduction can also cause a net loss for a year on that source. A taxpayer can count this loss against all other aggregated sources of income (or losses). However, losses from selling capital property, otherwise referred to as a capital loss, can only be counted against capital gains.

The process of assessing what is income and what is deductible has been the subject of many tax disputes in Canada considered in our courts system.

Income Tax

Canadians are taxed on their income from sources inside and outside Canada. There are various ways in which income is taxed, depending on the person or entity earning the income. And depending on who is earning the income and the type of income being earned, tax rates range from approximately 20% to approximately 53%, with federal and provincial rates combined.

Non-residents, although taxed on income earned in Canada, may benefit from lower tax rates as a result of tax treaties that Canada has with their country of residence.

Businesses, including corporations and partnerships not only have a broad range of deductions available to them, but their income is generally taxed at a more favourable rate than most or all individuals – especially if the business qualifies for the small business deduction. Partnership income differs from business income in that it is not taxed at the partnership level – instead partnership act as a "flow through", meaning that the income is first divided between partners who in turn pay income tax at their own rates.

Tax Filing Obligations

Canada is a self-reporting system which means that on an annual basis all taxpayers are required to report financial or property gains to the Canadian Government and pay tax on those amounts. Moreover, the self-reporting system includes providing the Canadian government with information on potential sources of income, or how their financial affairs are structured. These are referred to as information returns.

Pursuant to s. 3 of the Income Tax Act, when a Canadian taxpayer earns income from a source inside or outside Canada, they pay income tax on each of those sources. This is notwithstanding that hundreds of provisions in the ITA alter if, when, and how Canadians pay taxes on their respective sources of income.

Below is a table of different types of returns and deadlines, as well as personal schedules to file (these schedules are appended to one's tax return).

RETURNS (AND SCHEDULES TO)	DEADLINES
Personal Income Tax and Benefit Return	April 30, annually
Federal Amounts Transferred from Your Spouse or Common-Law Partner	April 30, annually, attached to personal return
Capital Gains (or Losses)	April 30, annually, attached to personal return

Amounts for Spouse or Common-Law Partner and Dependants	April 30, annually, attached to personal return
Canada Workers Benefit	April 30, annually, attached to personal return
RRSP and PRPP Unused Contributions, Transfers, and HBP or LLP activities	April 30, annually, attached to personal return
Canada Pension Plan Contributions and Overpayment	April 30, annually, attached to personal return
Donations and Gifts	April 30, annually, attached to personal return
Federal Tuition, Education, and Textbook Amounts	April 30, annually, attached to personal return
Employment Insurance Premiums on Self-Employment and Other Eligible Earnings	April 30, annually, attached to personal return
Climate Action Incentive	April 30, annually, attached to personal return
Information Return Relating to Controlled and Not-Controlled Foreign Affiliates	Within 15 months after the end of your taxation year
T4 return: Statement of Remuneration Paid (and relevant schedules)	The last day of February following the calendar year that the information return applies to. If the due date falls on Saturday, or a Sunday, your return is due the next business day.
T3 return: Trust Income Tax and Information Return (and relevant schedules)	Depends on the trust's tax year end; file no later than 90 days after the trust's tax year end

T2 return: Corporation Income Tax Return (and relevant schedules)	Within six months of the end of each tax year
T1204: Information return for Federal departments, agencies, and Crown corporations	File by March 31 of the year following the calendar year to which the information return applies. If March 31 falls on a Saturday or Sunday, the return is due the next business day
T5018: Statement of Contract Payments	Due six months after the end of the reporting period you have chosen or within 30 days of the day your business ends. Income from this slip must be reported on tax return.
NR4: Statement of Amounts Paid or Credited to Non-Residents of Canada	File by March 31 following the calendar year to which the information return applies or no later than 90 days after the year end of the fiscal year for an estate or trust. If this falls on a Saturday, Sunday or a public holiday recognized by the CRA, the information return is due the next business day. Be aware of a "loss restriction event" causing a tax year of a trust or estate to end early.
RRSP Contribution Information Return, Pooled Registered Pension Plan Information Return	File by March 1 of the year in which the contribution year ends. The contribution year is the period beginning on the 61st day of one year and ending the 60th day of the following year.
Part XVIII and Part XIX: Declaration of Tax Residence for Individuals	File before May 2 following the calendar year to which the information return applies. If May 1 is a Saturday or Sunday, your information return is due the next business day.

T5013: Partnership Information Return	Depends on the type of partners. If all partners are individuals or trusts, then March 31 after the calendar year in which the fiscal period of the partnership ended.

Below is a table of deadlines of various elections that can give taxpayers alternate tax treatment for income tax purposes. "N/A" indicates that there is no specific information regarding filing deadlines, but in most situations, these should be filed with their relevant tax return as a signed or jointly signed letter.

ELECTION	DEADLINE
Deferral on Non-Canadian controlled private corporation employee options	File with tax return each year that one has an outstanding balance of deferred security options benefit
Deemed outlay or expense	Signed letter for the year, next year, or any previous year
Available-for-use rules on long-term projects	File with return for the particular year
Amounts paid for undertaking future obligations	Made by notifying the Minster in writing on or before the earlier of the days on or before which either the payer of the recipient is required to file a return of income pursuant to section 150 for the taxation year in which the payment to which the election relates was made
Cost of borrowed money	With taxpayer's return
Exchanges of property	With taxpayer's return

Adjustments to cost base	On or before the day on or before which the taxpayer is required to file the taxpayer's return of income for the year under this Part for the year, or, where the property is acquired in the taxation year immediately following the year (see ss. 13(7.4) of the ITA)
Election where change of use	With taxpayer's return of income for the year
Debts established to be bad debts and shares of bankrupt corporation	In the taxpayer's return of income for the year
Amounts received or receivable under a restrictive covenant	Filing deadline is the same as the grantor's filing due date for persons resident in Canada (for non-residents, six months after the day on which the restrictive covenant was granted).
Successor rules for resource properties	When the property was acquired by amalgamation or windup, on or before the day in which the corporation is required to file a return of income for the tax year in which it acquired the property; or, in any other case, on or before the earlier of the day on or before which it, or the person from whom it acquired the property, is required to file a return of income for the tax year in which the corporation acquired the property
Transfers or distributions to a taxpayer's spouse, common-law partner, or spousal/partner trust on the death of the taxpayer	In the taxpayer's return of income

Transfer of farm and fishing property, or family farm or fishing corporations and partnerships, to a child	N/A
Election by legal representative and transferee regarding services	One copy with the deceased taxpayer's income tax return for the year of death, and another with the transferee's income tax return for the first taxation year ending after the death of the taxpayer
Inter vivos transfer of property	File an election with your income tax and benefit return
Deemed settlement on winding-up	The parent corporation has to complete one copy of this election and mail it separately from any other return to its tax centre, on or before the day on which the T2 Corporation Income Tax Return is required to be filed for the year in which the debt was settled
Expropriation assets acquired as compensation for, or as consideration for sale of, foreign property taken by or sold to a foreign issuer	For the day your income tax return has to be filed for the tax year in which you acquired any assets that are identified in s. 80.1
Dividends received by a taxpayer's spouse or common-law partner	N/A
Capital dividend	Mail one complete copy of this election, separately from any other return, to the processing site on or before the earlier of: the day the dividend becomes payable; and the first day on which any part of the dividend was paid.

Eligible distributions of foreign spinoff shares	Include a letter with the shareholder's income tax return for the year in which the distribution occurs
Preferred beneficiary election	Must be filed with the Minister within 90 days from the end of the trust's taxation year for which the election is made.
No rollover on election by trust	N/A
Deemed disposition on emigration	File one copy of this election and attach it to your tax return for the year in which you ceased to be resident in Canada
Departure tax adjustments for a returning former resident	You can make this election by sending your request in writing on or before your filing due date for the year you re-establish Canadian residency for income tax purposes
Departure tax adjustment for a returning trust beneficiary	Jointly so elect in writing and file the election with the Minister on or before the later of their filing-due dates for their taxation years that include the particular time, in respect of each property that the individual owned throughout the period that began at the distribution time and that ends at the particular time that is deemed by paragraph 1(b) to have been disposed of because the individual became resident in Canada...
Post-emigration loss on disposition	Elects in writing in the individual's return of income for the taxation year that includes the later time at which the property was taxable Canadian property of the individual

Allocation of income by communal organizations	Attached to T3 return
Home Buyers' Plan	N/A
Lifelong learning plan	N/A
Disposition of property by legal representative of deceased taxpayer	Claim these losses on the trust's T3 return. However, in the first tax year of a deceased person's graduated rate estate, you can elect to treat all or part of these losses as losses of the deceased on the deceased's final return. A net capital loss realized in the first tax year cannot be applied to any tax year before the year of death.
Realization of deceased employees' options	The letter shall be filed not later than the day that is the later of: the last day provided by the Act for the filing of a return that the legal representative of a deceased taxpayer is required or has elected to file under the Act in respect of the income of that deceased taxpayer for the taxation year in which he or she died, and the day the return of the income for the first taxation year of the deceased taxpayer's estate is required to be file under paragraph 150(1)(c) of the Act
Excess capital dividend or capital gains dividend	On or before the day that is 90 days after the day of sending of the notice of assessment in respect of the tax that would otherwise be payable

Time of day a loss restriction event occurs for a trust	If a trust is subject to a loss restriction event at a particular time during a day, the trust is deemed to be subject to the loss restriction event at the beginning of that day and not the particular time unless the trust elects in its return of income under Part I filed for its taxation year that ends immediately before the loss restriction event to have this subsection not apply
Date of acquisition of control	With T2 return
Election to include properties in Class 1	The election affects all properties on hand at the commencement of the tax year for which the election is made
Elections to include properties in Class 2, 4, or 17	The election affects all properties on hand at the commencement of the tax year for which the election is made
Elections to make certain transfers	Election can be made when, in the same year, (a) a property (new property) is acquired in the new class, (b) the property of the old class is disposed of, (c) property of the old class would have been in the same class as the new property if it were acquired at the same time and from the same person as the new property, and vice versa for the property of the new class, and (d) the new class is not a separate class described in Regulation 1101.
Earnings of a foreign affiliate	N/A

Taxpayer Rights

Get to know the taxpayer rights below. You may need to (try to) invoke them at some point or use them to your advantage.

A good place to start learning about one's rights is the Taxpayer Bill of Rights. And while this "Bill of Rights" is not a true legal "Bill", many of the individual rights listed below come from law. But the problem is that in order to actually assert one's rights it often involves maneuvering through a process that can be complicated at times and which requires specialized knowledge.

While some of these rights generally do not hold the force of law (I call them the Public Relations rights), and while the document is not a true "bill" of rights, as it has not been passed by Parliament, etc., it can be of use to be familiar with its contents.

The Taxpayer Bill of Rights was introduced in 2007 and outlines 16 rights that are theoretically meant to be guaranteed to every taxpayer, although this is not always the case. Below is a list of the Canadian Taxpayer's Rights:

1. You have the right to receive entitlements and to pay no more and no less than what is required by law.
2. You have the right to service in both official languages.
3. You have the right to privacy and confidentiality.
4. You have the right to a formal review and a subsequent appeal.
5. You have the right to be treated professionally, courteously, and fairly.
6. You have the right to complete, accurate, clear, and timely information.
7. You have the right, unless otherwise provided by law, not to pay income tax amounts in dispute before you have had an impartial review.
8. You have the right to have the law applied consistently.
9. You have the right to lodge a service complaint and to be provided with an explanation of our findings.
10. You have the right to have the costs of compliance taken into account when administering tax legislation.
11. You have the right to expect us to be accountable.
12. You have the right to relief from penalties and interest under tax legislation because of extraordinary circumstances.
13. You have the right to expect us to publish our service standards and report annually.
14. You have the right to expect us to warn you about questionable tax schemes in a timely manner.

15. You have the right to be represented by a person of your choice.
16. You have the right to lodge a service complaint and request a formal review without fear of reprisal.

In short, the problem is that a far better outcome can actually be achieved with the help of a professional like you or a tax lawyer. So those who cannot afford to prove that they were right or that their rights were offended often end up paying more tax than they should, which is not right. There is in fact a two-tiered system. And if you are in the bottom tier, get to know your rights.

For a perspective on this and our system in general, see below a re-print of my article "A Sad Story about Mr. X. from Country Y" – originally published in my tax column on the Lawyer's Daily.

Article - A Sad Story About Mr. X from Country Y

Originally published by the Lawyer's Daily

Meet Mr. X. Don't judge him by his country of residence. It is not his fault. It wouldn't be fair. He was taken there as a child by his parents who were fleeing another country for a better life. They could never have predicted how the government of Mr. X's adopted country would treat him when he grew up.

In fact, the government has been using its immense resources to conduct an ongoing investigation into the activities of Mr. X., which one night culminated in officials bursting into Mr. X's house without warning, bringing police with them and scaring his wife and children. That night the government took away all his computers and papers, as well as some cash that his family had been saving for a vacation.

Apparently, the investigation which had lasted two years, had uncovered evidence that Mr. X had been breaking the law. Armed with nothing more than circumstantial evidence at best, the government advised Mr. X of the fact that it believes he had been breaking the law. It gave him a 30-day period to respond to their allegations, but it didn't so much as read his response before forcefully and violently penalizing him without a trial. Mr. X was guilty.

Mr. X could not afford a lawyer nor was a lawyer even offered to him. The government didn't seem the least bit concerned with Mr. X's ability to defend himself against the action.

From the moment the government decided he was guilty and even before being afforded the opportunity to defend himself against the position of the state (which turned out to be incorrect), Mr. X found that the state had started to take away his possessions, freeze his bank accounts and make it impossible for him to transfer anything to his family members or pay his employees. In turn, he lost his business, his home, his wife and his dog. And since Mr. X was not and is still not able to afford the services of a lawyer, he has been forced to accept the government's punishment, which ultimately cost him 25 years of his life — the 25 years it took to get to this point in the first place.

Mr. X does not live in North Korea. And no, he does not live in a country without the rule of law. In fact, Mr. X lives in Canada. Just around the corner from you and me. Mr. X is Bob from around the corner. You know Bob from around the corner. And it is the Canada Revenue Agency who has been pursuing Bob from around the corner and trying to destroy him and his hardware store.

Arguably there are two major circumstances where the government uses its limitless resources against a citizen in a forceful and meaningful way. Those are during a criminal prosecution and during a tax audit and reassessment. Both a criminal prosecution and a tax audit are capable of destroying a person. The criminal justice system can lock a person away for years, while the tax audit can destroy and undermine years of hard work and leave a taxpayer flat broke.

A key difference between the two lies in the fact that when the government comes calling on criminal charges, the taxpayer is innocent until proven guilty and they have the right to legal representation. And when they cannot afford legal representation, they have access to legal aid. In the tax context, however, the taxpayer is deemed guilty until they prove themselves innocent. They have to spend their own money to prove their innocence and do not qualify for any government assistance. And in the case of disputed HST or payroll deductions where amounts are still payable while in dispute, taxpayers still face the punishing task of servicing debts, which often turn out to be incorrect, while dealing with abusive collections agents along the way.

If CRA auditors were actually always correct in their assessments (as they are deemed to be until proven otherwise), then there may be a way to justify and stomach a system where there is an assumption of guilt, an immediate assessment of penalties and the need to service trust debts. But as has been shown by many a taxpayer and their lawyer, the CRA auditors are not infallible. Their assessments are wrong. A lot. And the CRA knows this.
Isn't it about time to either do a better job on audits or flip the system on its side?

At the end of the day, what many don't realize is that Mr. X is forced to shoulder the cost of a bad audit or a bad system. Sometimes Mr. X has a large reassessment that he is incapable of challenging and his life is ruined by the inability to fight. Other times Mr. X has a small reassessment, and it is less expensive and troublesome to pay the bill than to challenge it. No matter what the reassessment, Mr. X's lack of access to justice and an unfair system make him ripe for the picking.

Tax Schemes and Shelters

Perhaps the most important tip you can take from this book is to be careful not to fall victim to a tax scheme or tax shelter.

Over the years I have spoken to thousands of individuals who were advised that they could reduce their taxes dramatically if they donated to a particular charity or participated in a particular tax shelter.

The one thing that these thousands of individuals have in common is that they were the subject of a CRA audit which either targeted those taxpayers who received a receipt from a particular charity, or those taxpayers who used certain tax preparers who offered to get them amazing tax refunds, or those taxpayers who all participated in a tax shelter which after having been audited by the CRA, resulted in tax reductions or deferrals which were offside.

Sadly, these thousands of people lost their homes, or their life savings, or were otherwise financially battered because of their participation.

What you have to remember is the golden rule:

If something appears too good to be true, it is.

This applies in tax as much as anywhere else. So, if somebody prepares your return and tells you that you will receive a tax refund which is much higher than you are used to getting, get a second opinion. And if you don't, you could be in for massive penalties.

02 PERSONAL CREDITS

Family

There are many different credits available to taxpayers which have to do with their family members. It is important to ensure that you understand these credits and take advantage of them. It can save you thousands in taxes. So, if you have children, or are a caregiver or pay support or have a disability or go to school, or are an individual taxpayer, pay attention to all the following personal credits.

Childcare

Childcare Expenses Deduction

If you spend money on childcare to enable you to work, carry on a business, or to attend school, you may be able to get a tax deduction on your return for the cost of childcare expenses. Under the tax rules, you can generally deduct money you paid to caregivers providing child-care services, day nursery schools, and daycare centres.

How to Qualify

The expense must be specifically incurred to allow the parent to work (or go to school). Further, the eligible child must live with you or the person making the expense claim to qualify. An eligible child can be your or your spouse or common-law partner's child or a child who was dependant on you whose net income was below $12,069. The child must have been under 16 years of age at some time in the tax year. This age limit does not apply to children with a physical or mental impairment.

The childcare expense deduction is limited to $8,000 annually for a child under the age of seven, $5,000 for other eligible children aged seven to 16, and $11,000 for a child who qualifies for the disability tax credit.

Supporting Documents Needed

Receipts showing information about the services provided by the individual or organization paid for childcare must be available in case the CRA requests such information, but they do not need to be included with the filed tax return. If the childcare services are provided by an individual, their social insurance number will be needed.

Use form T778 Childcare Expense Deductions to calculate your allowable amount of childcare expenses.

Tips

Child-care expenses incurred do not need to be paid for each eligible child. For example, let's say you have three kids. The 15-year-old and 13-year-old do not require any childcare, but you also have a toddler who is two and requires either daycare or the supervision of a nanny during the workday. You could still claim up to $18,000 of child-care expenses, based on the ages of your three kids and the respective limits (i.e., 2 X $5,000 + $8,000).

You cannot carry forward unclaimed expenses to another year.

Resources

For more information, see "Income Tax Folio S1-F3-C1, Child Care Expense Deduction" by visiting https://www.canada.ca/en/revenue-agency/services/tax/technical-information/income-tax/income-tax-folios-index/series-1-individuals/folio-3-family-unit-issues/income-tax-folio-s1-f3-c1-child-care-expense-deduction.html

Canada Revenue Agency / Agence du revenu du Canada

Protected B when completed

Child Care Expenses Deduction for 2019

Before you fill out this form, read the attached information sheet.

Part A – Total child care expenses

First and **last name** and **date of birth** of all your eligible children, even if you did not pay child care expenses for all of them.

Name	Year	Month	Day

First name of each eligible child for whom payments were made	**Child care expenses paid** (read note below)	**Name of the child care organization** or **name and social insurance number of the individual** who received the payments	Number of weeks for **boarding schools** or **overnight camps**
	+		
	+		
	+		
	+		
Total 67950	=		

Note
The maximum you can claim for expenses that relate to a stay in a boarding school (other than education costs) or an overnight camp (including an overnight sports school) is any of the following amounts:

- **$200 per week** for a child included on line 1 in Part B
- **$275 per week** for a child included on line 2
- **$125 per week** for a child included on line 3

Enter the amount of expenses included above that were incurred in 2019 for a child who was 6 or younger at the end of the year. 67954

Part B – Basic limit for child care expenses

Number of eligible children **born in 2013 or later**, for whom the disability amount cannot be claimed		× **$8,000** =		1
Number of eligible children **born in 2019 or earlier**, for whom the disability amount can be claimed *		× **$11,000** = 67960	+	2
Number of eligible children **born in 2003 to 2012**, (and born in 2002 or earlier, with an impairment in physical or mental function, for whom the disability amount cannot be claimed)		× **$5,000** =	+	3
Add lines 1, 2, and 3.			=	4
Enter the amount from **line 67950 in Part A**.				5
Enter your **earned income**.		× $\frac{2}{3}$ =		6
Enter the amount from line 4, 5, or 6, **whichever is least**.				7

If you are the person with the higher net income, go to Part C. Leave lines 8 and 9 blank.

Enter the amount that the **other person** with the higher net income deducted on line 21400 of his or her 2019 return.		–	8
Line 7 minus line 8. If you attended school in 2019 and you are the only person making a claim, also go to Part D. Otherwise, enter this amount on line 21400 of your return.	**Allowable deduction**	=	9

* Attach Form T2201, Disability Tax Credit Certificate. If this form has already been filed for the child, attach a note to your return showing the name and social insurance number of the person who filed the form and the tax year for which it was filed.

Part C – Are you the person with the higher net income?

Fill out this part **and** tick the boxes that apply if, in 2019, **another person** with lower net income was in a situation described below.

Name of person with lower net income	Social insurance number	Net income

- ☐ **a)** The other person attended school and was enrolled in a **part-time** educational program.
- ☐ **b)** The other person attended school and was enrolled in a **full-time** educational program.
- ☐ **c)** The other person was not capable of caring for children because of an impairment in physical or mental function. That person must have been confined for a period of at least two weeks to a bed or wheelchair, or as a patient in a hospital, or other similar institution. Attach a statement from the attending physician certifying this information.
- ☐ **d)** The other person was not capable of caring for children because of an impairment in physical or mental function, and this situation is likely to continue for an indefinite period. Attach a statement from the attending physician certifying this information.
- ☐ **e)** The other person was confined to a prison or similar institution for a period of at least two weeks.
- ☐ **f)** You and your spouse or common-law partner were, due to a breakdown in your relationship, living separate and apart at the end of 2019 and for a period of at least 90 days beginning in 2019, but you reconciled before March 1, 2020.

Enter the amount from line 4 in Part B.		× **2.5%** =	10
Multiply the amount on line 10 by the number of **months** in 2019 that the situation in **a)** existed (other than a month that includes a week that any of the situations in **b)** to **f)** existed).			11
Multiply the amount on line 10 by the number of **weeks** in 2019 that any of the situations in **b)** to **f)** existed.		+	12
Add lines 11 and 12.	67980	=	13
Enter the amount from line 7 in Part B or line 13, **whichever is less**. If you attended school in 2019, go to Part D. Otherwise, enter this amount on line 21400 of your return.	**Allowable deduction**		14

Part D – Were you enrolled in an educational program in 2019?

Fill out this part if, at any time in 2019, either of the following situations applied to you:

- You were the **only person supporting the eligible child**, line 7 equals line 6 in Part B, and you were enrolled in an educational program.
- You were the **person with the higher net income**, line 7 equals line 6 in Part B, and, at the same time in 2019, you **and another person** were enrolled in an educational program. **But first, fill out Part C.**

Part D does not apply to the person with the lower net income, since the other person will claim this part of the deduction for both of them.

Enter the amount from line 4 in Part B.		× **2.5%** =	15
Multiply the amount on line 15 by the number of **weeks** in 2019 during which you were enrolled in a **full-time** educational program. If there was **another person**, they must also have been enrolled in a **full-time** educational program during the **same weeks**.			16
Multiply the amount on line 15 by the number of **months** (other than any month that includes a week used to calculate the amount on line 16) in 2019 during which one of the following applies: • there was no **other person** and you were enrolled in a **part-time** educational program • you and the other person were enrolled in a **full-time** or **part-time** educational program during the **same months**		+	17
Add lines 16 and 17.	67990	=	18
Line 4 in Part B minus line 9 in Part B or line 14 in Part C, whichever applies to you			19
Line 5 in Part B minus line 9 in Part B or line 14 in Part C, whichever applies to you			20
Enter your **net income** (not including amounts on lines 21400 and 23500).		× $\frac{2}{3}$ =	21
If you filled out Part C: Line 13 in Part C minus line 6 in Part B			22
Enter the amount from line 18, 19, 20, 21, or (if it applies) 22, **whichever is least**.			23
Enter the amount from line 9 in Part B or the amount from line 14 in Part C, whichever applies to you.		+	24
Add lines 23 and 24. Enter this amount on line 21400 of your return.	**Allowable deduction**	=	25

Support Payments Made

If you are making deductible support payments under a court order or written agreement, you may be able to receive a tax credit.

How to Qualify

If you made support payments under a court order or written agreement, then you qualify for the deduction. Deductible support payments include the total amount of payments you paid under court orders or written agreements. Non-deductible child support payments should be included in the total amount.

Only the amounts specified in court orders or written agreements may be included with your deduction. You cannot deduct any amounts you gave directly to your children such as gifts or a weekly allowance.

Your court order or written agreement should also be registered with the CRA.

Supporting Documents Needed

Although supporting documents do not need to be submitted to the CRA, receipts must be retained by you and state your name, the date of payment, and the amount paid. Documents accepted to support your support payments claim may include cancelled cheques, bank or employer statements, or signed receipts from the recipient showing the total amount paid in the year.

Tips

You can request an adjustment in a year for which you have already filed a tax return if your court order or written agreement includes support paid.

Your situation may vary if you have more than one recipient to whom you are making support payments.

Legal and accounting fees cannot be deducted if incurred to get separated or divorced, to establish support payments, or to establish custody or visitation rights.

Resources

For more information see "Income Tax Folio S1-F3-C3, Support Payments" by visiting https://www.canada.ca/en/revenue-agency/services/tax/technical-information/income-tax/income-tax-folios-index/series-1-individuals/folio-3-family-unit-issues/income-tax-folio-s1-f3-c3-support-payments.html

Caregivers

Spouse or Common-Law Partner Amount

How to Qualify

Families living in the same household where one spouse is financially responsible for the other may claim a non-refundable tax credit. The maximum amount one could claim in 2019 was $11,809. This amount may change in future years.

This amount can be claimed for the entire year even if you were eligible for only part of it if you supported your spouse or common-law partner at any time during the year and their income was lower than $12,069 (2019).

You cannot claim this credit if you're claiming the amount for an eligible dependant.

Tips

Special rules apply if you filed for bankruptcy, immigrated to or emigrated from Canada, and if your spouse or common-law partner's net income is above the threshold because of dividends they received from taxable Canadian corporations during the tax year.

Remember to claim the corresponding provincial or territorial non-refundable tax credit to which you are entitled, on line 58120 of your provincial or territorial Form 428.

You may be entitled to the Canada caregiver amount for an impairment in mental or physical functions of your spouse, common-law partner, or eligible dependant 18 years or older.

Resources

For more information see "Income Tax Folio S1-F4-C1, Basic Personal and Dependant Tax Credits" by visiting https://www.canada.ca/en/revenue-agency/services/tax/technical-information/income-tax/income-tax-folios-index/series-1-individuals/series-1-individuals-1/income-tax-folio-s1-f4-c1-basic-personal-dependant-tax-credits.html

Canada Caregiver Amount for Spouse or Common-law Partner, or Eligible Dependant Age 18 or Older

How to Qualify

Anyone caring for a low-income dependant with an impairment in physical or mental function may qualify for the "Canada Caregiver Amount". This same amount is also available to anyone who cares for a dependant spouse or common-law partner.
Supporting Documentation

You'll need to get CRA-acceptable proof of the dependant's health condition. To support the claim, you may need a signed letter from a doctor describing the condition, although a completed Form T2201 [Disability Tax Credit Certificate] approved by the CRA would also do. But the letter from the doctor may be easier to get than the disability certificate.

Tips

While spouses, parents, or children are typically the dependants when it comes to caregiver claims, the credit can be applied even when the dependant is an infirm grandchild, aunt, uncle, nephew, or niece.

You may be able to claim the credit more than once if you have multiple qualifying dependants.

You can go back 10 years on the disability tax credit, medical expenses—anything that you want to amend.

Resources

For more information see "Income Tax Folio S1-F4-C1, Basic Personal and Dependant Tax Credits" by visiting https://www.canada.ca/en/revenue-agency/services/forms-publications/publications/rc4064.html

Amount for an Eligible Dependant

How to Qualify

If at any time in the year you supported an eligible dependant and you did not claim a spouse or common-law dependant amount, then you may be able to claim the amount for an eligible dependant under the age of 18.
You may qualify for this amount if you did not have a spouse or common-

law partner. You may still qualify if you did have a spouse or common-law partner but were not living with, supporting, or being supported by that person. You would also to have lived with the dependant in a home maintained by you.

Along with the above conditions, in order to qualify for this credit, the dependant must have been either your parent, grandparent, child, grandchild, brother or sister by blood, marriage, common-law partnership, or adoption. Further, any children claimed must be under the age of 18 or have an impairment in physical or mental functions.

Supporting Documentation

You may be asked to provide assorted documentation based on your specific circumstance. Documentation should only be provided to the CRA when requested.

Tips

Children living away from home while attending school still qualify if they ordinarily live with you when not at school.

Resources

For more information see "Income Tax Folio S1-F4-C1, Basic Personal and Dependant Tax Credits" by visiting https://www.canada.ca/en/revenue-agency/services/forms-publications/publications/rc4064.html

Canada Caregiver Amount for Other Infirm Dependants age 18 or Older

How to Qualify

As of the 2019 tax year, a claim of $7,140 can be made for each dependant child or grandchild was 18 years or older and was dependant on you because of an impairment of physical or mental functions.

Supporting Documentation

You may be asked to provide assorted documentation based on your specific circumstance. Documentation should only be provided to the CRA when requested.

Tips

You cannot claim an amount for dependants who do not have an impairment in physical or mental functions, including a parent or grandparent who was 65 years of age or older.

A child can include someone older than you who has become completely dependent on you for support and over whom you have custody and control.

Resources

For more information see "Disability-Related Information 2019" by visiting https://www.canada.ca/en/revenue-agency/services/forms-publications/publications/rc4064/disability-related-information-2016.html

Claim All Medical Expenses

Medical expenses are often overlooked but are a great way to reduce one's taxes.

These expenses can be claimed on line 33099 and 33199 of one's T1 personal tax return.

Medical expenses can be claimed on line 33099 as long as they exceed the minimum threshold of the lesser of $2,352 or 3% of one's income.

They can also be claimed on line 33199 as long as they exceed the minimum threshold of the lesser of $2,352 or 3% of one's dependant's income.

There are a great number of different types of eligible expenses which can be claimed. For a complete list visit https://www.canada.ca/en/revenue-agency/services/tax/technical-information/income-tax/income-tax-folios-index/series-1-individuals/folio-1-health-medical/income-tax-folio-s1-f1-c1-medical-expense-tax-credit.html

EXAMPLE

John and Jane have 2 children, Amanda and Andrew. They have reviewed their medical expenses and decided that the 12-month period ending in 2019 they will use to calculate their claim is July 1, 2018 to June 30, 2019. They had the following expenses:

John	$1,500
Jane	$1,000
Amanda (14-year-old daughter)	$1,800
Andrew (19-year-old son)	$1,000
Total	$5,300

Since Amanda is under 18, John and Jane can combine her medical expenses with theirs, for a total of $4,300. Either John or Jane can claim this amount on line 33099 of their tax return. Since Andrew is over 18, his medical expenses should be claimed on line 33199.

Jane's net income is $32,000. She calculates 3% of that amount, which is $960. Because the result is less than $2,352, she subtracts $960 from $4,300. The difference is $3,340, which is the amount she could claim on her tax return.

John's net income is $48,000. He calculates 3% of that amount, which is $1,440. Because the result is less than $2,352, he subtracts $1,440 from $4,300. The difference is $2,860, which is the amount he could claim on his tax return.

Disability Supports Deduction

A taxpayer with a physical or mental impairment can claim some medical expenses as a "Disability Supports Deduction" either on line 21500 or line 33099 or split between the two lines as long as the total claimed does not exceed the expenses paid.

Refundable Medical Expense Supplement

Individuals with low incomes and high expenses may also be able to access a refundable tax credit called the Refundable Medical Expense Supplement. As long as they were 18 or older by the end of the tax year, were resident in Canada throughout the year, and made a claim on their tax return on line 33200 for medical expenses or on line 21500 for the disability supports deduction.

Education Deductions and Credits

In 2017, the Canadian government eliminated the federal educational and textbook tax credits. However, they did not eliminate the tuition tax credit, allowing students the opportunity to apply tuition costs toward owing taxes.

The tuition tax credit is offered to Canadians by the CRA. It allows students 17 years of age and older who are enrolled in post-secondary education to use their tuition to reduce their taxable income. The tuition amount, can also be transferred to a spouse, common law partner, parent or grandparent

How to Qualify

In order to be eligible for the tuition tax credit, students must attend a post-secondary level course at an accredited institution in Canada – although individuals may qualify at school abroad as well.

Supporting Documents Needed

The accredited institution will issue an official tax receipt which will indicate the amount of eligible tuition fees for that calendar year.

Do not send any supporting documents to the CRA unless requested of you.

Tips

Examination fees for licensing or certification paid to education institutions, professional associations, or provincial ministries may be eligible for the tuition tax credit.

Although the federal government eliminated the textbook and education amounts in 2017, your province of residence may provide a credit.

If you moved more than 40 kilometres to attend a post-secondary program at a university, college, or similar, you can claim moving expenses.

The CRA maintains a list of recognized universities and higher educational institutions outside of Canada. This list can be found here: https://www.canada.ca/en/revenue-agency/services/tax/individuals/topics/about-your-tax-return/tax-return/completing-a-tax-return/deductions-credits-expenses/line-32300-your-tuition-education-textbook-amounts/recognized-educational-institutions-outside-canada/universities-higher-educational-institutions.html

Resources

For more information, see "Students and Income Tax" by visiting https://www.canada.ca/en/revenue-agency/services/forms-publications/publications/p105/p105-students-income-tax-2016.html

Disability Tax Credit

What is the Deduction / Credit?

The disability tax credit ("DTC") is a "non-refundable tax credit"[1] available to assist in reducing the amount of income tax payable for eligible individuals with severe or prolonged disabilities. The DTC may be claimed for a spouse, common-law partner, a dependant[2] or one's self. The credit assists in providing relief for additional expenses incurred for disability costs and may be claimed once eligible for the DTC, which requires CRA approval of Form T2201.

Once eligible for the DTC, the individual may become eligible for other provincial, territorial or federal programs, including the COVID-19 "special one-time tax-free payment"[3] for individuals eligible as of June 1, 2020 COVID-19 payment, the child disability benefit, the registered disability savings plan, and the working income tax benefit.

For eligible individuals under the age of 18 years at the end of the taxation year, the amount also includes a supplement.

How to Qualify

To qualify for the DTC, one must be an "eligible person with a disability"[4] by meeting the eligibility and certification criteria set out by the CRA.

To be eligible the individual must have "one or more prolonged impairments in physical or mental functions."[5] Such impairments, according to the CRA include being:

- in need of life sustaining therapy
- blind
- significantly restricted in two or more activities of daily living; o
- markedly restricted in at least one of the basic activities of daily living [6]

A medical practitioner must complete and certify Form T2201, Disability Tax Credit Certificate, indicating that one or more "severe and prolonged impairment"[7] in physical or mental functions exists and describe its effects.

An impairment is prolonged if the impairment has or can be expected to last for at least 12 months, as per paragraph 118.4(1)(a). The severity requirement requires that the impairment is "present all or substantially all of the time (at least 90% of the time)"[8].

To qualify, the effects must be such that the individual's quality of basic activities of daily living are "markedly restricted" or the equivalent thereof.

Basic activities of daily living include:

Walking;
- Dressing oneself;
- Feeding oneself;
- Hearing;
- Speaking;
- Eliminating (bowel and bladder functions); or
- "Mental functions necessary for everyday life:
  - Memory;

- Problem solving, goal-setting and judgement (taken together); and
- Adaptive functioning"

Activities are markedly restricted "or would be markedly restricted but for life-sustaining therapy" if the individual is unable to do a basic activity of daily living, or if it "takes an inordinate amount of time" to do the "basic activities of daily living, even with therapy (other than life-sustaining therapy) and the use of appropriate devices and medication. This restriction must be present all or substantially all the time (at least 90% of the time)."

One's basic activities of daily life are considered significantly restricted if the cumulative effect of the ability to perform more than one activity "is equivalent to being markedly restricted."

A disability amount may be transferred from a spouse, common law partner or dependent.

To claim your dependent's disability amount on line 31800, the dependent must be a resident in Canada at any time during the taxation year for which the claim is being made, be dependent on you for some or all of the basic necessities of life (such as food, shelter and clothing), and be eligible for the DTC. "In addition, one of the following situations has to apply:

- You claimed an amount on line 30400 of your tax return (Step 5 – Federal tax) for that dependant, or you could have if you did not have a spouse or common-law partner and if the dependant did not have any income.
- The dependant was your or your spouse's or common-law partner's parent, grandparent, child, grandchild, brother, sister, uncle, aunt, nephew, or niece, and you claimed an amount on line 30450 of your tax return for that dependant or you could have if they had no income and had been 18 years of age or older in 2019."

Supporting Documents needed (if applicable)

Approval of the DTC is based on the application and information given by the medical practitioner. Should the CRA require further information, they may contact the medical practitioner or the applicant directly. In case the CRA requests supporting documentation, it is recommended that the applicant maintain supporting documentation and receipts.

Tips

Prior to submitting the DTC application to the Disability Tax Credit Unit of your tax centre, to assist in determining one's eligibility, a self-assessment questionnaire is available in "Guide RC4064, Disability-Related Information."

It is recommended that you keep a copy of the application for your records. There is no deadline to submit the form, which may be sent at any time during the year, however, sending the form shortly prior to submitting your annual income tax return may delay your usual tax assessment.

While part A of Form T2201 is to be filled out by the taxpayer, a medical practitioner must complete part B of Form T2201 and certify the impairment. Medical practitioners eligible to certify the impairment include:

- occupational therapists;
- physiotherapists;
- medical doctors;
- optometrists;
- psychologists;
- speech language pathologists;
- audiologists; and
- nurse practitioners

Any fees incurred to pay the medical practitioner to complete the form may be claimed on line 33099 or line 33199 as medical expenses on your income tax return.

Once the CRA makes a determination, a notice of determination will be issued. If the determination is positive, indicating that the individual is eligible, another form should not be submitted unless the CRA requests that another form is required, or the prior period of approval has expired.

Once approved, the disability amount may be claimed on the corresponding line of your tax return. Adjustments for eligible years that were not previously claimed may be requested for up to 10 years under the CRA's taxpayer relief provisions.

If the determination is not in the taxpayer's favour, a notice of objection to appeal the decision may be submitted to the CRA. To dispute the determination, the objection should be filed no later than 90 days after the date of the decision provided in the notice of determination.

If the eligible individuals medical condition improves such that the individual is no longer eligible, there is a requirement to inform the CRA.

Resources

One may contact the CRA directly for assistance by calling 1-800-959-8281 or go to canada.ca/disability-tax-credit

Other useful CRA resources:

- "Disability deductions and credits," Date modified: January 21, 2020, https://www.canada.ca/en/revenue-agency/services/tax/individuals/topics/about-your-tax-return/tax-return/completing-a-tax-return/deductions-credits-expenses/disability-deductions-credits.html
- RC4064(E) Rev. 19, "Tax measures for persons with disabilities, Disability-Related Information," 2019, https://www.canada.ca/content/dam/cra-arc/formspubs/pub/rc4064/rc4064-19e.pdf
- Income Tax Folio S1-F1-C2, "Disability Tax Credit," Date modified: July 19, 2016, https://www.canada.ca/en/revenue-agency/services/tax/technical-information/income-tax/income-tax-folios-index/series-1-individuals/folio-1-health-medical/income-tax-folio-s1-f1-c2-disability-tax-credit.html
- Guide RC4064, "Disability-Related Information," Date modified: January 16, 2020, https://www.canada.ca/en/revenue-agency/services/forms-publications/publications/rc4064.html or go to canada.ca/disability-tax-credit.

Canada Revenue Agency / Agence du revenu du Canada

6729

Protected B when completed

Disability Tax Credit Certificate

Use this form to apply for the disability tax credit (DTC). The Canada Revenue Agency (CRA) will use this information to make a decision on eligibility for the DTC. See the "General information" on page 6 for more information.

Step 1 – Fill out and sign the sections of Part A that apply to you.

Step 2 – Ask a medical practitioner to fill out and certify Part B.

Step 3 – Send the form to the CRA.

Part A – To be filled out by the taxpayer

Section 1 – Information about the person with the disability

First name and initial | Last name | Social insurance number

Mailing address (Apt No. – Street No. Street name, PO Box, RR)

City | Province or territory | Postal code | Date of birth: Year Month Day

Section 2 – Information about the person claiming the disability amount (if different from above)

First name and initial | Last name | Social insurance number

The person with the disability is: ☐ my spouse/common-law partner ☐ my dependant (specify): ______

Answer the following questions for **all** of the years that you are claiming the disability amount for the person with the disability.

1. Does the person with the disability live with you? Yes ☐ No ☐

   If **yes**, for which year(s)? ______

2. If you answered **no** to Question 1, does the person with the disability regularly and consistently depend on you for one or more of the basic necessities of life such as food, shelter, or clothing? Yes ☐ No ☐

   If **yes**, for which year(s)? ______

Give details about the **regular** and **consistent** support you provide for food, shelter or clothing to the person with the disability (if you need more space, attach a separate sheet of paper). We may ask you to provide receipts or other documents to support your request.

Section 3 – Adjust your income tax and benefit return

Once eligibility is approved, the CRA can adjust your returns for all applicable years to include the disability amount for **yourself** or your **dependant under the age of 18**. For more information, see Guide RC4064, Disability-Related Information.

☐ Yes, I want the CRA to adjust my returns, if possible. ☐ No, I do not want an adjustment.

Section 4 – Authorization

As the **person with the disability** or their **legal representative**, I authorize the following actions:

- Medical practitioner(s) can give information to the CRA from their medical records or discuss the information on this form.
- The CRA can adjust my returns, as applicable, if the "Yes" box has been ticked in Section 3.

Sign here: ______ | Telephone | Year Month Day

Personal information is collected under the Income Tax Act to administer tax, benefits, and related programs. It may also be used for any purpose related to the enforcement of the Act such as audit, compliance and collection activities. It may be shared or verified with other federal, provincial, territorial or foreign government institutions to the extent authorized by law. Failure to provide this information may result in interest payable, penalties or other actions. The social insurance number is collected under section 237 of the Act and is used for identification purposes. Under the Privacy Act, individuals have the right to access, or request correction of, their personal information, or to file a complaint with the Privacy Commissioner of Canada regarding the handling of their personal information. Refer to Personal Information Bank CRA PPU 218 at **canada.ca/cra-info-source**.

T2201 E (18) (Ce formulaire est disponible en français.) Canada

Patient's name: ______________________________

Part B – Must be filled out by the medical practitioner

Step 1 – Fill out **only** the section(s) on pages 2 to 4 that apply to your patient. Each category states which medical practitioner(s) can certify the information in this part.

Note
Whether filling out this form for a child or an adult, assess your patient compared to someone of similar age with no impairment.

Step 2 – Fill out the **"Effects of impairment"**, **"Duration"**, and **"Certification"** sections on page 5. If more information is needed, the Canada Revenue Agency (CRA) may contact you.

Eligibility for the DTC is based on the effects of the impairment, not on the medical condition itself. For definitions and examples of impairments that may qualify for the DTC, see Guide RC4064, Disability-Related Information. For more information, go to **canada.ca/disability-tax-credit**.

Vision – Medical doctor, nurse practitioner, or optometrist

Your patient is considered **blind** if, even with the use of corrective lenses or medication, their vision meets any of the following criteria:

- The visual acuity in **both** eyes is 20/200 (6/60) or less, with the Snellen Chart (or an equivalent).
- The greatest diameter of the field of vision in **both** eyes is 20 degrees or less.

1. Is your patient **blind**, as described above? Yes ☐ No ☐

   If **yes**, when did your patient become blind (this is not necessarily the year of the diagnosis, as is often the case with progressive diseases)? Year ____

2. What is your patient's visual acuity **after correction**? Right eye ____ Left eye ____

3. What is your patient's visual field **after correction** (in degrees if possible)? Right eye ____ Left eye ____

Speaking – Medical doctor, nurse practitioner, or speech-language pathologist

Your patient is considered **markedly restricted** in speaking if, even with appropriate therapy, medication, and devices, they meet both of the following criteria:

- They are **unable** or take an **inordinate amount of time** to speak so as to be understood by another person familiar with the patient, in a quiet setting.
- This is the case **all or substantially all of the time** (at least 90% of the time).

Is your patient **markedly restricted** in speaking, as described above? Yes ☐ No ☐

If **yes**, when did your patient's restriction in speaking become a marked restriction (this is not necessarily the year of the diagnosis, as is often the case with progressive diseases)? Year ____

Hearing – Medical doctor, nurse practitioner, or audiologist

Your patient is considered **markedly restricted** in hearing if, even with appropriate devices, they meet both of the following criteria:

- They are **unable** or take an **inordinate amount of time** to hear so as to understand another person familiar with the patient, in a quiet setting.
- This is the case **all or substantially all of the time** (at least 90% of the time).

Is your patient **markedly restricted** in hearing, as described above? Yes ☐ No ☐

If **yes**, when did your patient's restriction in hearing become a marked restriction (this is not necessarily the year of the diagnosis, as is often the case with progressive diseases)? Year ____

Walking – Medical doctor, nurse practitioner, occupational therapist, or physiotherapist

Your patient is considered **markedly restricted** in walking if, even with appropriate therapy, medication, and devices, they meet both of the following criteria:

- They are **unable** or take an **inordinate amount of time** to walk.
- This is the case **all or substantially all of the time** (at least 90% of the time).

Is your patient **markedly restricted** in walking, as described above? Yes ☐ No ☐

If **yes**, when did your patient's restriction in walking become a marked restriction (this is not necessarily the year of the diagnosis, as is often the case with progressive diseases)? Year ____

2

Patient's name: ______________________________

Eliminating (bowel or bladder functions) – Medical doctor or nurse practitioner

Your patient is considered **markedly restricted** in eliminating if, even with appropriate therapy, medication, and devices, they meet both of the following criteria:

- They are **unable** or take an **inordinate amount of time** to personally manage bowel or bladder functions.
- This is the case **all or substantially all of the time** (at least 90% of the time).

Is your patient **markedly restricted** in eliminating, as described above? Yes ☐ No ☐

If **yes**, when did your patient's restriction in eliminating become a marked restriction (this is not necessarily the year of the diagnosis, as is often the case with progressive diseases)? Year ____

Feeding – Medical doctor, nurse practitioner, or occupational therapist

Your patient is considered **markedly restricted** in feeding if, even with appropriate therapy, medication, and devices, they meet both of the following criteria:

- They are **unable** or take an **inordinate amount of time** to feed themselves.
- This is the case **all or substantially all of the time** (at least 90% of the time).

Feeding yourself **does not** include identifying, finding, shopping for, or obtaining food.

Feeding yourself **does** include preparing food, **except** when the time spent is related to a dietary restriction or regime, even when the restriction or regime is needed due to an illness or medical condition.

Is your patient **markedly restricted** in feeding, as described above? Yes ☐ No ☐

If **yes**, when did your patient's restriction in feeding become a marked restriction (this is not necessarily the year of the diagnosis, as is often the case with progressive diseases)? Year ____

Dressing – Medical doctor, nurse practitioner, or occupational therapist

Your patient is considered **markedly restricted** in dressing if, even with appropriate therapy, medication, and devices, they meet both of the following criteria:

- They are **unable** or take an **inordinate amount of time** to dress themselves.
- This is the case **all or substantially all of the time** (at least 90% of the time).

Dressing yourself **does not** include identifying, finding, shopping for, or obtaining clothing.

Is your patient **markedly restricted** in dressing, as described above? Yes ☐ No ☐

If **yes**, when did your patient's restriction in dressing become a marked restriction (this is not necessarily the year of the diagnosis, as is often the case with progressive diseases)? Year ____

Mental functions necessary for everyday life – Medical doctor, nurse practitioner, or psychologist

Your patient is considered **markedly restricted** in performing the mental functions necessary for everyday life (described below) if, even with appropriate therapy, medication, and devices (for example, memory aids and adaptive aids), they meet both of the following criteria:

- They are **unable** or take an **inordinate amount of time** to perform these functions by themselves.
- This is the case **all or substantially all of the time** (at least 90% of the time).

Mental functions necessary for everyday life include:

- adaptive functioning (for example, abilities related to self-care, health and safety, abilities to initiate and respond to social interactions, and common, simple transactions)
- memory (for example, the ability to remember simple instructions, basic personal information such as name and address, or material of importance and interest)
- problem-solving, goal-setting, **and** judgment taken together (for example, the ability to solve problems, set and keep goals, and make the appropriate decisions and judgments)

  Note
  A restriction in problem-solving, goal-setting, or judgment that markedly restricts adaptive functioning, all or substantially all of the time (at least 90% of the time), would qualify.

Is your patient **markedly restricted** in performing the mental functions necessary for everyday life, as described above? Yes ☐ No ☐

If **yes**, when did your patient's restriction in performing the mental functions necessary for everyday life become a marked restriction (this is not necessarily the year of the diagnosis, as is often the case with progressive diseases)? Year ____

3

Patient's name: ____________________

Life-sustaining therapy – Medical doctor or nurse practitioner

Life-sustaining therapy for your patient must meet **both** of the following criteria:

- Your patient needs this therapy to support a vital function, even if this therapy has eased the symptoms.
- Your patient needs this therapy at least 3 times per week, for an average of at least 14 hours per week.

The 14-hour per week requirement

Include only the time your patient must dedicate to the therapy – that is, the patient has to take time away from normal, everyday activities to receive it.

If a child cannot do the activities related to the therapy because of their age, **include** the time spent by the child's primary caregivers to do and supervise these activities.

Do not include the time a portable or implanted device takes to deliver the therapy, the time spent on activities related to dietary restrictions or regimes (such as carbohydrate calculation) or exercising (even when these activities are a factor in determining the daily dosage of medication), travel time to receive therapy, medical appointments (other than appointments where the therapy is received), shopping for medication, or recuperation after therapy.

1. Does your patient need this therapy **to support a vital function**? Yes ☐ No ☐
2. Does your patient need this therapy at least **3 times per week**? Yes ☐ No ☐
3. Does this therapy take an average of at least **14 hours per week**? Yes ☐ No ☐

   If **yes**, when did your patient's therapy begin to meet the above criteria (this is not necessarily the year of the diagnosis, as is often the case with progressive diseases)? Year ☐☐☐☐

It is **mandatory** that you describe how the therapy meets the criteria as stated above. If you need more space, use a separate sheet of paper, sign it and attach it to this form.

Cumulative effect of significant restrictions – Medical doctor, nurse practitioner, or occupational therapist

Note: An occupational therapist can only certify limitations for walking, feeding and dressing.

Answer **all** the following questions to certify the cumulative effect of your patient's significant restrictions.

1. Even with appropriate therapy, medication, and devices, does your patient have a **significant restriction**, that is not quite a **marked restriction**, in **two** or more basic activities of daily living or in **vision** and **one** or more of the basic activities of daily living? Yes ☐ No ☐

   If **yes**, tick at least **two** of the following, as they apply to your patient:

   ☐ vision ☐ speaking ☐ hearing ☐ walking
   ☐ eliminating (bowel or bladder functions) ☐ feeding ☐ dressing ☐ mental functions necessary for everyday life

   Note
   You **cannot** include the time spent on life-sustaining therapy.

2. Do these restrictions exist together, **all or substantially all of the time** (at least 90% of the time)? Yes ☐ No ☐
3. Is the cumulative effect of these significant restrictions equivalent to being **markedly restricted** in **one** basic activity of daily living? Yes ☐ No ☐
4. When did the cumulative effect described above begin (this is not necessarily the year of the diagnosis, as is often the case with progressive diseases)? Year ☐☐☐☐

4

Patient's name: ______________________________

Effects of impairment – Mandatory

The effects of your patient's impairment must be those which, even with therapy and the use of appropriate devices and medication, cause your patient to be restricted **all or substantially all of the time** (at least 90% of the time).

Note

Working, housekeeping, managing a bank account, and social or recreational activities are **not** considered basic activities of daily living. Basic activities of daily living are limited to walking, speaking, hearing, dressing, feeding, eliminating (bowel or bladder functions), and mental functions necessary for everyday life.

It is **mandatory** that you describe the effects of your patient's impairment on his or her ability to do **each** of the basic activities of daily living that you indicated are or were markedly or significantly restricted. If you need more space, use a separate sheet of paper, sign it and attach it to this form. You may include copies of medical reports, diagnostic tests, and any other medical information, if needed.

Duration – Mandatory

Has your patient's impairment lasted, or is it expected to last, for a continuous period of at least 12 months? For deceased patients, was the impairment expected to last for a continuous period of at least 12 months? Yes ☐ No ☐

If **yes**, has the impairment improved, or is it likely to improve, to such an extent that the patient would no longer be blind, markedly restricted, in need of life-sustaining therapy, or have the equivalent of a marked restriction due to the cumulative effect of significant restrictions? Unsure ☐ Yes ☐ No ☐

If **yes**, enter the year that the improvement occurred or may be expected to occur. Year: ____

Certification – Mandatory

1. For which year(s) have you been the attending medical practitioner for your patient? ____
2. Do you have medical information on file supporting the restriction(s) for all the year(s) you certified on this form? Yes ☐ No ☐

Tick the box that applies to you:

☐ Medical doctor	☐ Nurse practitioner	☐ Optometrist	☐ Occupational therapist
☐ Audiologist	☐ Physiotherapist	☐ Psychologist	☐ Speech-language pathologist

As a **medical practitioner**, I certify that the information given in Part B of this form is correct and complete. I understand that this information will be used by the CRA to make a decision if my patient is eligible for the DTC.

Sign here: ______________________________

It is a serious offence to make a false statement.

Address

Name (print)

Date: Year Month Day

Telephone

5

Climate Action Incentive

The climate action incentive ("CAI") is a 2019 tax credit for residents of Alberta, Saskatchewan, Manitoba and Ontario. The CAI payment is a standard amount, which is increased by a 10% supplement for residents of small and rural communities. The payment is designed to assist with increased expenses in relation to the new federal carbon tax that residents of these provinces will be charged as of April 2019.

Only one member of the household may claim the credit. As well, to be eligible to claim the CAI, you must be a resident throughout the taxation year in one of the above-mentioned provinces, and be over the age of 17, unless you "were a parent that lived with their child" or "had a spouse or a common-law partner." The individual claiming the CAI credit may also claim additional amounts for eligible spouses or common-law partners.

For residents of small and rural communities, the supplement requires that you have resided outside of a census metropolitan area as of December 31, 2019.

Amounts may also be claimed in respect to qualified dependants. Only one CAI claim per child may be made and may not be split between parents. The requirements for eligibility for the CAI for a dependant are the same as above, with the exception that the child must be under the age of 18.

If at any time during the 2019 taxation year you were a non-resident of Canada, "confined to a prison or a similar institution for a period of at least 90 days during the year," were exempt from taxation as "an officer or servant of the government of another country, such as a diplomat, or you were a family member who lived with such a person or an employee of such a person," were "a person for whom a children's special allowance was payable," or passed away before April 1, 2020, then you are not eligible to claim the CAI payment. If any of the above apply to your dependant, then you are not eligible to claim the CAI payment for the dependant.

Standard CAI payments vary depending on which province you resided in, as well as personal aspects, such as the number of qualified dependants. The below chart highlights what can be expected when claiming the CAI.

PROVINCE	BASIC AMOUNT	SPOUSE OR COMMON-LAW PARTNER AMOUNT	QUALIFIED DEPENDANT AMOUNT	SINGLE PARENT'S QUALIFIED DEPENDANT AMOUNT
Alberta	$444	$222	$111	$222
Saskatchewan	$405	$202	$101	$202
Manitoba	$243	$121	$61	$121
Ontario	$224	$112	$56	$112

*These amounts do not include the supplement for residents of small and rural communities.

The CAI can be claimed on your 2019 income tax and benefit return by completing Schedule 14. Once assessed, the CAI payment will set-off any balance owing for the taxation year, and where applicable, may increase any refund entitlement.

File a Tax Return Even if You Are Not Required

What may people don't know is that if you do not owe the CRA any taxes you generally are not required to file a tax return. In fact, in many cases the CRA prefers that you do not file a tax return. And the reason is that after the "normal refund period," which is 3 years for individuals, the CRA will not provide any tax refunds.

So, in those cases where taxpayers would have otherwise received refunds but failed to file, after the 3-year period (from the end of the tax year in question) the CRA gets to keep the refund. So, they usually keep quiet in these cases and don't request returns from taxpayers who they know are in a refund position.

The very obvious tip here is to file your tax return (on time) even if you are not required to.

Not only will you receive your tax refunds, but you may receive credits like the GST/HST credit or the Canada Child Tax Benefit which you otherwise would not have received. You may also receive provincial credits for low-income earners if you file.

Also note that Guaranteed Income Supplement and Working Income Tax Benefit must be applied for every year.

Be Sure to Report all T-Slips Even Though the CRA Has Them Already

The whole idea behind T-slips (T4, T5, etc.) is that a copy is issued to the taxpayer and another copy is sent by the issuer to the CRA. So, the CRA already knows what T-slips are attributed to a taxpayer for a particular tax year. If you have received T-slips, there is no hiding.

This makes it easy for the CRA to identify taxpayers who have not included income which was reported on a T-slip. And failure to accurately report one's income is an offense punishable by penalties and possibly prosecution.

The flip side of the fact that the CRA has a copy of the T-slips is that if a taxpayer has lost theirs, a copy can always be obtained from the CRA.

Transfer Unused Credits Between Spouses

Tax credits (which directly reduce an individual's tax payable) can be transferred between married or common law spouses. If one's spouse is eligible for federal tax credits, and their federal taxable income has already been rendered "0" without using all of their credits, they can transfer their unused credits to their spouse. By attaching a form (https://www.canada.ca/content/dam/cra-arc/formspubs/pbg/5000-s2/5000-s2-19e.pdf) to their spouse's tax return, a taxpayer can transfer their unused credits to their spouse.

The following are credits eligible for transfer: up to $2,000 for eligible pension reported; up to $8,416 for the disability tax credit; up to $7,494 for low to medium income earners over 65 years of age; an amount for infirm or dependent children under 18 years of age; and credits for tuition, education and textbook amounts in certain years. In addition to being transferred to spouses, unused credits can be carried forward to future tax years.

For tuition, education and textbook credits, one may transfer a maximum federal credit of $5,000, minus the amount being claimed by the student in the year, to their spouse annually. For provincial credits, Ontario's maximum in 2017 was $7,033, minus the amount being claimed by the student in the year. Again, this must be after the federal and provincial taxable income is "0", respectively. Also, one can only transfer amounts in the first year that they are claimed. This means that if someone claimed a credit for $2,000 for tuition in 2017 and elected to carry that amount forward to future tax years, then they cannot transfer that credit.

The tuition, education and textbook credits are provided federally (education must cost more than $100) and provincially. However, for Ontario, the tuition and education tax credits have been discontinued. The tuition tax credit can be claimed for eligible tuition fees paid up to Sept. 4, 2017. The education credit can be claimed for months of study before September 2017. If one has not claimed credits for those years for tuition or education, then unused amounts can still be transferred to their spouse and otherwise carried forward to future tax years. The Federal Government canceled education credits as of January 2017. The above is to say that federal tuition and textbook tax credits are still available as well as provincial tax credits for textbooks. Both can be transferred to spouses.

Protected B when completed

Schedule 2

T1-2019

Federal Amounts Transferred From Your Spouse or Common-Law Partner

You may be able to claim all or part of certain amounts for which your spouse or common law partner qualifies if they did not need the whole amount to reduce their federal tax to zero.

Complete this schedule and **attach** it to your return to claim a transfer of the unused part of your spouse's or common-law partner's amounts as shown below.

If you were separated because of a breakdown in your relationship for a period of 90 days or more including December 31, 2019, your spouse or common-law partner cannot transfer any unused amounts to you.

If your spouse or common-law partner is filing a return, use the amounts that they entered on their return, schedules and worksheets.

If your spouse or common-law partner is not filing a return, use the amounts that they would enter on their return, schedules and worksheets as if they were filing a return and attach their information slips.

Age amount (if your spouse or common-law partner was 65 years of age or older in 2019): If their net income is $37,790 or less, enter $7,494. Otherwise, enter the amount from line 30100 of their return.	35200		1
Canada caregiver amount for infirm children under 18 years of age: Enter the amount from line 30500 of their return.	35300	+	2
Pension income amount: Enter the amount from line 31400 of their return. **(maximum $2,000)**	35500	+	3
Disability amount: (see **note 1** below) Enter the amount from line 31600 of their return.	35700	+	4
Tuition amount: (see **note 2** below) Enter the federal amount designated to you as shown on their Form T2202, TL11A, or TL11C.	36000	+	5
Add lines 1 to 5.		=	6
Spouse's or common-law partner's taxable income: Enter the amount of their taxable income from line 26000 of their return if it is $47,630 or less. Otherwise, complete Part B of Step 5 of their return and enter the result of the following calculation: amount from line 43 in Part C of their return divided by 15%.			7
Enter the total of lines 30000, 30800, 31000, 31200, 31217, 31220, 31240, 31260, 31270, 31285, and 31300 of their return plus line 11 of their Schedule 11.		−	8
Spouse's or common-law partner's adjusted taxable income: Line 7 minus line 8 (if negative, enter "0")	36100	= ▶ −	9
Line 6 minus line 9 (if negative, enter "0") Enter this amount on line 32600 of your return. **Federal amounts transferred from your spouse or common-law partner**		=	10

Note 1

If the amount on this line includes a **new claim** for the disability amount, attach a completed and certified Form T2201, Disability Tax Credit Certificate. Before assessing your return, the Canada Revenue Agency (CRA) will review your claim to see if your spouse or common-law partner is eligible for the disability tax credit. If your spouse or common-law partner **was eligible for 2018 and still meets the requirements in 2019**, you can claim this amount without sending the CRA a new Form T2201. However, you must send the CRA a new one if the previous period of approval ended before 2019 or if the CRA asks you to do this.

Note 2

The **maximum** tuition amount your spouse or common-law partner can transfer to you is **$5,000 minus** the current year amounts they use, even if there is still an unused part. Your spouse or common-law partner **cannot transfer** to you any tuition, education, or textbook amounts **carried forward from a previous year**.

Complete the provincial or territorial schedule (S2) to calculate your provincial or territorial amounts.

Transfer (or Carry Forward) Unused Tuition Credits

Tuition, education and textbook credits can be carried forward by a student indefinitely and can be used to offset their income when they start a job.

But these credits may also be transferred to spouse, parent or grandparent after they are maxed out to bring student's tax payable to zero. This means that if a student has excess credits, their family member could use the remaining credits to offset their income taxes. While this may hurt the student long-term, it may help their family member (who perhaps supported the student through school) in the short-term.

Deduct Your Student Loan Interest

Simple tip: student loan interest is deductible. So, if you have been paying interest on a student loan, ensure that you include the interest amount as a deduction when it comes time to preparing your tax return.

Deduct Out of Country Tuition Costs

Generally, tuition, education and textbook amounts, for those studying in a post-secondary institution in Canada, can be claimed as a deduction on line 32300 of your income tax and benefit return. For those studying out of country, the deduction is not as straight forward. Out of country tuition costs may only be deducted if certain eligibility requirements are met.

To receive the tuition tax credit, the educational institution must qualify in order to issue official tax receipts. The CRA has approved a number of institutions for this very purpose and maintains a list of "recognized universities and higher educational institutions outside Canada (excluding the United States, the United Kingdom and all of the Commonwealth countries) and a list of universities outside Canada registered as qualified donees for the purposes of the tuition tax credit." The lists should be referred to when determining if a foreign educational institution is approved to issue an official tax receipt.

For schools located in the United States, the United Kingdom, and the Commonwealth, the CRA asks that you refer to that country's list "of recognized universities and higher educational institutions."

The CRA places eligible schools into 3 categories:

1. Universities Outside of Canada (Form TL11A);

2. Commuter to the United States (Form TL11C); or
3. Educational Institutions Outside Canada for a Deemed Resident of Canada (Form TL11D).

Universities Outside Canada

For purposes of the tuition tax credit, the CRA considers an educational institution to be a "University Outside Canada" if it meets all of the following conditions:

- "it has the authority to confer academic degrees of at least the bachelor level (bachelor's degree or equivalent) according to the education standards of the country it is located in
- it has an academic entrance requirement of at least secondary school matriculation standing
- it is organized for teaching, study and research in the higher branches of learning"

For schools located in the Commonwealth, the institution must grant degrees of a bachelor level or greater. For the United States, the CRA accepts that schools that are recognized by the Council for Higher Educations Accreditation or Institute of Education Sciences National Center for Education Statistics is also considered to be a "University Outside Canada," provided that the school grants degrees of at minimum a bachelor level.

In no case may an educational institution that grants only associate degrees, certificates, diplomas or other degrees of a level below the bachelor equivalent be considered a University Outside Canada for tuition credit purposes. Similarly, the school does not qualify if the institution is merely affiliated with a university but in itself has no authority to confer degrees.

Commuter to the United States

Provided that you are a resident of Canada and commute to the United States on a regular basis for the purposes of taking courses at a qualified educational institution, such as a college, university or other institution that provides courses at a post-secondary school level, you should be able to claim your tuition fees.

Deemed Resident of Canada

Similarly, deemed residents of Canada, the qualified institution must be a college, university, or other institution that provides courses at a post-secondary school level.

Deemed residents are those that have not established significant residential ties with Canada, stay in Canada for 183 days or more in a calendar year, and are "not considered to be a resident in their home country under the terms of a tax treaty between Canada and that country."

It is important to note that in addition to the school qualifying to be eligible to issue official tax receipts, the specific course or program must still meet certain eligibility conditions in order to claim the tuition tax credit.

For instance, if attending school Outside of Canada, all of the following must occur:

1. you must be enrolled in full-time attendance;
2. for each course that is claimed the course must lead to a degree and last for 3 consecutive weeks (at minimum); and
3. the fees claimed must be eligible fees that have been paid for the calendar year indicated on Form TL11A.

For Commuters to the United States or Deemed Residents of Canada, the above conditions do not have to be met. There is no full-time requirement and the courses do not have to last for 3 consecutive weeks or more, however, the fees must be for $100 or more.

Forms for Students

One of the following tax forms has to be filled out and certified by a qualified foreign educational institution to support any claim for the Canadian tuition amount:

- TL11A, Tuition and Enrolment Certificate – University Outside Canada
- TL11C, Tuition and Enrolment Certificate – Commuter to the United States
- TL11D, Tuition Fees Certificate – Educational Institutions Outside Canada for a Deemed Resident of Canada

03 CHARITABLE CONTRIBUTIONS

What is the Deduction / Credit?

Section 118.1 of the Income Tax Act provides a non-refundable tax credit for charitable donations made to registered charities or other qualifying donees. The charitable donation credit is not unlimited, and restrictions do apply.

The amount claimed on gifts to qualified donees must be an eligible amount, to a limit of 75% of your net income, unless however the charitable gift is of "certified cultural property or ecologically sensitive land," which allows for a claim of up to 100% of your net income.

The credit may only be used to reduce taxes owing at the time of filing your income tax return; no refund will be received for those who do not owe any taxes.

The following are exceptions:

- If you are a resident of Quebec and are entitled to a refundable federal tax abatement, then your actual federal tax savings will be reduced.
- If you are required to pay provincial income surtax, then your actual saving will be more than the charitable tax credit calculated as the credit will reduce both your base income taxes and provincial surtax.
- If you made a donation of publicly traded securities, you may increase your tax saving by reducing your capital gains tax.

Once the donation amount is determined, the CRA's Charitable donation tax credit rates table is used to calculate the amount of the tax credit.

"There are two charitable tax credit rates for both the federal government and the provinces and territories. Any eligible amount you give above $200 qualifies you for a higher rate."

For taxation years after 2015, the first $200 of eligible donations is subject to a 15% credit and any amount thereafter is subject to a higher credit rate of between 29% and 33%. The highest tax credit rate of 33% corresponds with the personal tax bracket when an individual's income exceeds the top personal tax bracket.

How to Qualify

For a charitable donation to qualify as a tax credit, the gift to the organization must qualify as a charitable gift, the organization must be a registered charity or qualifying done, and the organization must issue an official donation receipt.

The types of gifts that qualify for the tax credit generally include voluntary donations of goods (such as personal use property like jewellery or paintings), inventory (such as art or antiques), cash, land, or listed securities. Not all gifts qualify as charitable donations; for instance, donations in the form of services, pledges (such as promises to make a gift) and the purchase of lottery tickets for the benefit of a charity do not qualify for the tax credit. Also, gifts cannot be made "as a result of a contractual or other obligation" and must be given freely.

If the donor receives an advantage in exchange for the donation, then part of or all of the gift will not qualify as a charitable donation. Where applicable, the charity may provide split receipting, whereby the eligible portion of the gift is determined based on subtracting the "fair market value (FMV) of the advantage from the FMV of the gift."

The donation must be made to a registered charity, as found in the CRA's List of charities ("the List") , or to a qualifying donee. A qualified donee is defined as an organization that may receive gifts from individuals, corporations and registered charities.

The CRA has published the following list of qualified donees :

- a registered charity (including a registered national arts service organization)
- a registered Canadian amateur athletic association
- a registered housing corporation resident in Canada constituted exclusively to provide low-cost housing for the aged
- a registered Canadian municipality
- a registered municipal or public body performing a function of government in Canada
- a registered university outside Canada, the student body of which ordinarily includes students from Canada
- a registered charitable organization outside Canada to which Her Majesty in right of Canada has made a gift
- Her Majesty in right of Canada, a province, or a territory
- the United Nations and its agencies

Note that "Her Majesty in right of Canada, a province, or a territory, and the United Nations and its agencies are qualified donees that do not have to be registered to be recognized as such."

At the time of claiming a charitable credit, one may include donations made up until December 31st of the applicable taxation year, as well as any donations that have previously been unclaimed by yourself or your spouse or common law partner during the prior five taxation years.

Supporting Documents needed (if applicable)

Official donation tax receipts must be included with your income tax return in the taxation year for which they are claimed.

Tips

If unsure if a charity is registered, it is recommended to verify that the charity is registered by referring to the List. The List is updated every business day by the CRA.

"The public can use this list to:

- confirm whether a Canadian charity is registered, revoked, annulled, penalized, or suspended (to help guide your donation decisions)
- view a charity's contact information, general activities, and financial information, including the public portions of a charity's annual information return

Charities can use this list to:

- confirm their registration
- review their contact information
- review the information filed on their annual returns to ensure it is accurate

You can ask the charity for its registration number and confirm its status in the List of charities . You can also call the Charities Directorate at 1-800-267-2384."

To determine the calculation for your charitable donation tax credit, the CRA provides a tool for donations made after 2015. The Charitable donation tax credit calculator tool may be used to calculate federal and provincial or territorial tax credits. It can be found by vising: https://www.canada.ca/en/revenue-agency/services/charities-giving/giving-charity-information-donors/claiming-charitable-tax-credits/calculate-charitable-tax-credits/calculator.html

It is always wise to beware of donation schemes and fraud when making charitable donations. The charity should always be registered, however, even with registered charities there are often issues of fraud. Red flags include a promise of receiving a tax receipt greater than the donation amount, pressure to donate immediately, overly friendly and eager canvassers, and requests to provide cash as opposed to cheques or credit cards. The CRA provides a list of warning signs that should be read prior to making large donations.

The CRA's client service representatives can be contacted directly to assist with information on registered charities, as well as other useful information such as how a charity should issue official donation receipts.

Resources

Income Tax Act, R.S.C. 1985 (5th supp.) c. 1, para. 110.1(1)(a), ss. 118.1(1) and 149.1(1) and 149.1(6.4), 188.1(5)

The Charities Directorate

CRA's client services can be contacted by phone at: 1-800-267-2384 or by TTY service for people with a hearing or speech impairment:1-800-665-0354, https://www.canada.ca/en/revenue-agency/services/charities-giving/charities/contact-charities-directorate.html

Other useful CRA resources include:

- "Claiming charitable tax credits," Date modified: February 24, 2020, https://www.canada.ca/en/revenue-agency/services/charities-giving/giving-charity-information-donors/claiming-charitable-tax-credits.html
- "List of Charities - basic search," Version May 8, 2019, https://apps.cra-arc.gc.ca/ebci/hacc/srch/pub/dsplyBscSrch?request_locale=en
- "Charitable donation tax credit calculator," Date modified: January 15, 2019, https://www.canada.ca/en/revenue-agency/services/charities-giving/giving-charity-information-donors/claiming-charitable-tax-credits/calculate-charitable-tax-credits/calculator.html
- "Charitable donation tax credit rates," Date modified: January 24, 2017, https://www.canada.ca/en/revenue-agency/services/charities-giving/giving-charity-information-donors/claiming-charitable-tax-credits/charitable-donation-tax-credit-rates.html
- CG-010, "Qualified donees", August 15, 2011, https://www.canada.ca/en/revenue-agency/services/charities-giving/charities/policies-guidance/qualified-donees.html

- "How can I donate wisely and avoid fraud?," Date modified: April 27, 2017, https://www.canada.ca/en/revenue-agency/services/charities-giving/giving-charity-information-donors/making-a-donation/donate-wisely-avoid-fraud.html
- Income Tax Folio S7-F1-C1, Split-receipting and Deemed Fair Market Value, Date modified: April 20, 2017, https://www.canada.ca/en/revenue-agency/services/tax/technical-information/income-tax/income-tax-folios-index/series-7-charities-non-profit-organizations/series/income-tax-folio-s7-f1-c1-split-receipting-deemed-fair-market-value.html

---

[1] CRA document, "Disability tax credit (DTC)", Date modified: January 21, 2020, https://www.canada.ca/en/revenue-agency/services/tax/individuals/segments/tax-credits-deductions persons-disabilities/disability-tax-credit.html#cmplt

[2] The Canada caregiver credit may also be claimed in certain instances to assist the caregiver with expenses incurred in caring for their spouse, common-law partner or dependant who has an physical or mental functions impairment. See CRA Guide RC4064(E) Rev. 19, "Tax measures for persons with disabilities,

[3] "Canada's COVID-19 Economic Response Plan", Date modified: July 3, 2020, https://www.canada.ca/en/department-finance/economic-response-plan.html

[4] Income Tax Folio S1-F1-C2, Disability Tax Credit
CRA document, at 2.2, "Eligibility for the credit", Date modified: July 19, 2016, https://www.canada.ca/en/revenue-agency/services/tax/technical-information/income-tax/income-tax-folios-index/series-1-individuals/folio-1-health-medical/income-tax-folio-s1-f1-c2-disability-tax-credit.html#N101E8

[5] Id at 2.4, "Prolonged impairment." Income Tax Folio S1-F1-C2, Disability Tax Credit

[6] CRA document, "Eligibility criteria for the disability tax credit," Date modified: January 21, 2020, https://www.canada.ca/en/revenue-agency/services/tax/individuals/segments/tax-credits-deductions-persons-disabilities/information-medical-practitioners/eligibility-criteria-disability-tax-credit.html

[7] Supra note 1

[8] Supra note 5

[9] Supra note 3 at 2.5 through 2.7

[10] Id. at 2.8 and 2.9

[11] Supra note 3 at 2.2

[12] It is a question of fact whether an activity takes an inordinate amount of time. Generally this would be considered 3x the time of that of an individual without the disability.

[13] Supra note 3 at 2.13

[14] Supra note 5

[15] Supra note 3 at 2.2

[16] Supra note 2

[17] CRA Form T2201 E (17), "Disability Tax Credit Certificate," https://www.canada.ca/content/dam/cra-arc/formspubs/pbg/t2201/t2201-18e.pdf

[18] Line 45110 – Climate action incentive, January 21, 2020, https://www.canada.ca/en/revenue-agency/services/tax/individuals/topics/about-your-tax-return/tax-return/completing-a-tax-return/deductions-credits-expenses/line-45110-climate-action-incentive.html

[19] Id.

[20] Id.

[21] "Recognized educational institutions outside Canada," Feb 25, 2020, https://www.canada.ca/en/revenue-agency/services/tax/individuals/topics/about-your-tax-return/tax-return/completing-a-tax-return/deductions-credits-expenses/line-32300-your-tuition-education-textbook-amounts/recognized-educational-institutions-outside-canada.html

[22] CRA Publication: "Information for Students – Educational Institutions outside Canada," RC 192(E) Rev. 20, November 19, 2020, https://www.canada.ca/en/revenue-agency/services/forms-publications/publications/rc192/information-students-educational-institutions-outside-canada.htmls

[23] Id.

[24] CRA, RC192 (E) Rev 19, "Information for Students – Educational Institutions outside Canada," 2020-02-25, https://www.canada.ca/en/revenue-agency/services/forms-publications/publications/rc192/information-students-educational-institutions-outside-canada.html

[25] CRA document, "How do I calculate my charitable tax credits?," Date modified June 27, 2016, https://www.canada.ca/en/revenue-agency/services/charities-giving/giving-charity-information-donors/claiming-charitable-tax-credits/calculate-charitable-tax-credits.html

[26] Ibid.

[27] CRA document, "Charitable donation tax credit rates," Date modified: January 24, 2017, https://www.canada.ca/en/revenue-agency/services/charities-giving/giving-charity-information-donors/claiming-charitable-tax-credits/charitable-donation-tax-credit-rates.html

[28] Supra note 1.

[29] CRA document, "What is a gift?," Date modified: November 16, 2016, https://www.canada.ca/en/revenue-agency/services/charities-giving/charities/operating-a-registered-charity/receiving-gifts/what-a-gift.html

[30] CRA document, "Split receipting," Date modified: May 22, 2018, https://www.canada.ca/en/revenue-agency/services/charities-giving/charities/operating-a-registered-charity/issuing-receipts/split-receipting.html

[31] CRA resource, "List of Charities - basic search," Version May 8, 2019, https://apps.cra-arc.gc.ca/ebci/hacc/srch/pub/dsplyBscSrch?request_locale=en

[32] CRA document reference number CG-010, "Qualified donees", August 15, 2011, https://www.canada.ca/en/revenue-agency/services/charities-giving/charities/policies-guidance/qualified-donees.html

[33] Id.

[34] Supra note 7.

[35] Id.

[36] CRA document, "How can I donate wisely and avoid fraud?," Date modified: April 27, 2017, https://www.canada.ca/en/revenue-agency/services/charities-giving/giving-charity-information-donors/making-a-donation/donate-wisely-avoid-fraud.html

[37] CRA's client services can be contacted by phone at: 1-800-267-2384 or by TTY service for people with a hearing or speech impairment:1-800-665-0354, https://www.canada.ca/en/revenue-agency/services/charities-giving/charities/contact-charities-directorate.html

04 PROVINCIAL AND TERRITORIAL TAX CREDITS

Provincial and Territorial credits are similar to their federal counterparts, however, instead of using the credit to offset your federal taxes payable, these credits are used to offset your Provincial / Territorial taxes instead.

Most Provincial governments have all of the same credits that are offered by the Federal government, however, the exact percentages, or entitlement amounts may be different.

Some provinces do offer their own unique tax credits that may not have a Federal counterpart. For example, Manitoba has a separate medical expense credit solely for individuals who incurred fertility treatment expenses.

How to Qualify

Depending on what province or territory you resided in for tax purposes in any given year, you will automatically qualify for these credits, and simply just need to

Supporting Documents needed

At the time of filing your return, you will not need to provide any supporting documents; however, if your return is subject to a review, then you may need to provide documents to show you incurred a certain expense.

Tips

Besides the basis credits that mirror the Federal tax credits, also take a look at your respective provinces or territory's unique tax credits so you make sure that you are getting all available credits.

Resources

A valuable link, which outlines all provinces and territories, and their respective credits can be found here:

https://www.canada.ca/en/revenue-agency/services/tax/individuals/topics/about-your-tax-return/tax-return/completing-a-tax-return/provincial-territorial-tax-credits-individuals.html

05 BUSINESS / SELF-EMPLOYMENT DEDUCTIONS (EXPENSES)

If you have a business or are self-employed, this section is of particular importance to you. In order to pay the least amount of tax possible it is important to take advantage of all the deductions available to you.

If you don't have any kind of business, you may want to consider starting some kind of a side hustle (See next section).

Business Deductions (Expenses)

Generally, all businesses can deduct from their income those expenses that are incurred not only to make the business operational, but also to maintain that business once it is up and running.

The important thing is that the expenses must be incurred to earn the business income and they must be reasonable under the circumstances

The CRA has a list of the common business expenses that you can deduct from the gross business income in order to arrive at the business's taxable income.

Advertising: You can deduct expenses for advertising, including advertising on Canadian radio and television stations and in Canadian newspapers. Digital advertising is also tax deductible.

Allowance on eligible capital property: As of January 1, 2017, you can no longer claim this allowance. Property that formerly would have been eligible capital property is now considered depreciable property under capital cost allowance Class 14.1.

Bed Debt: You could deduct an account receivable that won't get paid if you had already included it as income for the year.

Business start-up costs: You can deduct expenses that preceded the operation of the business. However, you can only claim expenses if you operated the business in the fiscal period in which the expense was incurred.

Business tax, fees, licences and dues: Tax, fees, licences and dues are deductible, but you can't deduct club membership dues including initiation fees if the main purpose of the club is dining, recreation, or sporting activities.

Delivery, freight, and express: The cost of delivery, freight, and express is deductible.

Non-Motor Vehicle Fuel Costs: Gasoline, diesel, propane, motor oil, and lubricants are deductible.

Insurance: You can deduct all ordinary commercial insurance premiums you incur on any buildings, machinery, and equipment you use in your business. Insurance costs related to your motor vehicle must be claimed as motor vehicle expenses.

Interest and bank charges: You can deduct interest incurred on money borrowed for business purposes or to acquire property for business purposes.

- **Fees, penalties, or bonuses paid for a loan:** You can also deduct any fees paid to reduce the interest rate on a loan and any penalty charged by your lender to pay off a loan before it is due.
- **Fees deductible over five years:** When obtaining a loan to buy or improve your business property, fees such as application, appraisal, loan guarantee, brokerage, and legal fees relating to financing are deductible. These fees are deducted over a period of five years.
- **Fees deducted in the year incurred:** Standby charges, guarantee fees, and service fees are deductible.
- **Interest deductible on property no longer used for business purposes:** Interest expenses for property once used for business purposes but are no longer using because the business ceased to operate may be deductible.
- **Interest Loans made against insurance policies:** Interest you paid on a loan made against an insurance policy is deductible under certain conditions.
- **Capitalizing interest:** Capitalized interest on money you borrow to either buy a depreciable property, buy a resource property, or for exploration and development is available to you.
- **Interest related to workspace in your home:** This can be claimed as business-use-of-home expenses.

Legal, accounting, and other professional fees: Fees incurred for professional advice, consulting, accounting and legal advice and help with keeping records, the preparation of income tax and GST/HST returns are deductible. Legal and accounting fees incurred to have an objection or appeal prepared against an assessment are also deductible.

Maintenance and repairs: The cost of labour and materials to maintain or complete minor repairs done to your property used to earn business income is deductible.

Management and administration fees: You can deduct management and administration fees, including bank charges incurred to operate your business. Bank charges include those for processing payments.

Meals and entertainment (allowable part): You can deduct 50% of the lesser amount incurred for this expense and only an amount that is reasonable. Food, beverages, and entertainment expenses such as tickets, entrance fees, room rentals, and gratuities are deductible.

- **Long-haul truck drivers:** You can deduct 80% of food and beverage expense incurred during eligible travel. Eligible travel is a period of 24 hours or more outside your residential area beyond a radius of 160 kilometres.
- **Extra food and beverages consumed by self-employed:** The cost of extra food and beverages consumed in an 8-hour workday by bicycle couriers, rickshaw driver, or workers on foot is deductible at a flat rate of $17.50 per day. A daily logbook should be maintained.

Motor Vehicle Expense: You can deduct motor vehicle expenses. To ensure no issues with the claim, you should maintain an accurate logbook of business travel for the entire year. The logbook should show each business trip, the destination and reason for the trip, and the distance travelled. Vehicle related expenses such as licensing, fuel, insurance, interest on vehicle loans, leasing costs, and maintenance/repairs are all valid expenses.

Office Expenses: You can deduct the cost of small items such as pencils, pens, stamps, paperclips, and stationery. Do not include desks, chairs, filing cabinets and calculators because they are capital items.

Prepaid Expense: Any expense you pay ahead of time is a deductible expense. Certain distinctions and rules apply depending on whether you're using the accrual method of accounting or the cash method.

Property Taxes: Property taxes incurred for property used in your business are deductible. Property tax related to a home office has to be claimed as business-use-of-home expenses.

Rent: You can deduct rent paid for property used in your business. For example, you can deduct rent for the land and building where your business is situated.

Salaries, wages, benefits: You can deduct gross salaries and other benefits, such as Canada Pension Plan and Employment Insurance premiums, you pay to employees.

Supplies: You can deduct the cost of items that your business used indirectly to provide goods or services. For example, drugs and medication used in a veterinary operation, or cleaning supplies used by a plumber.

Telephone and Utilities: You can deduct expenses for telephone and utilities such as gas, oil, electricity, water and cable, if you incurred the expenses to earn income.

Travel: You can deduct travel expenses such as public transportation, hotel, and meals incurred to earn business income. In most cases, the 50% limit applies to the cost of meals, beverages, and entertainment when you travel.

Other Business Expenses: Aside from the general and most common expenses listed above, there are other business expenses you might incur to earn income. These expenses are also deductible. Examples include disability-related modifications, equipment leasing costs, and private health service plans. These and other expenses incurred to earn income which do not fall into a specific category may be claimed as an "other expense".

For more information on the allowable business expenses, visit: https://www.canada.ca/en/revenue-agency/services/tax/businesses/topics/sole-proprietorships-partnerships/business-expenses.html

Supporting Documents Needed

All receipts, invoices, logbooks, and relevant documentation pertaining to any expense being claimed should be properly itemized, sorted, and maintained.

Do not send any supporting documents to the CRA unless requested of you. Keep your receipts at least for six years because they will be needed if there is an audit.

Tips

All claimed expenses must be supported by the original receipt, invoice, or other document. Credit and Debit card statements may not be sufficient to support a claim.

There is a lot that you can claim. It's about proportion and being reasonable You cannot deduct the clothing that you wear unless it is specialized work clothing such as a protective helmet for welding or PPE for a medical worker. The rule of thumb is that any clothing that you could wear outside of work (including steel-toed boots) cannot be deducted. These items are deemed to be personal expenses which are not deductible.

Resources

For more information, see "Business Expenses" by visiting https://www.canada.ca/en/revenue-agency/services/tax/businesses/topics/sole-proprietorships-partnerships/business-expenses.html#officeexpenses

Turn a Hobby into a Side Hustle

Having a side hustle can be awesome – especially if it allows you to do something you enjoy at the same time. You get to make a few extra bucks, but at the same time if you can also have fun and use the side hustle to help write off some expenses which you already had, that is even better. So, I always recommend that people look at their hobbies when considering a side hustle. If your hobby is 3D printing, you can start a 3D printing house in your part time and write off expenses related to the 3D printer, filament, and home office expenses, etc. Perhaps you love cooking, and your side hustle is a small catering business. The added benefit to you is that you can deduct all the expenses for the business and at the same time you can use the equipment and the leftovers for your personal use.

For more information about starting a business, read my book "A Quick and Dirty Business Start-Up Guide: From the Perspective of a Tax Lawyer and Serial Entrepreneur." It's available on Amazon: https://www.amazon.ca/Quick-Dirty-Business-Start-Up-Guide/dp/0986755907

Start a Corporation for Your Side Hustle

There are many good reasons to start a corporation for your side hustle. For one, a corporation protects you from liability in many circumstances. Generally, people cannot sue the owner of the corporation for something the corporation may have done. They sue the corporation itself. And probably my favourite reason to start a corporation is for tax reasons.

In cases where the side-hustle is providing you with surplus money that you are not spending on a monthly basis, it is advantageous to earn this money in a corporation.

The reason is that money earned by a corporation and kept in a corporation will be subject to lower taxes than if this same income were earned by an individual taxpayer. That means that in the short-term, there is less income tax being paid by income earned in a corporation, and the difference between the personal tax which would have been paid and the corporate tax which was paid is available for the corporation to use. See the following example:

EXAMPLE

Assume: $50,000 surplus side hustle income
Assume: Personal income tax rate is 50%
Assume: Corporate income tax rate is 15%

Scenario A: All the income is earned by the individual personally

Earnings = $50,000
Tax = $25,000
Remaining = $25,000 after tax

Scenario B: All the income is earned by the corporation

Earnings = $50,000
Tax = $ 7,500
Remaining. = $43,000

In Scenario B, $7,500 is paid in taxes immediately, versus Scenario A where $25,000 is paid. This means that in Scenario B where the income is earned by the corporation there is an immediate tax differential of $17,500. And instead of paying this $17,500 to the CRA immediately, a corporation could use this money to invest or to grow.

When a Corporation Doesn't Fit the Bill, Consider a Partnership Under Certain Circumstances

If two or more people form a business and start operating without having taken any steps to form an incorporation, whether or not they know it, they have formed a "partnership". While the sole proprietorship is the default business structure for an unincorporated individual, a partnership is the default business structure when multiple people work together with the intention of earning profit from a business.

Sharing many of the same characteristics of the sole proprietorship, the partnership is quick to start, it is low cost to maintain, and there is no legal distinction between the business and the people behind the scene. However, is one certain different characteristic of a partnership which needs to be explored very carefully. A particularly concerning pitfall of a partnership is that each partner may bind the partnership. That is to say that each partner may buy, hire, and perform transactions on behalf of the partnership. And if the partnership cannot satisfy the liabilities, the partners will find that they are jointly and severally liable for debts of the partnership.

Another matter of concern is that unless there is a partnership agreement which provides otherwise, general partnership between two parties end when one of the partners dies or otherwise leaves the business. Similarly, without an agreement that provides otherwise, when there are more than two partners, the death of one partner does not necessarily end the partnership, but it can leave the deceased partner without an interest to pass on to a surviving spouse.

General Partnerships

A General Partnership is formed when two or more people or companies get together to generate income. Sometimes this type of partnership is called a joint venture.

One of the benefits to a general partnership over a corporation is that it allows different people / entities who are in different tax brackets to work together without having to split post-tax income. If multiple people owned shares of a corporation and worked together, they would end up splitting income which was already taxed at the corporate level.

EXAMPLE

Let's assume that a corporation pays 20% tax. If $100,000 were earned by the corporation which was owned by two partners, the corporation would end up paying $20,000 tax, and each of the two partners would end up splitting the $80,000 which remained – each getting $40,000 which would be taxed at their own tax rate.

In the case of a general partnership, the $100,000 profit would be split equally between the partners. Each would get $50,000 which would in turn be taxed at their own tax rate. There would be no additional tax payable at the partnership level and the tax savings could be passed onto the partners.

Additionally, a general partnership structure allows people to team up with family members so that one can split income with lower income family members and in turn pay less tax. And the greater the difference between the two tax brackets, the more there is to gain.

EXAMPLE

If one were in a 50% tax bracket and they were to engage in a project on their own and earn $100,000, they would in turn pay $50,000 tax and be left with $50,000.

But: If they entered into a general partnership with their spouse who is in a 25% income tax bracket, and who actually contributed time and effort to the project, the results would be different.

The $100,000 would be split between them. The first spouse would get $50,000 less 50% of tax and be left with $25,000. The second spouse would also get $50,000 which would be taxed at their rate of 25% and they would be left with $37,500.

Between the two of them they would end up with $62,500 – a savings of $12,500 in taxes.

Limited Partnerships

A limited partnership is almost identical to a general partnership except that in a limited partnership there is one "general partner" responsible for the liabilities of the partnership and one or more "limited partners" with limited liability and limited control and decision-making capabilities. Unlike a general partnership, a limited partnership requires formal registration.

Often times a Limited Partnership is established to manage real estate. The general partner generally takes care of the day-to-day activities including collecting rent, managing and maintaining the real estate, and taking care of the books. The limited partners are often simply investors who contribute to the capital required to purchase the property and who simply want to make an investment in real estate.

Taxation of Partnerships

Since a partnership is not a legal entity, similar to the taxation of sole proprietorships, each partner will declare its own share of its income on their own T1 return if the partner is an individual or on their own T2 return if the partner is a corporation. So, in essence all the downfalls of the taxation of sole proprietorships are carried over for any partner who is operating as an individual. However, for certain partners who are non-profits or charities, it is beneficial to be a member of a partnership as no taxes are payable to the CRA "upstream" from them. So, they get to keep all of their share of the profits – tax free.

Pay Wages to Your Family Members from the Business

For Canadian business owners, paying a reasonable salary to children or a spouse is a means of legally splitting income and moving it from a high-income tax bracket to a low-income tax bracket. This increases the after-tax income of the entire family.

EXAMPLE

Consider a parent of two teenagers who is in the 53% tax bracket.

Their tax on $20,000 of their income would be $10,600. After tax this $20,000 would become $9,400.

If they were to employ their two teenagers in a part-time job and pay them $10,000 each, assuming the teenagers had no other income, the teenagers would not pay any tax at all. They would each keep the $10,000.

In this scenario there would be a total of $10,600 tax savings which could be used to pay for the teenagers' sporting activities, summer camps, or any other expenses.

But be careful! There are TOSI (Tax On Split Income) rules which make it difficult to split income with family members. These rules can be very punitive. So, if you are doing anything other than paying a reasonable salary to children or a spouse it is best to consult a professional. For more information on TOSI, read the section on Attribution and TOSI later on in Part 16.

So, as long as the amounts paid to your spouse and children are "reasonable" according to s. 67 of the Income Tax Act, you should be ok. And to determine what is reasonable, simply consider what you would pay a stranger to do the same job. If you would give a stranger $20 per hour to do certain work, then there is no reason why you can't pay that amount to your family member. And if a job would normally be a $20 per hour job, you can bet that you are on the wrong side of the law if you pay your family member $50 an hour to do the same job. In the case of an audit the expense may be deemed to be unreasonable and it may be denied and cost you extra tax.

Business Use of a Vehicle

The reality is that most small businesses, and certainly almost all sole proprietorships use a vehicle which is also used for personal purposes. Auditors know that people cannot generally substantiate the vehicle expenses that they have claimed. Many small businesses just pick a number – say 50% or 20%. You know this and the auditors know this.

It is perfectly fine to use a vehicle for dual purposes, but in order to make it through an audit it will be important to be able to distinguish the business use vs. the personal use.

What all auditors look for is a vehicle log. Plain and simple. If you have the vehicle log and it adds up, the auditor will allow your vehicle expenses. Otherwise expect that they will give you a hard time. A vehicle log is simple to keep. Throughout the year you will record each business trip in the vehicle log: where you went, starting odometer reading and ending odometer reading. You also need to take an odometer reading at the beginning and at the end of the year. Once all the business kms are added up, you determine the percentage of vehicle use which was for business purposes (e.g.: 15,000 km business / 20,000 km total = 75% business use).

As a sole proprietor you can claim the business percentage of auto expenses as an expense.

EXAMPLE

Odometer reading at beginning of month:	5,000 km
Odometer reading at end of the month:	7,500 km
Total of all the business trips taken during month	1,000 km
Total km driven in the month:	7,500–5,000= 2,500
Total business kms	1000
Business use of the vehicle	1,000 / 2,500 = .4

So, the vehicle was used 40% for business purposes during the month and 40% of the vehicle expenses could be used as a business deduction.

If you operate a corporation, you could have the corporation reimburse you for its share of the use of the vehicle expenses (lease cost, fuel, maintenance, insurance). This reimbursement is not taxable if it reflects the actual cost. In turn, the amount of the reimbursement to you becomes an expense to the corporation.

Meals and Entertainment

Meals and entertainment are another prime target on the CRA's list of items to be examined because of the frequent abuse in this area. Virtually every small business owner I have ever dealt with has written off an extra dinner here and there or a pair of tickets to the game or a concert which were actually used personally. This is normal. Not legal, but normal. Some business owners take this to an extreme level and attempt to expense a huge number of meals, and tickets. This is low-hanging fruit as far as the auditor is concerned.

When the auditor approaches these expenses, they want to see the original receipts as well as documentation for every single meal or ticket purchased to show the name of the client and what the purpose of the expense was. If the taxpayer cannot produce this information during the audit, the auditor is happy to reassess and disallow expenses.

Taxpayers also need to remember that only 50 percent of a restaurant receipt may be expensed (you can expense their meal, but not yours). These rules are different, however, when taxpayers have to travel for business.

Business Use of the Home

If you are claiming a home office expense:
Remember to keep records. This is an area which is highly audited.

The rule is that if your T2200 indicates that you are required to have a home office, you can claim a percentage of your carrying costs for your home. And the percentage that you can claim is related to percentage of your home used for business purposes. So, if you have a 1000 sq foot home and you use 110 sq ft room for your home office then you can claim 11% of your carrying costs. In the case of a rental home, you can claim 11% of your rent, heat and power. If you own your home you could claim 11% of your mortgage interest, property tax, heat and power. It is best not to claim 11% of your gardening expenses and swimming pool maintenance, etc. as well as other questionable items which are likely to be denied in the case of an audit.

Taxpayers routinely get into trouble with the CRA in respect of home office expenses. Most times people don't bother to take actual measurements to determine the percentage of the home used for business purposes. Oftentimes people just "eyeball it" or inflate the actual square footage (or percentage) or they arrive at the figure using absurd logic. I once had a client claim their entire basement (1/2 of the square footage of his house) when its only business use was to store about a dozen banker's boxes of old files. The CRA auditors see through this during an audit and unless the taxpayer can support their claim, they can expect the auditor to deny expenses.

To satisfy the auditor, one needs to show their actual expenses (e.g., property tax bills, mortgage statements, and electricity bills), plus demonstrate the percentage of the home being used for business purposes. Not a crazy percentage, but the real percentage. And in case taxpayers move and are not able to show their home office to the auditor, it is important to document the home office with photos and floor plans.

Union / Professional Dues

An overlooked and often forgotten income tax deduction is payments made during the year for annual union and professional dues. The deductions available include:

- annual dues for membership in a trade union or an association of public servants;
- professional board dues required under provincial or territorial law;
- professional or malpractice liability insurance premiums or professional membership dues required to keep a professional status recognized by law; and
- parity or advisory committee (or similar body) dues required under provincial or territorial law.

There are, of course, limitations on the kinds of expenses which may be claimed and the circumstances in which a taxpayer is entitled to claim those expenses. The most important such restriction is that amounts paid must be those which are necessary in order for the taxpayer to obtain or maintain his or her professional standing.

The cost of maintaining membership in voluntary associations, even if related to one's trade or profession, is not deductible.

06 EMPLOYMENT EXPENSES

Make Sure You Have a T2200 Form

In order to claim employment expenses (those expenses which you had to pay for as a part of doing your job), you require a T2200 form from your employer – See the sample form reproduced below.

And if you are required to pay for certain expenses in order to do your job – other than the normal costs of buying clothes shoes and getting to work – you may be able to claim deductions for these “employment expenses” which will cause a reduction in your taxable income and which will in turn reduce your tax bill.

Expenses such as tools, home office, cell phone, vehicle, and the costs of an assistant are all things which can be deducted if your employer designates them as employment expenses on the T2200.

Article:

So You’re Working from Home: Deduct Expenses and Pay Less Tax

By Dale Barrett
Published on the Lawyer’s Daily: Aug 17, 2020

Almost all of us have been working from home during the Covid-19 pandemic and many of us will continue to work from home for some time to come. Google just announced that it is going to have its employees to work from home for at least the next year, and personally I have no immediate plans to bring all my employees back to my office. I may decide to have some employees work from home forever.

If you are working from home, and even if you have just worked from home for a period of time and have since returned to your place of employment, you will want to take advantage of all the possible ways in which you can reduce your taxes.

If you are an employee

Just because you are an employee of a company does not mean that you do not have the opportunity to reduce your taxes by working from home. Au contraire my friend. In fact, as an employee who is required to work from their home you may be entitled to claim a number of deductions in respect of working from home.

But before we go into the deductions you would be entitled to claim, we first need to ensure you are in fact able to claim the deductions at all.

Not all employees can claim deductions in respect of "Employment Expenses." This privilege is reserved for those who have a T2200 form, otherwise known as a "Declaration of Conditions of Employment" form, completed and executed by their employer.

What is this T2200 form you ask? Good question.

If an employer requires an employee to pay for certain expenses while carrying out the duties of employment, then the T2200 form outlines which expenses an employee is required to pay for and whether (and how much) reimbursement is provided. Once completed and signed by the employer an employee can deduct from their income, the expenses outlined by the employer – which of course are subject to any reimbursements or allowances which the employee has received in respect of these expenses.

These deductible expenses may include travel expenses, vehicle expenses, office rental, assistants' wages, costs for supplies used directly in your work, cell phone, internet, phone line, home office costs, and any other expenses for which you did not receive an allowance or reimbursement.

So, as you can see, the sky is the limit in terms of how working from home can save you tax dollars.

For example, if you normally have an assistant at work who helps you accomplish your daily tasks, and if you have been deprived of the assistant due to working from home, you may be able to hire your otherwise unemployed spouse as your assistant. You can do the same with your kids. The first $10,783 (Ontario 2020) of their income will be tax free in their hands if they have no other income, and this will reduce your overall tax. The more you pay your spouse and your kids, and the higher your tax bracket, the more tax you can save. But you must pay a reasonable amount for the work done (i.e., the same that you would have paid somebody who is not your spouse). And the work done has to be legit.

If you are claiming home office expenses remember to keep records. This is an area that is highly audited.

The rule is that if your T2200 indicates that you are required to have a home office, you can claim a percentage of your carrying costs for your home. And the percentage that you can claim is related to percentage of your home used for business purposes.

So, if you have a 1,000-square-foot home and you use a 110-square-foot room for your home office, then you can claim 11 per cent of your carrying costs. In the case of a rental home, you can claim 11 per cent of your rent, heat, power and insurance. If you own your home you could claim 11 per cent of your heat, power and insurance.

While there are many items that you can claim and justify in the case of an audit, it is best not to claim 11 per cent of your gardening expenses and swimming pool maintenance, etc. as well as other questionable items that are likely to be denied by an auditor.

Taxpayers routinely get into trouble with the Canada Revenue Agency (CRA) with respect to home office expenses. Most times people don't bother to take actual measurements to determine the percentage of the home used for business purposes. Often people just "eyeball it" or inflate the actual square footage (or percentage) or they arrive at the figure using absurd logic.

I once had a client claim their entire basement (half of the square footage of his house) when its only business use was to store about a dozen banker's boxes of old files. The CRA auditors see through this during an audit and unless the taxpayer can support their claim, they can expect the auditor to deny expenses.

To satisfy the auditor, one needs to show their actual expenses (e.g., property tax bills, mortgage statements and electricity bills), plus demonstrate the percentage of the home being used for business purposes. Not a crazy percentage, but the real percentage. And in case taxpayers move and are not able to show their home office to the auditor, it is important to document the home office with photos and floor plans.

Conclusion

Since you are working from home anyway, you might as well take advantage of your options. Claim everything you possibly can (and should) and if you are an employee, get a T2200 form in order to be eligible to claim deductions. Regardless who you are, be well organized and keep all your backup documents in case you are ever audited. While taxpayers are only typically audited up to three or four years in the past, you must keep your records for six years from the end of the calendar year to which the documents relate.

And in the worst-case scenario where an auditor denies some or all of your expenses, you have 90 days from the date of reassessment to challenge the outcome of the audit.

Make Sure You Take Reimbursements and Allowances into Consideration

But be careful. The T2200 also has a place for employers to record any reimbursements and allowances which you were provided in respect of your employment expenses. If you received reimbursements, you may not be able to claim all your employment expenses.

So, if you were provided a reimbursement or an allowance, just remember to subtract that amount from your total expense.

According to the CRA, vehicle allowances are taxable unless they are based on a reasonable per km rate, which in 2020 is 59¢ per kilometre for the first 5,000 kilometres driven and $53¢ for the remainder. So, you can receive this amount per km from your employer without being taxed. But if you receive in excess of this reasonable rate, then you will have to declare the allowance as part of your income. But you will be able to deduct the vehicle expenses.

EXAMPLE

Vehicle employment expenses = $2,000
Vehicle allowance = $5,000

Since you received a larger allowance than your actual cost, the allowance is not at the "reasonable rate" and thus is taxable. But you can deduct your expenses.

So: You will have $5,000 of income and $2,000 of expenses which you can deduct, and thus you will pay taxes on $3,000.

EXAMPLE

Vehicle employment expenses = $4,000
Vehicle allowance = $1,000

Since you received a smaller allowance than your actual cost, the allowance is at the "reasonable rate" and thus is not taxable if you don't want to make a claim to deduct your expenses.

So, if you do want to deduct your expenses (which you should): You will have $1,000 of income and $4,000 of expenses which you can deduct. And thus, you will have a total of $3000 of expenses which you can claim on your tax return as "employment expenses."

Canada Revenue Agency / Agence du revenu du Canada

Declaration of Conditions of Employment

Protected B when completed

The **employer** must complete this form for the employee to deduct employment expenses from their income.

The **employee** does not have to file this form with their return, but must keep it in case we ask to see it. For details about claiming employment expenses, see Guide T4044, Employment Expenses, or interpretation bulletins IT-352, Employee's Expenses, Including Work Space in Home Expenses, and IT-522, Vehicle, Travel and Sales Expenses of Employees.

Part A – Employee information (please print)

Last name	First name	Tax year	Social insurance number
Home address	Business address		
Job title and brief description of duties			

Part B – Conditions of employment

1. Did this employee's contract require them to pay their own expenses while carrying out the duties of employment? ☐ Yes ☐ No

   Answer "**yes**" even if you provide an allowance or a reimbursement in respect of some or all such expenses.

   If **no**, the employee is **not** entitled to claim employment expenses, and **you are not required to answer any of the other questions**.

2. Did you normally require this employee to travel to locations that were not your place of business or between different locations of your places of business, during the course of performing their employment duties? ☐ Yes ☐ No

   If **yes**, what was the employee's area of travel (be specific)? ____________________

3. Did you require this employee to be away for at least 12 **consecutive** hours from the municipality and metropolitan area (if there is one) of your business where the employee normally reported for work? ☐ Yes ☐ No

   If **yes**, how frequently? ____________________

4. Indicate the period(s) of employment during the year: From Year Month Day to Year Month Day

   If there was a break in employment, specify dates: ____________________

5. Did this employee receive or were they entitled to receive a motor vehicle allowance? ☐ Yes ☐ No

   If **yes**, indicate:

   - the amount received as a fixed allowance, such as a flat monthly allowance $__________
   - the per km rate used ________ ($/km), and the amount received $__________
   - the amount of the allowance that was included on the employee's T4 slip $__________

   Did this employee have the use of a company vehicle? ☐ Yes ☐ No

   Was the employee responsible for any of the expenses incurred for the company vehicle? ☐ Yes ☐ No

   If **yes**, indicate the amount and type of expenses:

Amount	Type of expense
$	
$	
$	

T2200 E (19)

(Ce formulaire est disponible en français.)

Canada

Protected B when completed

6. Did you require this employee to pay for expenses for which they **did** or **will** receive a reimbursement? ☐ Yes ☐ No

If **yes**, indicate the amount and type of expenses that were:

	Amount	Type of expense	Included on T4 slip
- received upon proof of payment	$		☐ Yes ☐ No
- charged to the employer, such as credit card charges	$		☐ Yes ☐ No

7. Did you require this employee to pay other expenses for which they **did not** receive any allowance or reimbursement? ☐ Yes ☐ No

If **yes**, indicate the type(s) of expenses: ______________________

8. Did you pay this employee wholly or partly by commission according to the volume of sales made or contracts negotiated? ☐ Yes ☐ No

If **yes**, indicate the commissions paid ($ ____________).

and the type of goods sold or contracts negotiated (______________________).

Is there a business development account or other similar commission income account available from which the employee's employment expenses are paid or reimbursed? ☐ Yes ☐ No

If **yes**, is the commission income from this account included in box 14 of the T4 slip? ☐ Yes ☐ No

9. Did this employee's contract of employment require them to:

- rent an office away from your place of business? ☐ Yes ☐ No
- employ a substitute or assistant? ☐ Yes ☐ No
- pay for supplies that the employee used directly in their work? ☐ Yes ☐ No
- pay for the use of a cell phone? ☐ Yes ☐ No

Did you or will you reimburse this employee for any of these expenses? ☐ Yes ☐ No

If **yes**, indicate the type of expense and amount you did or will reimburse:

Amount	Type of expense	Included on T4 slip
$		☐ Yes ☐ No
$		☐ Yes ☐ No
$		☐ Yes ☐ No

10. Did this employee's contract of employment require them to use a portion of their home for work? ☐ Yes ☐ No

If **yes**, approximately what percentage of the employee's duties of employment were performed at their home office? ______ %

Did you or will you reimburse this employee for any of their home office expenses? ☐ Yes ☐ No

If **yes**, indicate the type of expense and amount you did or will reimburse:

Amount	Type of expense	Included on T4 slip
$		☐ Yes ☐ No
$		☐ Yes ☐ No
$		☐ Yes ☐ No

Protected B when completed

11. Did this employee work for you as a tradesperson?	☐ Yes ☐ No
If **yes**, did you require this employee, as a condition of employment, to purchase and provide tools that were used directly in their work?	☐ Yes ☐ No
If **yes**, do all of the tools itemized on the list provided to you by the employee satisfy this condition? **Please sign and date the list.**	☐ Yes ☐ No
12. Did this employee work for you as an apprentice mechanic?	☐ Yes ☐ No
If **yes**, was this employee registered in a program established under the laws of Canada or of a province or territory that leads to a designation under those laws as a mechanic licensed to repair self-propelled motorized vehicles?	☐ Yes ☐ No
Did you require this apprentice mechanic, as a condition of employment, to purchase and provide tools that were used directly in their work?	☐ Yes ☐ No
If **yes**, are all of the tools itemized on the list provided to you by the employee used in connection with the employee's work for you as an apprentice mechanic in the program described **in this question**? **Please sign and date the list.**	☐ Yes ☐ No
13. Did this employee work for you in forestry operations?	☐ Yes ☐ No
Did this employee, as a condition of employment, have to provide a power saw (including a chain saw or tree trimmer)?	☐ Yes ☐ No

Employer declaration

I certify that the information provided on this form is, to the best of my knowledge, correct and complete.

Name of employer (print) ______________ Name and title of authorized person (print) ______________

Date ________ Telephone number ________ ext. ____ Signature of employer or authorized person ______________

Note: Please clearly print the name and telephone number of the authorized person in case we need to call to verify information.

See the privacy notice on your return.

Working from Home: The COVID-19 Deductions

Contributed by Michael Alexander and Simon Townsend

On September 11, 2020 the Canada Revenue Agency ("CRA") conducted a consultation hosted by the Canadian Chamber of Commerce. At this consultation, the CRA provided guidance on the deductibility of home office expenses as a result of the COVID-19 pandemic. This memorandum explains (1) what the law is on the topic of home office expense deductions for employees; and (2) how a draft "short-form" T2200 presented at the consultation, have clarified and changed requirements for compliance with the law, according to the CRA.

The CRA has indicated that they will accept employment income deductions for home office expenses if the expenses were required during specific periods of employment when employees were principally required to work

from home. This is different than the Income Tax Act ("ITA") which does not refer to taxpayer-delineated periods under the relevant provision, subparagraph 8(13)(a)(i).
This shifting compliance requirement speaks to the context of living in a global pandemic and the reality of having multiple Government-mandated shutdowns.

The Legal Framework of Salaried Employment Deductions

Eligible deductions of employment expenses for employees derive from s. 8 of the ITA. "Write-offs" according to that section include eligible motor vehicle expenses, travel expenses, parking, supplies, computers, cell phones and other equipment, special clothing and tools, as well as salaries and office rent. Pertinent to the present topic, "office rent" includes workspace in the home, referred to in ss. 8(13) of the ITA. For any expense to be eligible for deduction, it cannot be reimbursed.

Similar to other employment expenses, for home office expenses to be deductible they must be required by an employment contract. The home office must also be where the individual principally performs their duties. Moreover, all employers must fill out a Form T2200 for an employee to deduct expenses. This form is consulted by the CRA to assess whether an employment expense was required by the employees' contract. It can later be used as primary evidence in court, although is non-determinative of whether an expense was required by an employment contract.

As a result of COVID-19, many Canadians are required to maintain home offices to perform their employment duties, and that is likely where they perform the majority of those duties. This spurred the CRA to provide comments on home office expenses and propose a new short-form T2200.

The CRA's Changes and Clarifications for Home Office Expenses During COVID-19

The following are considerations on deductions that independent contractors and salaried employees may count against their income due to the current COVID-19 pandemic.

If salaried employees are required by contract (written or implied) to maintain a home office, they fulfill over 50% of employment duties in their home office, and their employer completes a Form T2200, then they may deduct expenses for that home office. Employees may also deduct expenses for supplies used in their employment duties, not reimbursed by their employer.

For independent contractors, expenses can be deducted from your income, if those expenses were incurred for the purpose of earning income from a business or property.

Independent Contractors

Deductions for independent contractors are broader than those for employees. For independent contractors, the legal source of deducting expenses from their business income is ss. 9(1) of the Income Tax Act ("ITA"). Subsection 9(1) defines profit from a business or property as a net concept, meaning that it includes what is deductible from a commercial trading or business practice standpoint.1 Subsection 18(1)(a) on the other hand expressly disallows certain expenses if they were not incurred for the purpose of earning income from a business or property.

Legal rules have not altered expenses available to independent contractors due to COVID-19; however, independent contractors should be aware of how COVID-19 has altered expenses attributed to their income-earning process. For example, if an independent contractor travels longer with a motor vehicle to access income streams as a result of the present pandemic, then they can include those vehicle expenses, including fuel, oil changes, repairs, toll charges, insurance, depreciation (etc.) in their annual tax return.

Salaried Employees

Eligible deductions from employment expenses for employees derive from s. 8 of the ITA. "Write offs" according to that section include eligible motor vehicle expenses, travel expenses, parking, supplies, computers, cell phones and other equipment, special clothing and tools, as well as salaries and office rent. "Office rent" includes workspace in the home, referred to in ss. 8(13) of the ITA. For an expense to be eligible for deduction, it cannot be reimbursed.

In order for an employment expense to be deductible, it must be required by an employment contract. This requirement is found in each provision under s. 8 except for those that deal with expenses outside the scope of employment, such as suing an employer for wages. All employers must fill out a Form T2200 for an employee to deduct expenses.

For home expenses to be deductible, they must comply with ss. 8(1)(i)(ii) and be "required by the contract of employment." They also must fulfill one of two conditions under ss. 8(13)(a). Either the location is:

1. where the individual principally performs the duties of the office or employment; or

2. used exclusively during the period in respect of which the amount relates for the purpose of earning income from the office or employment and used on a regular and continuous basis for meeting customers or other persons in the ordinary course of performing the duties of the employment.

Due to COVID-19, the first condition is met for many Canadians. The CRA considers an amount in excess of 50% to fulfill the term "principally."[2] As such, if an employee is required by contract to incur home office expenses and performs an excess of half of their duties from home, then they can deduct a percentage (measured in terms of square feet and divided by total square feet of the home) of their home office expenses, such as electricity. For renters, they can deduct a proportion of rent based on home office space, from their employment income. Employees can also deduct expenses for maintaining their home office, which could include cleaning materials or paint.

In order for any employment expense to be deductible, it must be "required" by an employment contract as indicated in a Form T2200 and in the ITA. According to case law in federal courts, including the Tax Court of Canada ("TCC"), strong evidence of an employment "requirement" is as follows. An employment requirement under the ITA may be found if not doing that task would lead to an "unfavorable assessment by an employer."[3] Employment requirements "by contract" can be implied as well as written, and whether one exists is a question of fact. Therefore, case law in the TCC[4] shows that, even where no "requirement" is laid out in the words of an employment contract, employees can still be required to incur certain expenses and legally deduct those amounts from their employment income.

The CRA's draft short-form T2200 for home office expenses has two notable elements. First, the CRA affirms that a formal contract is not required between an employee and employer to find an employment requirement exists. This is present in recent case law and is otherwise recognized by the CRA – but not clear on the current form T2200.

The second notable element is that the draft short-form T2200 asks whether an employee was required to work principally (meaning more than 50% of the time) from their home office space for one or more periods in 2020 during COVID-19. The draft form goes on to ask the taxpayer to identify those periods. This is distinguishable from subparagraph 8(13)(a)(i) of the ITA which requires that the home office space be where the employee principally performs their duties, without referencing any specific time period. The time period subparagraph 8(13)(a)(i) relates to is presumably the taxation year in question.

If the proposed short-form T2200 is made official, then employees can prove compliance with subparagraph 8(13)(a)(i) during periods that they delineate — not necessarily the entire tax year that a form T2200 relates to. In other words, during the current pandemic, employees can apply the concept of "principally" (i.e., greater than 50%) to more than one window of time. To illustrate, taxpayer-employees can indicate that they spent more than 50% of their time fulfilling employment duties in their home office from March to May, and August to October, excluding months that they may have performed employment duties at an office. This speaks to realities of work closures relating to COVID-19 and creates greater opportunity for eligible deductions.

Two other considerations arising from the CRA's feedback on home office expenses are that: (1) a regular Form T2200 will still have to be filed for non-home office or supplies expenses, as the general form includes expenses not considered in the draft short form; and (2) the new short-form T2200 will not need to be filed with an employee's income tax return but must be signed by the employer and kept by the employee in case it is requested by the CRA.

As the draft form was only released in September of 2020, it is important to stay up to date on this issue. The CRA will likely provide more clarifications on the topic of home office expenses during COVID-19, as requested by accountants, tax lawyers, and other interested taxpayers.

Moving Expenses

The CRA allows for a deduction for moving expenses in some cases. Not all moving expenses are deductible.

Moving expenses are only deductible if you either (1) moved to establish a new home to work or to run a business at a new location, or (2) you moved to be a full-time student of a post-secondary program at an educational institution. In both cases, you have to move at least 40 kilometres closer to your new place of work or school.

If you have concluded your move is eligible for the deduction, you may claim the following expenses:

Travel expenses such as meals, accommodation, and vehicle costs to move your and the members of your household;

Temporary living expenses, such as meals and temporary accommodation, near the old or new place for you and your family members (no more than 15 days);

Transportation and storage expenses for household goods, including packing, movers, in-transit storage, and insurance;

Other incidental expenses, such as replacing driving licenses and other documents, utility installation and disconnections, legal costs directly related to the move, changing your address, and so on.

The Story of Johnny Konecny - The Man Who Moved in a Canoe (in his own words)

From 1984-1989, I moved between Ottawa, ON and Kingston, ON as a student. My landlord had told us we must sign our fuel oil contract with her heating oil distributor; therefore, I included the cost of the fuel oil as "rent" in my taxes. CRA balked. I explained to them my landlord's arrangement with her Kingston, ON Fuel Oil Delivery Company, and provided the CRA with my rent contract and forced fuel oil receipts. The CRA allowed me the fuel oil deduction (to be included in my total cost of rent) and then went after both the landlord and the fuel company. My landlord had done this with over forty of her homes. I believe they were the bigger "fish." This, and ensuring my remainder of my tuition deduction went to my father, were my only early dealings with the CRA.

Self-representation on self-reported tax filings can be very daunting. Over and over again, --particularly from Justice Canada (representing The CRA) lawyers—one will see, read, and hear it is not a recommended practice. Perhaps because I am overly stubborn, my annual claims for "moving expenses" were relatively low dollar amounts, and what became years and years of ongoing interaction with The CRA, I did learn a very great deal. It was naïve of me to believe that this process was somehow a friendly and collegial meeting of the minds—between conscientious tax-paying citizen and a friendly Government lawyers (representing friendly helpful CRA workers)—objectively working together to help solve an otherwise simple and straightforward tax dispute. Access to Information requests and responses revealed solving disputes with CRA and other government employees in these matters could be--behind the scenes--highly vindictive, sometimes highly careerist oriented, and a bloodsport—where the "so-called" "conscientious tax-paying citizen was viewed as an "enemy," "adversary." There are chains of emails in various government departments (Statistics Canada, The CRA, Finance, and Justice) which document this. Particularly in the "General Procedure," Tax Court contitutional motions and countermotions, some Toronto Justice Department lawyers acted and talked as if I was a near-criminal.

In 1989, I moved from Ottawa, to Toronto for June Supply teacher work in the, then; Board of Education of the City of Scarborough. I; then, moved back to Ottawa to teach summer school and worked as a waiter in The Ottawa Byward Market. Caroline (my wife) and I married in August of 1989 and we moved to Toronto, ON for her banking career as well as my teaching (Scarborough, ON) career. For the 1989 tax year, I deducted the student move and the employment moves between Kingston and Ottawa, Ottawa and Toronto, Toronto and Ottawa, and back to Toronto. This pattern continued for thirty-one years. In Summer--I moved from Teaching in a Toronto day school to Teaching Summer School in Ottawa. I moved back to Toronto (Whitby) each year in late summer.

Teacher Contracts (they are ten months) run for 190 days between September 1st and June 30th in a given school year (the school year calendar is then made by The Board within Provincial Guidelines). Summer School Contracts generally run from July 1 (or later) to July 31 (or earlier). Boards do not wish to pay Canada Day or August Civic Holiday pay; therefore, usually attempt to fit 90 to 110 hours of instructional time into each July—between the two Statutory Holidays.

CRA, Heron Road, Ottawa conducted a full audit on my 1994 Tax year, in 1996. After extensive mutual sharings (writings, and telephone calls), The CRA had requested teaching contracts, collective agreements, T4 Slips, every receipt, cancelled cheques, credit card statement, bank statement--every receipt for every cent of expenses I had claimed. In the end, The CRA wrote a decision that supported my 1994, claimed "moving expenses." The senior employee that made the final decision cited the 1966 Carter Commission, and that I was "unemployed" and between teaching contracts--and that I worked rather than attempt Employment Insurance (Teachers are actually Statute Barred from attempting this claim, if they are in possession of a future teaching contract). The CRA senior employee wrote of the BNA Act, intent of Parliament out of the late 1960s Tax Reforms, and "Mobility" (between intercolonial Canadian trading colonies). The CRA communicated that what I was doing was exactly what the 1972 "Tax Reform," had both intended and anticipated?

From 1994 until the 2004 tax year The CRA permitted the twice a year "moving expenses," deductions. In 2006, CRA Sudbury, ON (CRA Re-assessment Review) following a "Re-assessment," took a heavy hand and a dim view of what I had now been doing (previously, with their blessing?) for fifteen (working) to twenty (if one includes five years of university) years. The CRA employee on my file, initially made statements like: "I can't believe they let you do this before?" and "Did you put your television and couch on your Hyundai, roof rack, for your one trip?" However, after months of interaction, letters from my employers, and her thorough scrutiny--she wrote a T20 decision citing the then; recent Tax Court of Canada decision: (Cavalier v The Queen [2002] 1 CTC 2001 (TCC)), and in my favour. Kenneth Cavalier was a law teacher. He left his wife in Delta BC, while he moved alone to Fort McMurray to teach for four months. He flew on a plane and returned back to the exact residence and career, he was at previously. The case law, apparently, fit. Cavalier did not sell his home. He did not buy a new one. He knew before he left that he would be returning back to where he started. Justice Eric Bowie (Tax Court of Canada) ruled in Cavalier's favour (including a Constitutional reference on "Mobility").

I had cited: CRA--internal documents from Headquarters to Appeals Branch included internal instructions on how to handle "Cavalier"-like claims and deductions. Obtaining these documents have been the focus of four of my forty CRA (ATIP) Access to Information, requests. The Government has now been found in contempt of Access to Information laws by a recent Information Commissioner of Canada, decision. I still do not have any of this information beyond all the completely redacted CRA Headquarters, papers. The Canadian Government has cited National Security and Lawyer / Client privilege (Justice Canada / CRA), and a potential appeal to Privy Council. I still do not have the internal CRA information. A CRA employee in Surrey BC—Tax Appeals Office, informed me of and read me these documents on the telephone. "Mr. Konecny, there are instructions atop your file to all CRA employees to not give you future "moving expenses," deductions under any circumstances, in any tax year, despite any of your potential counter-arguments."

Starting in the 2007 tax year, and in every year until 2011, the CRA went through full Re-assessment / Review. 2007 to 2010 tax years all went in my favour. That was now a 26-year successful "moving expense" claim track record for me. In 2007, and 2008: Federal Finance Minister James Flaherty {(my friend, and my MP), I was his campaign manager}, and CRA Minister Gordon O'Conner intervened on my behalf. I was granted the 2007, and 2008 "moving expense" deductions. I was given the 2009, and 2010 "moving expense" tax deductions.

In the 2011 tax year: I was given an unusual (even for myself) level of documentation scrutiny. All information was requested, all receipts, all documents, employers, all employer information, bank, driver's license, mail (at both Whitby, and Ottawa addresses). T-4s issued to separate addresses. Union membership in each city, Library Cards, bank information, The location of my drug prescriptions, email addresses, and voting enumerations. The

CRA accessed my personnel file at both employers School Board Head Offices and asked for both Union Collective Agreements. I even provided the CRA with the documentation of my location of my future burial spot. The CRA; then, confirmed (a "Notice of Confirmation") their negative decision (from CRA, Summerside PE, Appeals).

I filed a 2011 "Notice of Appeal" with the Principal Tax Court in Ottawa. Justice Canada informed me in the summer of 2013, that the hearing of my "Reply" to their challenge of Constitutional Motions on "Mobiltiy," (Charter 6) "Economic Liberty,"(Charter 7) and the protection of my "Marriage" (Charter 15), would be "moved" to Toronto. When I informed Justice Canada I would prefer the hearing be in Ottawa, they said, that I was presently living in Whitby, and they would seek compensation for their time, travel, meals and hotel. At Toronto, Her Honour Tax Court Justice Diane Campbell (Konecny v The Queen: 2013 TCC 334) seemed uneasy that a "moving expense" deduction had come to Constitutional Questions: "This is about "moving expenses?"" Her honour, Justice Campbell ruled against "economic liberty"—"a tax deduction is not an economic right—it is a privilege granted to a tax-payer, by The Crown." She pointed out that I had moved, and that my wife had not; however, neither had my wife been forced to stay, or prohibited from moving; therefore, each of our "mobilities" had not been in any way impinged. Justice Campbell also explained that in her view I had inadequately explained the need for the protection of my wife and marriage. CRA had been writing to my wife to ask her to explain where she lived and have her employer write letters documenting her time at work, while I worked in Ottawa. My argument was that the "moving expense" deduction is an individual deduction, and not a family or joint deduction. I argued that just because I moved; didn't require my wife to. I further argued my wife and my wife's employer did not have to respond to CRA requests of their documents, made to me, in an investigation of my personal taxes (We supplied all the requested documents). Much to my personal happiness, Justice Diane Campbell did put this argument about the "INDIVIDUAL," in her ruling. This point alone later became very important in a Justice Guy Smith, 2016 Ruling (on tax year 2014) (A "Consent to Settlement") in my favour.

On behalf of The CRA, The Justice Canada, Constitutional Motions lawyer decided to call me "near treasonous," in open Federal Tax Court, at Toronto. I objected! Her Honour Diane Campbell heard and encouraged the eleven points of my objection, while the government; then, objected to my objection.

John Konecny: "Your Honour, "I object.""
Justice Diane Campbell: "Go ahead, Mr. Konecny."
John Konecny: "Your Honour, my father dug himself into a coal train to leave The Czech Republic and get to this country. I am sincere, loyal, and seeking a "moving expense," tax deduction. I didn't create the process to appeal one's taxes; however, I am appealing. I served in The Canadian Armed Forces, I was on Parliament Hill cheering as Her Majesty The Queen, and Prime Minister Trudeau when they signed the Constitution. The copy I received that day proudly hangs in my Ontario Public School, Classroom. I have been an election officer in Municipal, Provincial, and Federal elections. I am not a member of the movement of people who reject the Tax System, its authority to collect tax, or who plan vexatious activities to waste The Court's time..." "I am now more greatly offended being called "near treasonous," than I am upset about not obtaining a tax deduction I had been given previously, for twenty-six years."

There was an $11,000.00 bill for photocopies (I had cited everything from Magna Carta to Thomson, 1946 (Thomson v. Minister of National Revenue, [1946] S.C.R. 209). There was a $36,000.00 bill for their eight government lawyers. I had thought because I was introducing Constitutional Arguments I had to use "General Procedure." This put me at a huge jeopardy for the Government's request for "costs." The judge took a night to write her decision. Before the end of the hearing the judge asked me if I understood, and was aware for what the Government was asking for? Kindly, Justice Campbell ruled that I should pay the court fees which she set at a maximum of $1,500, on the $1,496 appeal of my CRA refused, 2011 "moving expenses," tax deduction. She noted, that any of my arguments on the worthiness of "moving expenses," will be considered by a different Tax Court Judge, at a separate, future hearing. My advice: "use the "Informal" process."

His Honour, Tax Court Justice Randal Bocock (Konecny v The Queen: 2014 TCC 114)—to me--did not seem to grasp my argument that Ontario teachers are unemployed between July 1 and August 30th. He labeled my practice of seeking work when unemployed, a "working vacation:" "You're "double dipping," while on your holiday." He was not interested that I "moved" more than 40 km, rented an Ottawa apartment, had two different employers, brought my family with me, or many of the facts I attempted to introduce to his court. Tax Court Judge Bocock suggested I was somehow a "commuter." I assured him that Whitby to Ottawa and back, daily was neither practical nor economically feasible. When I asked His Honour Bocock (because I understood Tax Court Judges had to live in Ottawa, within 40 km of the court) if he was a "commuter" to the Toronto Court Room we found ourselves in, in 2014, he seemed to take offence. He assured me he flew, stayed at a downtown hotel, had restaurant meals, and a limousine drive to court. I was upset that I was not convincing him of my argument; however, he seemed to demean the significant day in, day out work of: preparing, teaching, and marking. He pointed out that I visited my boyhood neighbourhood and went fishing on the weekend.

Judge Bocock had asked me how I had moved previously: West-Jet, walked, taxi, Uber, Go-Train, OC Transpo, Durham Transit, Greyhound, Via Rail, car, truck, my brother gave me a free ride. He asked me: "Mr. Konecny? Could one move on a bicycle?" I responded that my opinion--"because the legislation is for "Travel," and The CRA form allows for "vehicle" expenses, it was my opinion one could?" Tax Court Justice Randal Boscock asked me if one could move in a day. I explained that someone had. From Quebec to Alberta, and the judge ruled that the second the woman and her two children touched the ground in Alberta, she was "ordinarily resident," in that province (de Hann v. Gracia 2004 ABQB 74 (AQB) and Proia v. Proia 2003 ABQB 576 (AQB)). In the case law: Justice Sommervell, in Nova Scotia (1949) had ruled, one could be "ordinarily resident," in a day (Macreae v. Macrae, [1949] P. 397, [1949] 2 All E. R. 34 Somervell L.J. said a pp. 36-370). Family law, and tax law borrow definitions from each other, in Canada—and are mutually influencing. "Mr. Konecny?" "Could you move in a canoe?" "Yes, your honour, one could." At the time—and before the recent Muskoka, ON, unfortunate death (of a child) in a canoe, ruling in Oshawa, ON (R. v. Sillars, 2019 ONCJ 57) with the supervising adult deemed to be intoxicated, confirmed this, I had already understood a canoe to be a "vehicle," (particularly if it had a motor attached). Individuals in Nova Scotia, Quebec, Nunavut, and Ontario had all been charged with "Impaired," in the operation of their (vehicles) canoes. Since the tax legislation and CRA documents only read "travel," perhaps it just doesn't matter how one travels?" At the time, nonsensical, and farce-like, it popped into my head: "Why not sometime do this?—Move in a canoe" I lost the Spring 2014 Tax Court decision, on my 2011 tax year.

However; His honour Bocock said at the closing of the hearing: "John! Change your driver's licence, change your Bank information." "Go out of your way to demonstrate that you have, actually, moved." Moving forward: I made a list of every criteria I ever found under the tax case law on "moving," Justice Bocock's decision, and many others, included.

For 2012, I was granted the "moving expenses" deductions without any further scrutiny

For 2013, I was fully audited and an appeal's officer CRA Appeals Winnipeg went through everything and ruled in my favour. Although he did not permit my youngest son a moving meal--the youngest son was helping me; however, he did not move. I accepted this.

For 2014, I was fully audited again. I attempted to argue this was a CRA reprisal. I "appealed" to the Tax Court of Canada in 2016. The two lawyers for Justice Canada telephoned to advise me that they had informed the CRA—they could not win their CRA case. His honour Justice Guy Smith asked for Notice of Confirmation: He ruled that I was entitled to "all claimed moving expenses," I had claimed in the Notice of Appeal. The Lawyers for Justice Canada did verify and allow all my claims.

For 2015: There was no further scrutiny after The CRA accepted my filing.

For 2016: I was subject to a full audit (Sudbury, ON Tax Center) again. I was issued a "Notice of Confirmation." I appealed again. It took over six months for the Sudbury TO to read (now) thousands of pages of my tax Documents: 1977 to 2016. I was granted all moving expenses. Notably: This was the move on a bicycle where I successfully claimed three days of food, park fees, firewood, ice and the $17.50 bicycle fuel (the bike courier food allowance).

For 2017: I moved on a Via Rail train: I claimed $44.00 train tickets and two $17.00 meals. I was aiming for my "lowest cost move."

For 2018: I moved in a canoe. All receipts were available, plus all Facebook posts and Photos. I actually wanted a fourth session of tax court. I wanted this one on the books. What upset me about His Honour Justice Guy Smith's, previous Confirmation, of my "Consent for Settlement," was that it would not be written up as an elaborated, detailed, Tax Court of Canada, decision. I claimed ice (I am diabetic and carry two refrigerated insulins), firewood (for heat and cooking only / I did not transport [move] firewood), meals, and Ontario Provincial Park fees (trailer spots to obtain electrical outlets for charging my devices), On the one full day, when I towed the canoe by bicycle on a trailer, I successfully claimed ($17.50) the bike—food as fuel—courier allowance.

In 2019, I Retired: I was not permitted (as per Ontario Teacher's Pension Plan Rules) to negotiate teacher any future teacher employment while negotiating retirement. Therefore, I was not able to apply and interview for Ottawa summer school.

In 2020: I was hired as a "Virtual Teacher in an Ottawa Google Classroom." I "moved" to Ottawa June 29th. I "moved" with my dog. A Tax Court Justice has ruled "a dog is the member of a family." I want to test this by deducting the dog's lunch in Peterborough on the way from Whitby, to Ottawa. On December 26th and 27th 2020, I completed Dog Sled, snowshoe, ski, skate, snow board, toboggan, sled, ice climb, snowmobile, in return "move" from Ottawa, to Whitby, ON.

John Konecny

07 REFUNDABLE TAX CREDITS

Federal Refundable Tax Credits

Unlike non-refundable credits which can only serve to decrease your taxes payable, but can never result in a tax refund, refundable tax credits can serve to decrease your income and may result in a tax refund if all taxes have been eliminated.

At the Federal level there are only three refundable tax credits, however, each province and territory also has their own different credits. At the Federal level there is the Goods and Services Tax / Harmonized Sales Tax Credit, and Working Income Tax Credit, and the Refundable Medical Expense Supplement Credit.

The GST/HST credit is simply a payment by the Federal government on a quarterly basis that changes depending on your income. If your family's income is below $36,976, then you are entitled to full amount which changes each year. Once you earn more than $36,976, the maximum amount that you can receive begins to slowly decrease until your family income increases beyond $48,000 at which point you stop being entitled to the credit.

The Working Income Tax Benefit

The working income tax benefit is a credit for employed, low-income individuals who are over 19 years of age, and for those who are not full-time students. The benefit is calculated as 26% of income exceeding $3,000 to a maximum of $1,355 for you, and $2,335 for a family. The maximum is reduced by 12% of net income over $12,820 for single individuals and $17,025 for families.

The Refundable Medical Expense Supplement

The Refundable Medical Expense Supplement is a credit available to low-income individuals who have paid medical or disability support expenses. In order to qualify for the full benefit, you must have employment income over a $3,645, but below $27,639. The government will reimburse you for 25% of these expenses up to a maximum of $1,248, however this amount is reduced by 5% of your family's income in excess of $27,639.

How to Qualify

The GST/HST credit and Working Income Tax Credit are both automatically applied for when you file your tax returns.

In order to qualify for the Refundable Medical Expense credit, you simply need to put the total amount of the credit that you qualify for on line 45200 of your T1 return.

Supporting Documents needed

At the time of filing your return, you will not need to provide any supporting documents; however, if your return is subject to a review, then you may need to provide documents to show you incurred medical or disability support expenses or were a full-time student.

Resources

https://www.canada.ca/en/revenue-agency/services/tax/individuals/topics/about-your-tax-return/tax-return/completing-a-tax-return/deductions-credits-expenses/line-45200-refundable-medical-expense-supplement.html

https://www.canada.ca/en/revenue-agency/services/tax/individuals/topics/about-your-tax-return/tax-return/completing-a-tax-return/deductions-credits-expenses/line-45300-canada-workers-benefit-cwb.html

https://www.canada.ca/en/revenue-agency/services/child-family-benefits/goods-services-tax-harmonized-sales-tax-gst-hst-credit/goods-services-tax-harmonized-sales-tax-credit-calculation-sheet-july-2019-june-2020-payments-2018-tax-year.html

British Columbia Refundable Tax Credits

What Refundable Tax Credits Do They Offer?

The British Columbia government offers seven refundable tax credits, which include:

- Home renovation tax credit for seniors and persons with disabilities
- Mining exploration tax credit
- Sales tax credit
- Shipbuilding and ship repair industry tax credit
- Training tax credit (Individual)
- Training tax credit (Employers)
- Venture capital tax credit

Home Renovation Tax Credit for Seniors and Persons with Disabilities

This tax credit is available for residents of British Columbia who were a resident of British Columbia, and either you or on behalf of someone incurred an eligible renovation expense. Additionally, either yourself, or a family member that you reside with had to have been over the age of 65 or living with an eligible disability.

The credit provides up to lessor of $10,000 or the total amount of eligible expenses, which were incurred in the year.

The list of eligible expenses extensive, but effectively it includes anything to make the individuals life easier such as:

- lever handles on doors and taps, instead of knobs
- lowering of existing counters and cupboards
- non-slip flooring in the bathroom

In order to claim this credit you need to complete a Schedule BC(S12) form and include it with your return. The amount of the credit determined by this schedule is then added onto line 60480 of your BC479, and 10% of this amount is added onto line 14 of your BC479.

Venture Capital Tax Credit

The venture capital tax credit is a new refundable tax credit that you can claim if you acquired shares from a venture capital corporation, or an Eligible British Columbia corporation that was registered in British Columbia in 2020. The corporation that you purchased shares from would need to be able to issue a form SBVC 10 which is provided to the corporation itself by the Government.

The credit can provide a maximum credit of up to $60,000 for shares acquired before February 20, 2019, or $120,000 if purchased after February 20, 2019.

In order to claim the credit you need to enter the certificate number, and tax credit amount found on your SBVC on on line 18 of your Form BC479. You also need to include the certificate with your tax return.

British Columbia Mining Exploration Tax Credit

The mining exploration tax credit is a refundable tax credit that refunds up to 20% of the qualified mining exploration expenses incurred in a given tax year. These expenses would include things like prospecting, surveying, drilling, and trenching.

In order to claim this credit you will need to fill out a form T88, and provide your free miner certificate number. The amount determined on the form is then entered on line 60510 of your BC479.

Training Tax Credit (Individual)

The training tax credit provides a flat refund for completing different levels of your Red Seal and non-Red Seal apprenticeship programs.

In order to claim this credit you will need to fill out a form T1014. The amount determined on the form is then entered on line 60550 of your BC479.

Training Tax Credit (Employer)

This training tax credit is similar to the previous credit; however, it applies to the employer of an eligible employee, instead of the individual. The credit can range depending on the level of the employee, and the total amount paid to them. The maximum that can be received range from $2,500 - $4,000

In order to claim this credit you will need to fill out a form T1014-1. The amount determined on the form is then entered on line 60560 of your BC479.

If you are an employer of individuals in a red seal or non-red seal apprenticeship program it is strongly recommended that you consult with a tax professional to make sure you are claiming the full credit.

British Columbia Shipbuilding and Ship Repair Industry Tax Credit

The Shipbuilding tax credit is essentially an enhanced version of the training tax credit. The credit provides individual who employ eligible employees for the purposes of construction, repairs or conversions of ships in British Columbia.

In order to claim this credit you will need to fill out a form T1014-2. The amount determined on the form is then entered on line 60570 of your BC479.

How to Qualify

In order to qualify for any of the abovementioned credits you will need to fill out the required line numbers on your BC479.

Supporting Documents needed

At the time of filing your return, you will not need to provide any supporting documents except for the venture tax credit; however, if your return is subject to review, then you may need to provide documents to show you incurred the required expense.

Resources

https://www.canada.ca/en/revenue-agency/services/forms-publications/tax-packages-years/general-income-tax-benefit-package/british-columbia/5010-pc/information-residents-british-columbia.html#L14

Ontario Refundable Tax Credits

What Refundable Tax Credits Does Ontario Offer?

The Ontario government offers a grand total of eight refundable tax credits, however, 3 of these are administered under the Ontario Trillium Benefit. The refundable tax credits include:

- Ontario Child Care Credit (ON479-A)
- Ontario Focused Flow-Through Share Tax Credit (T221-19)
- Ontario Senior's Public Transit Tax Credit (ON479)
- Political Contribution Tax Credit (ON479 if over $3,149, if under you need to include a Worksheet ON479)
- Ontario Co-operative Education Tax Credit

The three refundable tax credits administered under the Ontario Trillium Benefit include:

- Northern Ontario Energy Credit (ON-BEN)
- Ontario Energy and Property Tax Credit
- Ontario Sales Tax Credit

Ontario Childcare Credit

The Ontario Childcare Credit is a credit aimed at helping low to moderate income families pay for certain childcare expenses. The amount ranges from reimbursements of 75% of eligible childcare expenses if your family's adjusted net income is less than $20,000, to as low as 1% if your family's adjusted net income is between $146,400 to $150,000.

Ontario Focused Flow-Through Share Tax Credit

The Ontario Focused Flow-Through Share Tax Credit is a niche refundable tax credit, which reimburses you for 5% of eligible expenses related to flow-through shares. Eligible expenses can include:

- transportation of supplies
- shipment of samples, assays and chemical analyses of samples
- food and lodging
- mobilization and demobilization of equipment and crew within the Province of Ontario
- certain overhead costs related to carrying out the project, but not head office costs
- determining the existence, location, extent or quality of a mineral resource

Ontario Senior's Public Transit Tax Credit

The Ontario Senior's Public Transit Tax Credit provides seniors who have paid for eligible public transit services a credit of 15% of amount paid up to a maximum of $450.

Political Contribution Tax Credit

The Political Contribution Tax Credit is available to Ontario residents who contributed to a registered Ontario political party, or candidate in an Ontario election.

The credit provides a maximum benefit of $1,384 if you donated over $3,149 in the tax year. Any amounts lower than that are taxed on a progressive basis with any amount up to $415 providing a credit of 75% of the amount donated, 50% of any amounts contributed between $415, and 1,384, and 33.33% of any amounts contributed between $1,384 and $3,149.

Ontario Co-operative Education Tax Credit

The Ontario Co-operative Education Tax Credit is a credit that allows individuals who have hired one or more co-op students enrolled in college or university to be reimbursed for eligible expenditures. The current rate is 30% of eligible expenditures such as salary and wages up to a maximum of $3,000.

In order to claim this credit, the student must have worked in a permanent establishment in Ontario and have worked for you for a minimum of 10 weeks.

Northern Ontario Energy Credit

The Northern Ontario Energy Credit is a credit designed to help low to moderate-income individuals pay for the higher energy costs while living up North. The amounts offered each year varies, but currently provides a maximum amount of $157 for single individuals, or $241 for a couple or single parent. In order to qualify one of the following must apply:

- rent or property tax for your principal residence in Northern Ontario was paid by or for you;
- accommodation costs for living in a public or non-profit long-term care home in Northern Ontario were paid by or for you; or
- home energy costs (for example, electricity, heat) for your principal residence on a reserve in Northern Ontario.

If you earn over $42,201 as single individual, or $54,258 as a single parent or couple, then the amount is reduced by 1% of the amount you earn above those amounts. This means that if you earn over $57,901 as a single individual, or $78,358 as a family unit you will not be entitled to any amounts under this credit.

Ontario Energy and Property Tax Credit

The Northern Ontario Energy Credit is a credit designed to help low to moderate-income individuals pay for the higher energy costs while living up North. The amounts offered each year varies, but currently provides a maximum amount of $1,085 for non-seniors, and $1,236 for seniors. In order to qualify one of the following must apply:

- rent or property tax for your principal residence in Ontario was paid by or for you;
- accommodation costs for living in a public or non-profit long-term care home in Ontario were paid by or for you;
- home energy costs (for example, electricity, heat) for your principal residence on a reserve in Ontario were paid by or for you; or
- you lived in a designated university, college, or private school residence in Ontario.

The benefit is calculated automatically when you meet one of these criteria, and the Ontario government does not provide any formula for how they determine this benefit, but they do look at things such as your age, marital status, property taxes paid, and rent paid in Ontario.

Ontario Sales Tax Credit

The Ontario Sales Tax Credit is a credit designed to assist low to moderate-income individuals with the sales tax they pay. The amounts offered each year change slightly and currently max out at $313 for each adult and child in a family.

If you earn over $24,115 as single individual, or $30,0143 as a family unit, then the amount is reduced by 4% of the amount you earn above those amounts. This means that if you earn over $31,940 as a single individual, or $37,968 as a family unit you will not be entitled to any amounts under this credit.

How to Qualify

In order to qualify for the Ontario Child Care Credit, you need to fill out and submit a form ON479-A with your T1 return. In order to qualify for the Ontario Senior's Public Transit Tax Credit, or the Political Contribution Tax Credit, or the Ontario Co-operative Education Tax Credit you need to submit a form ON479 with your T1 return.

In order to qualify for the Ontario Focused Flow-Through Share Tax Credit, you need to fill out and submit a T221-19 with your T1 return.

Finally, in order to qualify for any of the credits administered under the Ontario Trillium Benefit, you need to fill out and submit a form ON-BEN with your T1 return.

Supporting Documents needed

At the time of filing your return, you will not need to provide any supporting documents; however, if your return is subject to review, then you may need to provide documents to show you incurred the required expense.

Manitoba Refundable Tax Credits

What Refundable Tax Credits Do They Offer?

The Manitoba government offers six major refundable tax credits, which include:

- Fertility Treatment Tax Credit
- Education Property Tax Credit
- Homeowner's School Tax Assistance
- Seniors' School Tax Rebate
- Primary Caregiver Tax Credit

- Green Energy Equipment Tax Credit

The Manitoba government also offers several smaller refundable tax credits which can be found at https://www.canada.ca/en/revenue-agency/services/forms-publications/tax-packages-years/general-income-tax-benefit-package/manitoba/5007-pc/information-residents-manitoba.html#mb479.

Fertility Treatment Tax Credit

The Fertility Treatment Tax Credit, is a credit aimed at assisting Manitoba residents in conceiving a child. It covers up to 40% fertility treatment costs paid in Manitoba to a licensed medical practitioner or fertility treatment clinic, or prescription drugs, net of any reimbursements from private insurance. The credit covers up to $20,000 of these expenses, so the maximum refund that you can receive is $8,000.

It should be noted that the eligible treatment costs do not include reversing a vasectomy, or tubal ligations.

In order to claim the credit enter your eligible medical expenses on line 63 of your form MB479.

Education Property Tax Credit

The Education Property Tax Credit is a credit that is designed to help offset the property taxes paid that relate to school taxes. It is equal to the sum of: 20% of total rental payments; and school taxes paid up to maximum of $750.

In order to claim the credit you must fill out lines 20-22 on Form MB479 with your tax return.

Homeowner's School Tax Assistance

The Homeowner's School Tax Assistance Tax Credit is a credit that is designed to help offset the property taxes paid that relate to school taxes if you receive rental assistance or social assistance and your total family income is less than $23,800. The amount is on sliding scale, and ranges between $175 if your family income is below $15,100, to as low $1 if your family income is $23,700.

In order to claim the credit you must fill out lines 44, 54, and 58 on Form MB479 with your tax return.

Seniors' School Tax Rebate

The Senior School Tax Credit is a credit that is designed to help offset the property taxes paid for seniors that relate to school taxes. It is equal to the sum of: 20% of total rental payments; and school taxes paid up to maximum of $750. The difference between this credit and the traditional Education Property tax credit is that this credit allows for a higher family income before becoming ineligible.

In order to claim the credit you must fill out line 32 Form MB479 with your tax return.

Primary Caregiver Tax Credit

The Primary Caregiver Tax Credit is a credit of $1,400 designed to help individuals who take care of an individual who requires caregiving without receiving compensation. The individual must be assessed as requiring Care Levels 2, 3, or 4 while living at home. Examples include those with a disability, people with life threatening illnesses and others needing care and supervision for periods of more than 90 days.

The individual must reside in a private residence, and only one individual may claim this credit of $1,400 per individual who requires care.

In order to claim the credit you must fill out line 61 Form MB479 with your tax return.

Green Energy Equipment Tax Credit

The Green Energy Equipment Tax Credit provides for a refundable tax credit if you installed a geothermal ground source heating system, or a solar heating system. The credit is equal to 15% of the eligible capital installation cost of the geothermal unit, plus an addition 7.5% if the pump was manufactured in Manitoba; or 10 of eligible capital cost of a qualified solar thermal heating equipment.

In order to claim the credit you must fill out lines 69-70 Form MB479 with your tax return.

How to Qualify

In order to qualify for any of the abovementioned credits you will need to fill out the required line numbers on your MB479.
Supporting Documents needed

At the time of filing your return, you will not need to provide any supporting documents; however, if your return is subject to review, then you may need to provide documents to show you incurred the required expense.

Resources

https://www.canada.ca/en/revenue-agency/services/forms-publications/tax-packages-years/general-income-tax-benefit-package/manitoba/5007-pc/information-residents-manitoba.html#P223_56788

https://www.gov.mb.ca/finance/personal/pcredits.html#caregiver

08 CLEVER (AND CHEEKY) DEDUCTIONS

The Trip to Hawaii (to Check on the Rental Property, Of Course)

Perhaps you have a rental property. Perhaps it is somewhere you like to travel. Perhaps you don't yet have a rental property, but you are considering acquiring one.

In that case, say you love to travel to Hawaii, and you do so year after year (or whenever you can afford it).

If you purchased a rental property in Hawaii with you and your spouse on title, you could quite conceivable both travel to Hawaii, stay in your rental property, rent a car and eat meals, with the entire expense being deductible from your rental income.

If you were going to spend the money on a trip either way, the best way to do it is to have a trip to the rental property so that you can take care of annual maintenance and do a check-up, etc. This way your entire trip is deductible – as long as both of you are on title. If only you are on title and you and your spouse both travel to Hawaii, only your trip will be deductible.

But be ready to justify the expense of a trip to Hawaii to the CRA. Be ready to explain why you had to travel there and why you had to be there personally.

The Trip to Vegas (to Go to the Convention)

Perhaps you like to gamble. Perhaps your spouse likes to go see Cirque de Soleil. Perhaps you do too. Perhaps you want to have the government help finance your trip to Vegas.

Easy. Attend a convention.

The nice thing about Las Vegas is that (until COVID hit), Las Vegas has a convention for virtually every type of business once a year. So, if you and your spouse are in the electronics business or the printing business or the automotive business, or if you are in virtually any other business at all, there is a convention in Las Vegas which has your name written all over it.

So, if both you and your spouse work in your business – even your side business – even the Hawaii rental house business – and you both attend the rental house business convention in Las Vegas, you can deduct the cost of your airfare, car rental, meals, and accommodation. Again, if only one of you is part of the business then only their travel expenses can be deducted from business income.

And this is how the government can help finance your trip to Las Vegas or wherever you have to be for business purposes. Get creative. There are conferences around the world. There are seminars and learning opportunities around the world. If these trips have a legitimate business purpose, then you are on your way to writing off trips around the world. Instead of paying for these trips with your after-tax dollars you are paying for them with your pre-tax dollars. Cheaper trips and less tax owed to the government. Win-win (for you and your spouse. Not the government).

The Kids' Activities (Paid by Their Part Time Job with Before Tax Dollars)

Instead of paying for your kids' activities with after tax dollars, imagine being able to pay them with before tax dollars – to make them a write off?

While it is not possible to write off the activities themselves, it is possible to use your kids to obtain a tax advantage in order to do the equivalent of paying for their activities with before tax dollars.

Here's how it works:

Say you have teenagers. And say you have a business. Perhaps you have rental properties, one of which is in Hawaii. What you do is have your teenagers do some work for the business. They can help take reservations, answer emails, file documents, send faxes, process payments, clean the office, go to the office supply store for paper, etc. You catch my drift. And for doing these tasks, you can pay them a fair wage – say $14 per hour, which is the minimum wage in Ontario. And if they work 2 hours per day (averaged over the year), over the course of the year they would have earned about $10,000 from you.

And wouldn't you know it? Canadians are allowed to earn about $10,000 without paying any tax at all. What this means is that you can transfer about $10,000 from your company to each of your kids tax free on an annual basis. They can in turn use the $10,000 to pay for their activities.

Be sure to have them complete time sheets and document what they have done in case there is a CRA audit.

EXAMPLE

Assume your kid's activities cost $4,000 per year.
Assume you are in a 50% tax bracket.

Scenario A: Kid is not employed. $10,000 paid to owner of business (you)

Paid to you	$ 10,000
Tax	$ 5,000
Remaining after tax	$ 5,000
Cost of Activities	$ 4,000
Remaining	$ 1,000

Scenario B: Kid is employed by your company. $10,000 paid to the kid.

Paid to your kid	$ 10,000
Tax	$ 0
Remaining after tax	$ 10,000
Cost of Activities	$ 4,000
Remaining	$ 6,000

In this example, paying your kid the $10,000 versus paying yourself the $10,000 results in $5,000 being saved in taxes. This can pay for more activities.

You can do this with each kid where reasonable (And NO. It is not reasonable to pay your 3-year-old to be the model on the company web site).

The Family Get Together (the Day After the Office Party)

A way to deduct the cost of your party or family get-together is to use leftovers from a business function the day before.

Remember – all the costs associated with a business function can be written off. They are legitimate expenses. You can have cocktail parties and you can have elaborate functions for your clients and staff. Every cent is a deduction to the business.

And when you do have business events, remember to purchase a little extra of this and a little extra of that.

And if the leftovers are enough to take home and have your own little party, then why not?

Voilà. The costs of your personal function are zero to you and fully deductible to your business.

09 TIPS TO SAVING MONEY IN AN AUDIT

Audits are feared by Canadians. This is because everybody knows that an audit can cost you thousands of dollars if the auditor disagrees with the way that your tax return was filed. So, it is very important to be prepared for an audit and to be able to justify your position. Every penny that you save during an audit will add up.

Be Aware of and Try to Mitigate Audit Risk Factors

Sometimes a taxpayer is randomly selected for an audit. It's like winning the worst lottery in the world. It's just random. Nothing you can do to change that. But apart from a random audit, the odds of being targeted for an audit are dependent on a variety of risk factors.

In short, the odds of being audited depend on who you are, where you are located, what your business does, who you do business with, what types of expenses you have, and so on. You get the idea.

Various pieces of a taxpayer's profile may help uncover risk factors. And the more risk factors a taxpayer has, the greater the odds of that taxpayer being audited.

Audit Risk Factors

1. Being Self-Employed (running a sole proprietorship)

Self-employed individuals do not have taxes withheld at source. Their tax is more likely to have been incorrectly reported than in the case of an employee who receives a T4. For the CRA, this group is a great category to target.

2. Running a Cash Business

Various types of businesses are by their nature, reliant on cash, and when there is a lot of cash being received by a merchant there is obviously more opportunity for the CRA to recover taxes on undeclared cash income.

Since there is more opportunity to reassess and recover taxes from cash business versus other businesses, this makes cash businesses a better and more frequent target for CRA auditors.

3. Being in Certain Industries

A taxpayer may find that an audit occurred for no other reason that the taxpayer's industry.

Certain industries are targeted by the CRA, because there is a large number of cash transactions, such as the restaurant and construction industries.

Other industries are audited from time-to-time in special projects to help recover missing HST and income tax dollars. There are HST projects addressing missing trader scams which have occurred and are ongoing in variety of industries, such as employment and gold and which have caused the disappearance of hundreds of millions of tax dollars.

4. Higher expenses than others in the industry

If a taxpayer shows expenses which are dramatically different from others in the industry, it may be a cause for scrutiny on the part of the CRA.
It is important to remember that the CRA computer matches and compares many pieces of taxpayer information. If a taxpayer sticks out, they can expect to be audited. If a restaurant declares 15% cash sales and all its neighbours are showing 24-28% cash sales, this is a red flag.

Moral of the story: Blend. Blend. Blend.

5. Large Vehicle Expenses

Vehicle expenses are often arbitrarily determined. When preparing their tax return, often times taxpayers and their accountants pick a reasonable (but arbitrary) figure to quote for vehicle expenses, based on an estimate of the percentage of the vehicle usage used for business purposes. The problem is when this deduction is based on an estimate. Auditors jump on estimates.

Few taxpayers and accountants actually keep a log of every trip. This means that few taxpayers can prove to the auditor with absolute certainty, the relative use of the vehicle between personal and business purposes. This makes auditors happy. It makes it easy for them to deny vehicle expenses, and this increases the size of their reassessments.

Moral of the story: Keep detailed logs to support your vehicle expense claims.

6. Large Home Office Expenses

The CRA loves auditing home office expenses.

Home office expenses are often arbitrary and often over-declared. Some people inappropriately include a percentage of their cleaning, snow clearing, and landscaping costs.

The CRA knows this.

People often overstate the percentage of their home which is dedicated to business use. I had a client who claimed the square footage of his entire basements as part of his home office so that he could store a small piece of equipment. I have seen a taxpayer claim all his kitchen as part of his home office because when the taxpayer has guests to his home office, he prepares drinks and food for the clients in his kitchen. The same taxpayer also claimed part of his living room because he entertained clients there and had meetings there. CRA auditors have seen it all and they know what to look for. Home office expenses are low-hanging fruit for the auditor.

So, if a taxpayer is declaring home office expenses which appear to be large in compared to the overall costs of running the home or in comparison with others in the industry, there is an increased possibility of an audit.

7. Discrepancies

The CRA compares many things and when there are discrepancies, it is a red flag for the CRA.

One discrepancy in particular leaves taxpayers with a marked increased likelihood of an audit, and that discrepancy is between figures on a GST/HST return and the figures on a T2 return. If the two returns don't match the CRA will likely have some questions.

Some discrepancies are within the taxpayer's control, such as discrepancies between an HST return and a T2 return. It is important to be as diligent as possible to avoid such discrepancies. Other discrepancies unfortunately are simply out of the taxpayer's control.

Control What You Can

While the CRA claims to uniformly interpret and apply the law when auditing, the reality is quite different. If one compared audits or auditors, one would see that the outcomes of audits have a great deal to do with the type or size of a business, whether the taxpayer is legally represented or even the auditor's mood.

Concerning the size of a business being audited, the smaller the business, the less the CRA is likely to learn from the audit, and the easier it is to find the discrepancies. Small businesses often receive cursory audits from inexperienced junior auditors. These audits are often left unchallenged because these small business taxpayers cannot afford to have proper representation to fight the CRA. However, big corporations usually have highly trained auditors assigned to their audits--auditors who are Chartered Public Accountants. These auditors have a smaller caseload and can audit effectively.

Similarly, large corporations can afford proper legal representation. Thus, when the CRA auditor makes an error, it will be identified. This improves the likelihood a large corporation will achieve a fair outcome.

There is no way to prevent the CRA from reassessing you for additional taxes owed, but if an audit is appropriately handled, you can reduce your taxes owing, and you may be able to avoid penalties. In many cases, if they have the correct documentation, the taxpayers can obtain positive results without any representation. However, sometimes when the taxpayers have something to hide, or when they have been sloppy with their record-keeping--especially when the discrepancy is more than $100,000--they are best to seek legal advice before proceeding with the audit.

Get Off to a Good Start

Don't avoid the auditor. I know... It's a normal human tendency to hide from horrible things, but once you receive that audit letter it is best that you get in touch with the auditor right away to schedule the appointment.

And while it is a good idea to get in touch with the auditor soon after you receive their letter, you don't want to get the audit started too quickly. You want to be ready for this.

Consider Getting Assistance from a Tax Lawyer or an Accountant

Many people ask me whether they can have their accountant represent them during an audit. The answer is YES. Your accountant knows your books and your records and is likely in the position where they CAN handle your audit.

The question is SHOULD they? If your books and records are clean and you have a competent accountant, then there is likely no reason why your accountant shouldn't represent you. But if your books and records are less than perfect. Or if you have been less than 100% honest. And especially if you are hiding something from the CRA, it is a terrible idea to have your accountant represent you through an audit. The primary reason being that there is no privilege between an accountant and their client. So, if the accountant learns something which you don't want the CRA to know about, there is always a risk that the CRA will force the accountant to divulge information. There is never such a risk with a lawyer.

And oftentimes it is best to work with a tax lawyer and your accountant. There is a way to do so such that the accountant's work product falls under lawyer-client privilege. For more information, consult a tax lawyer (cheap plug: BarrettTaxLaw.com).

Stay on Track

Do not give the auditor more than they need (i.e.: don't give them the QuickBooks file with 10 years of data for a 3-year audit. In fact, don't give the QuickBooks file at all. Just the journals that are required).

Ensure That the Charity you are Donating to is Legitimate

While official charity receipts are examined during audits, oftentimes the CRA performs specialized audits on people who have contributed to certain charities which are suspected of acting fraudulently in one way or another. In such cases all the people who donate to the charity can be audited and reassessed with interest and penalties. The key to a charitable donation is as follows: If a tax preparer or somebody asks you to contribute to a charity and promises that it will reduce your taxes and that you will get a financial benefit, the odds are that it is a scam and that years down the road you will be reassessed. If you are just donating to a random charity on your own volition, the odds are that you are not being scammed. But either way, in order to claim a charitable contribution, it is important to ensure that a) you keep the receipt and are able to show it to an auditor and b) you ensure that the charity is legitimate.

Document Your Home Office

Many people claim deductions in respect of home office expenses (heat, hydro, insurance, property tax, mortgage interest, etc.). Many people also move from house to house. And when audited, many people find themselves unable to prove to the auditor exactly what percentage of the square footage of their previous house was actually used for business purposes. Whether you plan on moving or not, document your home office. Take pictures. Make a floorplan and square footage calculation. Take pictures of those. Send those all to yourself by email and hope that you never have to use them. But keep the evidence just in case.

Keep and Show Your Vehicle Log

If you are going to claim vehicle expenses, be prepared to show your vehicle log. By presenting a log of all business use of the vehicle and comparing that to the remainder (i.e., personal) of the use of the vehicle (as determined by odometer readings at the beginning and end of the month or year), you will be able to justify your vehicle expense deduction. Without the log you are up the creek without a paddle.

Provide Organized Records

To the extent possible, provide the auditor with documents which are clear and organized. They should be separated by year or by month and by expense type or vendor. Your cheque stubs should be neat and organized, as should your bank statements and all financial records. Do not expect to do well in an audit where you provide the auditor with a shoebox of receipts, gum wrappers and invoices.

Don't Discuss Personal Matters or Have Personal Conversations with the Auditor

A seemingly innocuous mention of your latest trip to Hawaii may get the auditor thinking about how you afforded the trip. While you are at it, park your Bentley in the back, and don't let the auditor see anything flashy.

If You Have Hired a Representative, Avoid Dealing Directly with the Auditor

There is nothing wrong with having a representative. It's not a sign of guilt, and it is your right. The nice thing about having a representative deal with the auditor is that they can handle the difficult questions for you. If a question was posed directly to you by the auditor, it is hard to come up with a clever answer on the spot. You may seem cagey or like you are lying

– even when you're telling the truth! A representative can just answer the question with "I don't know. Let me find out". This can buy time to get your ducks in a row.

Do Not Sign CRA Waivers

If you are presented with a waiver by an auditor (or anybody else at the CRA), DO NOT SIGN IT WITHOUT LEGAL COUNSEL. Sometimes an auditor runs out of time during an audit. In these instances, it is common practice to get the taxpayer to sign a waiver allowing the auditor further time to complete their audit. And some auditors can be quite insistent. Don't give in. Don't be intimidated.

Do Challenge Bad Audits

Remember, after the auditor issues their reassessment, there are still 4 more opportunities to challenge it (counting the Supreme Court of Canada). Don't get frustrated if the auditor doesn't see things the way you do. It doesn't mean that they are right. Sometimes you have to object to the auditor's findings. And sometimes you have to appeal the appeals officer's findings to Tax Court. That's just the way it goes sometimes.

Know Your Rights

Make sure you know your rights and recourses and make sure the auditor knows that you know. This will prevent you from being pushed around by the auditor.

Keep Good Records

Whether you plan on selling your business and need to show immaculate records to a buyer or whether you just want to ensure that an audit goes smoothly and that you are able to justify every last expense, you will need to keep good records. Not just good records – great records.

Ironically, there is no requirement in the Income Tax Act (the "ITA") a taxpayer to have an original receipt in order to claim a business expense, yet if an auditor requests the original receipt and all one has is a copy or a scan or a credit card statement, etc., the auditor may disallow the expense altogether. So, it's best to keep everything that the auditor may want to see – and that includes original receipts. And of course, we all know that some receipts fade over time. Even auditors get this. So, you may want to keep a copy or a scan of those.

While taxpayers are only typically audited up to 3 or 4 years in the past, as a general rule, keep your records for six to seven years. According to the ITA, the six-year retention period begins at the end of the tax year to which the records relate. For corporations, the tax year relates to the fiscal period, and for individual taxpayers such as sole proprietors, the tax year relates to calendar years.

I suggest keeping records for a year or two longer than required even though the "CRA" may only reassess personal/corporate tax returns for up to three years and GST/HST returns for up to four years. And the reason for my recommendation is that if the auditor suspects fraud or gross negligence on the part of the taxpayer, they can open up and reassess years beyond the normal reassessment period. So, it is best to be ready in case.

There are times when records shouldn't ever be thrown out, such as things related to the disposal of property or major acquisitions. Examples include purchase/sale agreements, stock transactions and share registries. Without having access to these documents in the future at the time of disposition, it is impossible to ensure that the correct capital gain is being recorded, which could lead to more taxes being paid than necessary.

There are also some special circumstances where taxpayers must keep records beyond the standard time period.

In the case of an objection to the CRA's Chief of Appeals, or subsequent appeals to the Tax Court of Canada (TCC), all records should be kept until the six-year period has passed, or until the matter has been concluded (whichever is later).

If a taxpayer files a late income tax return, records should be kept for six years from the date the return is assessed following filing.

If a business is unincorporated and operations have ended, records must be kept for six-years beginning at the end of the tax year that operations ended.

If the taxpayer is deceased, their executor should maintain all records until a time a clearance certificate is granted.

If there is a corporate merger/amalgamation, the resulting/acquiring company must retain corporate records as if the original business was still in existence.

When dissolving a corporation, after the dissolution, records must be maintained for two-years, and long enough that if the business is audited during the normal reassessment period (three-years for income tax returns and four-years for GST/HST returns), that it is able to prove its figures during an audit.

CRA information: IC78-10R5, "Books and Records Retention/Destruction," provides additional guidance for record retention.
For electronic records, information circular IC05-1R1, "Electronic Record Keeping," provides further guidance.

For those who don't know what records they should keep, CRA document RC4409, "Keeping Records," provides the requisite guidance.

The Importance of Maintaining Complete Records

Other than claiming Input Tax Credits or charitable contributions there is no positive requirement for a taxpayer to keep actual receipts.

In most cases auditors deny expenses when there are not perfect records and receipts. If you provide photocopies or scans or if you show bank statements and cancelled cheques, but are not able to provide the actual receipt, chances are that your expenses will be denied.

The single most important reason for maintaining complete records is that if you are ever audited in the future, unless you are operating a large company and get a competent, senior CRA auditor, your auditor may be less competent, they may be very junior, they may be inexperienced, and they will not have time to do a complete, thorough audit, and as a result of all of this, they will likely make many errors and disallow many expenses. Only with the proper records can the taxpayer properly defend themselves against this.

And remember, if you keep electronic records, you may be asked to show documentation to support your records. It's important to keep all of your receipts, bank statements, deposit slips and cancelled cheques. Don't find yourself in the position with your back against the wall after having lost data to a computer crash. Back up your business records. Keep a copy offsite. Auditors can use missing records as a reason to disallow expenses, which is much more costly than a backup hard drive.

10 TIPS TO REDUCE TAXES BY CHALLENGING AN INCORRECT REASSESSMENT

Don't Be in a Rush to Provide Details About Your Objection

If you feel that you have been unfairly reassessed, it is vital that you act immediately because if you wait too long an assessment can no longer be challenged and it becomes permanent.

If a taxpayer disagrees with any tax assessment – GST/HST, corporate tax, or personal tax, they have an option to appeal the decision. The first step of the appeal begins by the filing of a notice of objection (T400A), which can also be filed online.

The filing of the notice of objection begins the entire process. It must be filed within 90 days and has to clearly explain in writing the grounds for the appeal. If the objection is late, you may request an extension for up to a year.

Once the Notice of Objection is filed, you generally will wait for up to a year for an appeals officer to be assigned to the case. Given that there is so much waiting time, I often chose to file a notice of objection simply indicating that "the assessed tax owing amount is incorrect" and indicating that once an appeals officer is assigned to the case, I will provide further details.

By filing an objection immediately without providing your entire case right away you have accomplished three things:

1. You have started the process early and have not delayed starting it in order to write a lengthy notice of objection. You get the clock started sooner.
2. You have not rushed to prepare an objection in 90 days, possibly missing things, and possibly doing a sloppy job; and
3. You have provided yourself with the better part of a year to gather all necessary information in order to build your case and gather all your evidence.

Generally, I like to take the first 2-3 months after the objection is filed to prepare the case and leave myself a few extra months for clients to obtain hard-to-get documents, such as statements and legal documents from foreign countries.

The goal is that by the time the appeals officer is assigned you have produced a package which is comprehensive and detailed. It should outline your position and provide all supporting documentation in an organized fashion. You need to make it easy for the appeals officer to decide in your favour.

The appeals officer will consider your position, arguments and evidence and will render a decision. Either the appeals officer agrees with you in whole or in part, in which case a reassessment is issued. In other cases, the appeals officer disagrees altogether, and a "Notice of Confirmation" is issued. During this entire time, interest continues to accrue on the debt, as the CRA is presumed to be correct until proven otherwise.

File an Objection to Stall Collections Activity

One of the consequences to filing an objection in respect of a personal tax debt or a corporate income tax debt is that it causes a "stall code" to be applied to the debt in the CRA computer, and as a result collections action ceases in respect of the debt. The amounts in question, considered to be "disputed amounts", are non-collectible.

The same is not true of HST and Payroll debts. Even once a notice of objection is filed the amount remains collectable and a CRA collector can take necessary action to recover the debt.

Skip Directly to Tax Court if the Objection Takes Too Long

If is important for you to get your CRA dispute closed as quickly as possible, especially if you feel that you may end up having to go to Tax Court anyway, this section is for you. It can help save you time and help reduce interest charges.

It should be noted that for income tax cases, a taxpayer has the right to skip over the appeals officer and appeal directly to the Tax Court of Canada once 90 days have elapsed from the filing of the notice of objection. For GST / HST cases, a taxpayer must wait 180 days from the filing of the objection, and they can then skip directly to the Tax Court of Canada.

For taxpayers who want to save time, skipping directly to court is often a good solution. In particular it is helpful for those who are objecting to an HST assessment which is incorrect, and which has to be serviced on an ongoing basis until such time as the reassessment is reversed.

An objection to an assessment or reassessment concerning a non-trust tax debt will result in a "stall code" being applied in the CRA's computer. This means that if the CRA has already started collections action, it will stop. And if they have not yet initiated collections, they won't begin. But remember that while an objection to an income tax debt stops collections activity, this is not the case for an HST debt. So, a terribly incorrect HST assessment will take a year or two to correct, and in the meanwhile the incorrect debt is fully collectible by the CRA collections department.

Even if Your Debt Is Not Collectible, Pay Anyway

It is important to realize that even while a stall code has been applied, and even while a CRA statement of account will show the amount a "disputed item", and even though the CRA may not be able to take collections action, it is in your best interest to voluntarily service the debt while you are waiting for the objection to be heard.

There are three primary reasons for this:

1. Interest still accrues on a daily basis. Voluntary payments reduce the debt and thus reduce the interest;
2. Every payment you make will reduce the debt. It is better to start paying what you can and reduce the debt over the year or two, rather than be faced with a debt at the end of the process which has not been serviced; and
3. If there is any amount owing at the end of the objection / court process, and if this amount does go to the collections department, you will be one of the only taxpayers in the collection officer's inventory who has been paying voluntarily. This will go a long way to building good faith and negotiating a reasonable payment plan which you can manage.

11 PENSION & RETIREMENT

Max out your RRSP contribution

Unless you have a better place to park your money, max out your RRSP contribution. TFSA and RRSP accounts both grow tax-free, but it is better to start to max out your RRSP contributions prior to the TFSA. Contributing as much as you can to the RRSP will result in larger tax refunds which you can then in turn use for the TFSA.

Also, if the purpose in putting money away is retirement versus a large purchase (perhaps a round-the-world trip or an investment property), putting the money in the RRSP preferentially vs. the TFSA will result in the money more likely still being there at retirement. For one thing, removal of money from an RRSP is taxable, and for another thing, returning the money (except when borrowed for a first-time house down payment or continuing education) is not an option, and the contribution room in the RRSP disappears permanently. This is not the case with the TFSA. You can always take money out and put the money back in with no tax consequences, which makes it an attractive place to look when renovating one's bathroom.

Make a $2000 Over Contribution to your RRSP

Generally, one is penalized by being charged a tax of 1% per month on excess contributions which exceed their RRSP contribution limit. However, this tax is only levied if the over contribution exceeds $2000. This leaves the door open for Canadians to overcontribute $2000 to their RRSP without such a tax.

And while one cannot deduct the $2000 from their taxable income, this money can sit in one's RRSP and grow tax free. The earlier that one makes the over contribution the longer the amount grows tax free.

Contribute to a Spousal RRSP if it Makes Sense

It is possible for Canadian spouses to contribute funds to their spouse's (or common-law partner's) RRSP, but it doesn't always make sense to do so. In the case where only one spouse has a pension, the other spouse should have more RRSPs to make up for not having a pension. In the case where neither spouse has a pension to draw from upon retirement, it is a good idea for them to both have similar amounts contributed to their RRSP.

The cases where it makes the most sense to contribute to a spousal RRSP is when a higher income earner contributes to a lower income earner's RRSP. In this case the high income earner gets a tax deduction for the contribution amount, and in the future when the RRSP amount is withdrawn by the lower income earning spouse, it is taxed at their rate.

One must remember, however, that if one contributes to their spouse's RRSP, that spouse may not withdraw the money until 3 years later or they may face the adverse consequences of the attribution rules which will then tax the withdrawal at the tax rate belonging to the contributor.

Don't Withdraw from RRSPs Early if You Can Avoid It

Remember, when you withdraw money from RRSPs, it counts as income. And while the banks hold back some taxes (typically 15%), invariably they do not hold back enough and at the end of the year this leads to additional taxes payable. The higher your tax bracket, the greater the amount you will have to pay at the end of the year.

Borrow Tax-Free and Interest Free from Your RRSP under the Home Buyer's Plan

An exception to the rule of RRSP withdrawal counting as income is when you borrow money from their RRSP to make a down-payment on your first home.

So, you can decrease the amount of your mortgage and increase the amount of your down-payment by borrowing interest-free from your RRSP. This will save you money in bank interest. As long as the bank interest is higher than the interest you were receiving on your RRSP account then you are ahead.

Conditions:

- First repayment within 24 months of the RRSP withdrawal
- You must repay the amount within 15 years.
- You must be a first-time homebuyer (you must not have lived in a house owned by you or your spouse in previous 4 years)

Take Advantage of the Home Buyers' Amount

First-time homebuyers are eligible to claim $5000 on line 31270 of their T1 personal tax returns, for the home buyer's amount - regardless of the cost of their new home. This results in tax savings.

In order to qualify the following conditions must both be met:

1. You or your spouse or common-law partner acquired a qualifying home
2. You did not live in another home owned by you or your spouse or common-law partner in the year of acquisition or in any of the four preceding years (first-time home buyer)

Virtually any type of home can be a "qualifying home". It may be a single-family home, a semidetached home, a townhouse, a mobile home, or a condo, or an equity share in a co-op.

Borrow Tax-Free and Interest Free from Your RRSP (Lifelong Learning Plan)

Instead of using bank financing to pay for the costs of going back to school, you can borrow tax-free and interest-free from your RRSP. This saves big bucks in interest over the 10-year lifespan of the repayment.

If you or your spouse are going back to school, you can borrow money from your RRSP to pay for allowable full-time education or training programs. If disabled, the full-time requirement is waived.

Each year you may borrow $10,000 for a total lifetime loan of $20,000. Repayments of a minimum of 10% of the loan amount must be repaid each year.

Make Sure to Convert RRSP to a RRIF by Age 71

The benefit of an RRSP is that it allows your investments to grow tax-free. However, the tax sheltering benefits of the RRSP terminate at age 71. In the calendar year when you turn 71, you must make a decision:

You can either convert your RRSP into an RRIF (Registered Retirement Income Fund), purchase an annuity, or withdraw your money.

If you don't need all your money, there are tax benefits to an RRIF. Earnings in the RRIF are tax-free, while amounts paid to you from the RRIF are taxable in your hands. Simply put, the RRIF is a vehicle to let your capital grow tax-free.

Split CPP Retirement Benefits With your Spouse (If it Makes Sense)

The Canadian Pension Plan (CPP) income can be split between spouses. As long as certain criteria are met spouses may split their CPP income by completing the joint election on Form T1032.

By filing Form T1032, spouses may jointly elect to split pension income. This form does not affect payments under the Canadian Pension Plan (CPP) or from old age security. Jointly electing using this form simply can cause the following annuity income to be split: from a superannuation, from a pension fund or plan, form an annuity and registered retirement income fund, from a registered retirement savings plan, and form a retirement compensation arrangement. A spouse under this rule includes married and common law spouses.

This election needs to be made on an annual basis. These criteria include:

1. You and your spouse or common-law partner were not living separate and apart from each other, because of a breakdown in your marriage or common-law partnership, at the end of the tax year and for a period of 90 days or more beginning in the tax year.
2. You and your spouse or common-law partner were residents of Canada on December 31, 2019 (or on the date of death).
3. You received pension income in the tax year qualifying for the pension income amount or you were 65 years of age or older and received certain qualifying amounts distributed from a retirement compensation arrangement.

Pension splitting is accomplished "on paper," and no money needs to actually be transferred between spouses. In order to actually share your CPP payments (and not just split the payments on paper), one must complete an application ISP-1002 through Service Canada.

Splitting pension income makes sense if one spouse is in a higher tax bracket than the other, and splitting pension income, causes them to pay less income tax as a family unit. Throughout a Canadian taxpayer's life, they face harsh rules for splitting income including those found in s. 74.1-74.5 and 75.1 of the Income Tax Act, as well as the new Tax on Split Income rules under 120.4(1) of the ITA.

However, harsh income splitting rules do not apply to pension income. Section 60.03 of the Act permits pensioners to split up to half of their pension income with a spouse or common law partner, by election. The pensioner must include the split income as a subdivision e tax deduction from income. The spouse or common-law partner must include the split income as a subdivision d amount. As mentioned, they must also file a Form T1032.

The CPP payments can be received by eligible Canadians from 60 years of age. Splitting CPP payments makes sense if one spouse is in a higher income bracket than the other and they can benefit as an economic unit from shifting money between them. Conversely, if your spouse is in the same tax bracket, then splitting your pension does not make sense — it may even cause you to pay more income tax as an economic unit because you could be shuffling income to a higher tax bracket.

Also consider how CPP payments affect Old Age Security (OAS) payments. OAS payments begin at the age of 65 for Canadians earning less than $128,149 annually. The maximum monthly payment amount is $614.14. If one's income is higher than $77,580 (as of 2019), then they will have to repay a portion of their OAS.

If one's income from CPP and OAS (or otherwise) is higher than $77,580 and their spouse has a lower income, then applying to share CPP payments could ensure that OAS payments need not be repaid. It is important to note that Canadians must apply for OAS in most cases (they will not always be granted these payments automatically), and if one has been remiss to apply since they turned 65, then they may receive payments retroactively.

The Economic Consequences of Splitting Pension

EXAMPLE

If spouse A earns $60,000 of income, and spouse B earns $20,000 of income, then spouse A is in the third lowest tax bracket and spouse B is in the lowest bracket.

If spouse A received annuity payments of $40,000 in the tax year considered, then pursuant to s. 60.03 that can be split in half.

Electing to split that income in half, Spouse A now earns $40,000 and Spouse B earns $40,000 for tax purposes.

It is important to note that this only happens on paper; the annuity payments were still earned and may have been spent by Spouse A. However, as an economic unit Spouse A and B have effectively reduced their tax bill by around $800.

This considers all income besides the pension amounts is employment income, and CPP and EI are accounted for.

EXAMPLE

The amount saved on a tax bill becomes more substantial if Spouse A is a higher earner.

If Spouse A were in the highest tax bracket, then they would be saving approximately 30% tax on annuity payments, by transferring them to Spouse B in the lowest tax bracket.

This is if they were shifting income over $220,000 (taxed at the combined federal and provincial rates of ~53%) to the bracket of their Spouse under $44,740 (taxed at ~20%).

If Spouse A earned $200,000 plus $40,000 pension and split their pension with Spouse B earning $20,000 before the pension split, then Spouse A and B would save more than $6,000 after tax.

Again, this includes EI and CPP premiums paid on employment income. The following is a breakdown of how this income splitting benefits Spouse A and B.

SPOUSE A INCOME	SPOUSE A INCOME	SPOUSE B INCOME	SPOUSE A AFTER TAX INCOME	SPOUSE B AFTER TAX INCOME	SPOUSE A AND B TOTAL AFTER TAX INCOME
Non-Splitting Example 1	60,000	20,000	45,844	17,760	63,604
Splitting Example 1	40,000	40,000	32,208	32,208	64,416
Non-Splitting Example 2	240,000	20,000	146,393	17,760	164,153
Splitting Example 2	220,000	40,000	137,096	33,300	170,396

12 TIPS TO DEFER TAX

Earlier on we discussed the benefits of deferring tax to a future date. As noted, if there is $100 of tax to be paid, it is preferential for us to keep our $100 invested and pay the tax later on after our $100 has grown and when a $100 bill has less buying power than has today.

Use a Corporation to Defer Taxes

The way a corporation works is as follows: A corporation is owned by shareholders. Each of these shareholders own shares, and most shares allow their owners to vote at shareholder meetings. One of the things that shareholders do at the meetings is decide upon important business and this is also where they elect the directors of the corporation. The directors of the corporation are not involved in the day-to-day operation of the corporation. Instead, the board of directors meets regularly to make important decisions about the corporation and its direction, including the hiring of officers of the corporation such as the President, the Vice-President, the Treasurer, etc. who are the day-to-day managers of the corporation.

So, to recap: the shareholders own the corporation and elect the board of directors who in turn appoint / hire officers of the corporation like the president and vice-president who in turn manage the company for the shareholders.

As far as I am concerned, ninety-nine times out a hundred I would recommend a corporation as the vehicle of choice for a business. There are just so many clear advantages over say a sole proprietorship or a partnership – especially when it comes to tax deferral.

What makes a corporation great for many things, and especially for tax deferral, is that it is its own entity. And generally (with some exceptions), what happens in the corporation stays in the corporation (or was that Vegas?).

So, being its own separate identity in the eyes of the law means that it is separate from its owners or shareholders or directors. This creates a liability shield for the shareholders, and there are very few items which can penetrate this liability shield, among them certain taxes like unpaid GST/

HST and payroll remittances. Otherwise, shareholders and their assets are immune from creditors action and lawsuits against the corporation.

And while a shareholder is generally immune from actions against the corporation, if a shareholder receives payment of dividends when the corporation has not paid its taxes, this payment is considered a non-arm's length transfer of assets. And in this case the CRA may claw-back the dividend payment made to the shareholder.

If you are planning on opening a corporation and you will not be the sole shareholder, it is important to draw up a unanimous shareholders agreement (a "USA") to keep everybody in check. There are many reasons why a USA is an essential part of a corporation, and it is important to negotiate and sign the USA while everything is new and fresh and while all shareholders are still friends.

The USA governs what the shareholders can and can't do. It provides dispute resolution mechanisms to help end problems between shareholders. It provides minimum numbers of votes which are required in order to do certain things. It provides very clear rules and mechanisms for the transfer of shares and can prevent shareholders from disposing of or offering their shares as collateral. The USA also may provide mechanisms to force minority shareholders to sell their shares along with the majority when there is a takeover bid, or to allow shareholders to "piggyback" on a deal where another shareholder is selling their shares to a third party.

There are so many clauses in a USA which protect shareholders from each other, and which make the operation of the corporation that much clearer. I think that it is a mistake for any corporation with more than one shareholder to overlook the USA.

Taxation of Corporations

Corporations are taxed on their net taxable income each year. Like sole proprietorships, expenses are deducted to arrive at the taxable income. Unlike a sole proprietorship, for larger amounts of active income, the corporation is typically taxed at a far lower rate.

And for qualified corporations, active income up to $500,000 per year is subject to the small business deduction, which effectively reduces the rate to 12.2% for Corporations in Ontario this year. The difference can be considerable. Consider for example, the example provided above. If the individual had incorporated and the business had earned the $128K in income and had paid $28K of expenses, the corporation would have earned the $100K. It would have in turn paid the shareholder $66K, leaving the $34K in the corporation.

The difference between having the money in the corporation versus in the taxpayer's pocket is easily seen in the following example which demonstrates why a corporation is a great vehicle for tax deferral.

EXAMPLE

Assume the taxpayer earns a total of $150,000 per year in total between this business and everything else.

The tax rate above $150,000 is 48.19% in Ontario in 2020.
So, on the $34K, the taxpayer would be left with almost $18K, while if earned by the corporation, the tax would be much less, and the corporation would retain almost $30K after tax.

The difference is that the extra $12K, which isn't immediately payable to the CRA may be used within the corporation to grow the corporation. It can also be invested by the corporation for many years to come.

If or when the $34K and whatever it grows to gets paid out to the taxpayer, it will be taxed in the taxpayer's hands. But for now, this $12K of found money (money which would otherwise have been paid directly to the government) sits in the corporation's bank account for the corporation's benefit.

So, as you can see, among other benefits, a corporation offers an opportunity to defer taxes and use what would have otherwise gone to the CRA to the corporation's advantage. And besides the tax advantages and the liability shield, there are so many advantages to adopting a corporate structure.

Take Advantage of Tax-Free Rollovers

In Canada, when certain property is transferred to another related entity (be it a person, corporation or trust), a taxable event occurs whereby the property is considered to be disposed of at fair market value, and the recipient is considered to have received the property at fair market value. If the value of the property at the time of the disposition is greater than its adjusted cost base, a capital gain has occurred. This gain is taxable to the transferor.

Often times a taxable event occurs even when the property is not sold. Such is the case with deemed dispositions; the assets are assumed to be sold at fair market value, thereby creating a taxable event.

In certain situations, it may be possible to defer the taxable event by utilizing a tax-free rollover. What the rollover does is effectively defer the taxable event and cause it to be taxable in the hands of the recipient. With the rollover, in certain cases it may be possible for the recipient to receive the property at the initial cost base (the price paid for the property), as opposed to at fair market value. In such a case, the taxable event would only occur once the recipient eventually disposes of the asset.

Subsection 73(1) Rollover

For Canadian residents who are transferring property to Canadian recipients, it may be possible to transfer property via a sub. 73(1) rollover, provided that the property is capital property, meaning that it is depreciable property of the transferor, and any other property that when disposed of would result in a capital gain or capital loss to the transferor. The rollover allows for the capital property to be "to be transferred between living persons on a tax-deferred rollover basis to:

a. the spouse of a taxpayer ... ;
b. he former spouse of a taxpayer, in settlement of rights arising out of their marriage;
c. a spousal trust ...; or
d. in certain cases, to a former "common-law" spouse ....

Unless the taxpayer (the transferor) elects not to have the rollover apply..., the realization of accrued gains and losses, including any terminal losses or the recapture of capital cost allowance, is postponed until the recipient (the spouse, former spouse or trust) disposes or is deemed to dispose of the property."

If the conditions of subs. 73(1) are met, the rollover is automatic. For instance, in settlement of a divorce or separation, or when gifting property to your spouse, the rollover automatically occurs, thereby eliminating the taxable event and transferring the asset at adjusted cost base. To avoid the rollover, an election would have to be made.

Keep in mind that although the rollover defers taxation, attribution rules apply to spouses or related minors, whereby any income from the property or gain on the subsequent sale of the property is deemed to be attributed to the transferor. That means that the income is deemed to be the transferor's and not taxable as that of the recipients. One way to avoid the attribution rules when transferring property, such as a gift is to elect-out of the subs. 73(1) spousal-rollover and to have the property transferred at fair market value.

Spousal rollover on death

When a Canadian taxpayer dies, all of the assets of the estate are deemed to be disposed of at fair market value. If, however, the taxpayer is married at the time of death, a spousal rollover automatically occurs, as per subsection 70(6) of the Income Tax Act, thereby transferring the assets to the spouse at cost base, thereby eliminating any immediate tax event.

No election is required for the spousal rollover, however, in certain cases, it may be optimal to elect out of the rollover to utilize capital losses or capital gains, as to maximize the lifetime capital gains exemption. Proper planning could effectively limit or eliminate taxes for the deceased and allow for the spouse to receive the property instead at an adjusted cost base that is equivalent to fair market value. A proper plan could potentially minimize taxation to both spouses, as opposed to merely defer taxation by use of the rollover.

Qualified Farm of Fishing Property

Certain qualified farm property may be rolled over from a parent to a child, such as via subsections 73(3) and (3.1). Certain conditions need to be met, including that the property must be principally used in a farming or fishing business for more than 50% of the time over the course of ownership.

Subsection 73(3):

"Subsection (3.1) applies to a taxpayer and a child of the taxpayer in respect of property that has been transferred, at any time, by the taxpayer to the child, where

a. the property was, before the transfer, land in Canada or depreciable property in Canada of a prescribed class, of the taxpayer;
b. the child of the taxpayer was resident in Canada immediately before the transfer; and
c. the property has been used principally in a farming or fishing business in which the taxpayer, the taxpayer's spouse or common-law partner, a child of the taxpayer or a parent of the taxpayer was actively engaged on a regular and continuous basis (or, in the case of property used in

> the operation of a woodlot, was engaged to the extent required by a prescribed forest management plan in respect of that woodlot)."

What's interesting is that unlike transfers of regular property to a spouse, where the transfer is done at either adjusted cost base or fair market value (without an ability to elect an amount between the two), farm and fishing property or shares can be transferred to children or grandchildren at an elected value between the adjusted cost base and the fair market value. This is the case whether the rollover is done at the time of death via subsection 70(9.01) election, or during life, inter vivos, via subsection 73(3).

Eligible Small Business Corporation Shares

Without going into great detail, in certain instances, capital gains can be deferred when an individual disposes of shares in an eligible small business corporation. To qualify for the deferral, the proceeds would need to be replaced by investing in another eligible small business corporation within 120 days from the end of the taxation year of the original disposition. One must first verify that the issuing corporation is an eligible small business corporation and that the carrying value of all assets of the corporation and any related corporation does not exceed $50 million immediately before and after the shares were issued. Other requirements must be met, including that shares must be held for more than 185 days prior to the disposition.

Section 85 rollover

For certain individual Canadian taxpayers or partnerships, trusts or corporations, eligible property that would otherwise be taxable on a disposition may be rolled over to a taxable Canadian corporation. The joint election is done through Form T2057 (or T2058 for partnerships), Election on Disposition of Property to a Taxable Canadian Corporation. The transfer may be done at an elected amount, subject to certain constraints imposed by the Act.

The tax rollover is fairly beneficial when sole proprietorships or partnerships later incorporate the operation of the business. For businesses that have grown in value, what would otherwise trigger a capital gain when transferring eligible company assets to the corporation may instead be done on a rollover basis, deferring capital gains tax. The business owner must receive at least one share in the corporation in return for the transfer, becoming a shareholder of the corporation. The business owner may also receive "boot", which is non-share consideration (payment) such as cash, other assets, new debt or the assumption of old debt. Boot has the effect of altering the elected amount, whereby the elected amount cannot be less than the fair market value of the boot.

The rollover can also be beneficial when accomplishing an estate freeze.

The elected amount cannot be greater than the fair market value of the property and cannot be lesser than the lesser of the cost base or fair market value.

EXAMPLE 1 – ROLLOVER WITHOUT BOOT:

You transfer capital property to your corporation with an adjusted cost base ("ACB") of $100,000 and fair market value of $200,000.

The agreed upon elected amount of the cost of the property cannot be greater than $200,000.

In this case, an election of $100,000 has been chosen and you receive as consideration 10 common shares. There would be no gain on the transfer.

The cost of the 10 common shares would be $100,000 and the corporation's cost of the property would be $100,000.

If much later on, you sell your 10 common shares for more than $100,000 (the ACB), you would incur a capital gain at the time of sale, effectively deferring taxation from the date of transfer until the date of the sale later on.

If the fair market value of the corporate share has increased to more than $200,000, you may incur a greater capital gain than had the rollover not been utilized.

If you have current capital losses available to offset any capital gain, it may be advisable to elect an amount greater than cost base or to potentially avoid the rollover to begin with.

EXAMPLE 2 – ROLLOVER WITH BOOT:

Looking at the same facts as the previous example, except that the corporation has paid you boot in the amount of $150,000. The elected amount must then not be less than the boot or $150,000.

If the elected amount if $150,000, a taxable capital gain has been incurred by you in the amount of $50,000 (the elected amount of $150,000 less the ACB of $100,000). If you do not want to incur an immediate capital gain, then the boot should not exceed the cost of the transferred property.

One must be careful when utilizing a section 85 rollover, as it has the potential to create double taxation of capital gains, such as when there is a quick disposition of the asset by the corporation and the taxpayer simultaneously sells their shares. In such a scenario, the taxpayer and the corporation would concurrently incur a gain on the difference between the fair market value and the elected amount.

Keep in mind, that when possible, taxes should attempt to be reduced, and when that is not possible it may be best to have them deferred. Create a strategy that works best for you to determine if a rollover is right for you.

Defer Taxes with an Estate Freeze

A great planning tool is the estate freeze. It is a common succession tool, the purpose which is to take a snapshot of the taxpayer's business assets at a point in time and freeze their tax liability on the basis of that snapshot. Not only is their liability frozen, but the value of their asset on their net worth statement remains constant. All future increases in the value of the business are transferred through the estate freeze, to others such as children, grandchildren and key employees.

In the freeze transaction, the transferor retains the current value of his/her shares and defers the income taxes on the capital gain to the time of their actual or deemed disposition.

In a nutshell, an estate freeze converts a taxpayer's shares in their business into preferred shares with value equal to the value of the shares they traded in. After the freeze the taxpayer is left with preferred shares that will never increase in value.

The corporation then issues a few new common shares worth $1 to family members or a family trust. They pay $1 for shares that are worth $1 and there is no taxable event at that point. And as the business and its assets increase in value over time, that increase is attributed to the common shares owned by the next generation, which at the time of the freeze were only worth, say, $1, but which could turn out to be worth millions of dollars down the road. And voilà, tax on any further increase in value of the business is paid by the next generation many years in the future when they sell the $1 shares that were given to them — and not by the taxpayer who had frozen their estate.

Article :

Estate Freezes: A Silver Lining of COVID-19

Originally Published by the Lawyer's Daily

With the world in flux and an unprecedented shutdown of the world's economy, those who were planning to transfer businesses to the next generation have been given what is (hopefully) a once-in-a-lifetime opportunity to defer additional taxes for many years. As valuations of investments and businesses — both public and private — have reduced sharply, unless you are in the hand sanitizer business, right now is arguably the best time ever to freeze one's estate.

The Estate Freeze

Since capital gains tax is imposed at the time of death, owners of closely held corporations are assessed a capital gains tax on the growth of their shares on their terminal return. The idea behind an estate freeze is to limit the tax payable upon death by limiting the growth of the taxpayer's interest in the company. It is not that we want to freeze the taxpayer's business itself. Rather we want to stop the growth of the taxpayer's shares while allowing the business (and somebody else's shares) to keep growing.

In a nutshell, an estate freeze converts a taxpayer's shares in their business into preferred shares with value equal to the value of the shares they traded in. After the freeze the taxpayer is left with preferred shares that will never increase in value. The corporation then issues a few new common shares worth $1 to family members or a family trust.

And as the business and its assets increase in value over time, that increase is attributed to the common shares, owned by the next generation, which at the time of the freeze were only worth, say, $1, but which could turn out to be worth millions of dollars down the road. And voilà, tax on any further increase in value of the business is paid by the next generation many years in the future when they sell the $1 shares that were given to them — not by the taxpayer who had frozen their estate.

Why Freeze Now?

While the crisis is still its infancy, it is important to take advantage of the fact that business valuators have still not figured out how to go about performing a meaningful valuation. Until more is known about the duration and the severity of the recession/depression, valuators are likely going to be approaching valuations very conservatively. So, while it is going to be a good time to perform an estate freeze at any point during the crisis, it may be best to act sooner than later to take advantage of the uncertainty.

Audits and Valuations

There is always a possibility that the Canada Revenue Agency will audit a freeze transaction. And there may be an increased likelihood of attracting CRA attention and scrutiny for freeze transactions with very low valuations. So, if the CRA comes calling, it is always best to be prepared. And being prepared means being ready to either a) support the valuation or b) in the case where one cannot successfully oppose the CRA's challenge of the valuation, one needs to be able to avail themselves of a price adjustment clause, which will allow them to retroactively adjust the valuation of the preferred shares.

But one of the requirements in order to be able to invoke the price adjustment clause is that the original valuation was arrived at using a methodology that was fair and reasonable. So, one can't just be cheeky and value a $1 million business at $100,000, then do an estate freeze on that basis and expect to be able to use the price adjustment clause if the CRA audits. If it is determined by the Canada Revenue Agency that the valuation that the taxpayer is relying upon was not performed in a fair and reasonable manner, the CRA won't allow the price adjustment clause to be invoked and there will be tax consequences, plus penalties could be applied.

In either case — whether one wants to challenge the Canada Revenue Agency by supporting their valuation or whether they want to accept the CRA's valuation and invoke the price adjustment clause and revalue the preferred shares — a taxpayer will require a proper valuation upon which they can rely. And the gold standard is to get a valuation performed by a certified business valuator (CBV). As long as one has a CBV valuation they stand a far greater chance of either supporting their valuation or of invoking a price adjustment clause and ultimately having a successful estate freeze.

Moral of the story: Freeze your estate now and get a proper valuation performed by a CBV.

A complete discussion of exit plans is beyond the scope of this book, but I want to leave you with a few nuggets of advice. Not legal advice, but just plain old good advice. Firstly, organize your company as if it were going to take on partners or be sold one day. That means you should keep your minute book up to date and organized. You should ensure that you always have proper books and records for a valuation or for a bank loan. You should keep all memberships, licenses, domain names, etc. up to date and in good standing. You should have all the proper organizational documents and resolutions prepared. And once you decide to take on other shareholders as partners you should also very seriously consider having a shareholders' agreement prepared so that everybody's rights and responsibilities are properly defined.

And as important as it is to ensure that everything has been properly set up and organized, it is just as important to re-evaluate the plan and the structure with a professional every few years. Tax laws change. Your family changes. Your goals change. Your needs for capital change. And your tax plan and your exit plan should reflect that.

Finally, you should consider that your business is capable of considerable growth. It may not be the next Amazon, but then again it may be. The moment before Amazon was founded, it was the next Amazon. So, you never know. And as your business evolves and grows, accept the change and accept that your exit plan may also change along the way.

Use the Capital Gains Reserve Mechanism to Defer Capital Gains When You Get Paid Over Time

Capital Gains Reserve

Sometimes one sells a capital property which would give rise to a capital gains tax, yet they don't receive all the money at once. And when this occurs it is sometimes difficult to make the tax payment given that the proceeds have not all been received.

In such circumstances one is allowed to claim a "capital gains reserve" which exempts the seller from paying the entire capital gains tax bill until they have received the entire payment from the buyer. This can help defer the capital gain for up to five years.

In order to claim the capital gains reserve, one must complete form T2017 and submit it with the T1 individual tax return for the year of the sale.

EXAMPLE

One sells a capital property and makes a gain of $500,000

An agreement is made with the purchaser to have the payment split over 5 years at $100,000 per year.

By claiming the capital gains reserve using form T2017 only $100,000 of capital gains is reported each year for five years.

A word of caution:

While the capital gains reserve allows one to claim the capital gains over a number of years, this can be detrimental if one's income is likely to increase over the duration of the deferral. In such a case one may be in a higher tax bracket in future years and have to pay more tax than they otherwise would have had to pay without the reserve.

13 ESTATE PLANNING TAX TIPS

Do an Estate Freeze

As noted previously in Part 11, the estate freeze is a tool which can be employed to limit the capital gains tax payable upon the death of a taxpayer.

If a taxpayer has an asset which is likely to increase in value over the remainder of their life, rather than paying a capital gains tax on the deemed disposition of their assets at the time of death, the estate freeze allows a taxpayer to put the future growth of their assets in the hands of their children. As such, in the course of the estate freeze, the taxpayer "freezes" and limits the amount of capital gains tax which shall be paid at their death. The taxes to be paid on the future (post-freeze) gains shall be paid only when their child disposes of the assets in the distant future.

EXAMPLE 2 – ROLLOVER WITH BOOT:

Let's assume that the taxpayer has an asset which is going to increase in value by $1,000,000 over the remainder of their life. Let's also assume that the taxpayer will live another 20 years and plans on leaving their estate to their children. Without an estate freeze, a capital gains tax of approximately $250,000 would be payable at the time of death.

However, if an estate freeze were performed, rather than having to pay $250,000 in year 20 (the year in which the taxpayer dies), the increase in value of $1,000,000 will be an increase in the hands of the children – and will only be taxed at the time the children dispose of the asset. And if the children dispose of the asset 25 years after their parent's death, assuming that the asset has not further increased in value, they will have to pay a capital gains tax on that $1,000,000 – still $250,000.

And due to the decreasing value of money over time, paying $250,000 25 years later at the time of disposition is far less costly than paying $250,000 at the time of death of the parent.

Sell Shares, Not Assets

Whenever possible, you want to sell the shares of your corporation rather than the assets. Gains on the sale of assets cannot be shielded with the LCGE. Only shares. The problem is that buyers prefer asset sales in most situations. An asset sale is cleaner because you are not buying anything which has a potential liability. When you buy an "used" company there could be skeletons in the closet. After purchase, a lawsuit could arise for something which happened in the past. The CRA could audit and reassess for a time period before the purchase. And besides this there are many other possible liabilities which could arise. And of course, these possible or contingent liabilities may be addressed with the appropriate guarantees and indemnities in the agreement of purchase and sale. Nonetheless it always seems to be something which needs to be sold to the buyer.

Take Advantage of the Lifetime Capital Gains Exemption

A major consideration when planning for one's exit is the lifetime capital gains exemption (the "LCGE"). Here's how it works: When one disposes shares of a "Qualified Small Business Corporation" (a "QSBC"), if certain tests are met, each taxpayer has a LCGE which essentially wipes out capital gains taxation on the disposition of their shares – up to the LCGE limit, which is currently $883,384, and which is indexed and increases on an annual basis.

The LCGE is available to individuals upon the disposition of either:

- Qualified farm property.
- Qualified fishing property (post 2016).
- Qualified small business corporation shares (QSBC).

QSBC Shares

- The shares must be shares of a Canadian-Controlled Private Corporation (CCPC).
- At the time of sale, the share of the capital stock must be part of a small business corporation, and was owned by you, your spouse, or common-law partner, or a partnership of which you were a member. Additionally, during the 24 months immediately before the sale of the shares, more than 50% of the fair market value of the assets must have been used in an active business carried on primarily in Canada.
-

- Hardest condition to meet is that to qualify as a QSBC, on the date of sale more than 90% of its assets must be used in an active business in Canada.
- The amount of capital gain that is eligible for the capital gains deduction may be affected by the balance in your cumulative net investment loss (CNIL) account and if you have ever claimed an allowable business investment loss (ABIL)

Purification

Sometimes a business does not qualify as a QSBC at a given point in time, but often this can be remedied through a process called "purification". For a company to qualify as a QSBC at the time of a future sale, it may be necessary to take steps now to remove from the company non-active business assets, such as excess cash or portfolio investments. This can be as easy as having the company use its excess cash to pay off debts or pay dividends to its shareholders, or it may involve a corporate reorganization to transfer the non-active assets into a separate company.

Opt out of Automatic Spousal Rollover if there is LCGE Room

When one dies, certain of their capital assets, like shares in a corporation, are automatically passed to their surviving spouse on a tax-free basis through a spousal rollover. This is usually a good thing, but sometimes this can be a bad thing.

For example, if the deceased spouse had some remaining space in their Lifetime Capital Gains Exemption (the "LCGE"), then the automatic rollover would deprive them of taking advantage of the LCGE space.

Under section 73(1) of the Income Tax Act there is an automatic tax-free spousal rollover upon death. Sometimes this acts in the best interests of the long-term family wealth of a deceased taxpayer and their family. Sometimes it does not. The election for 73(1) to NOT automatically apply is used in those circumstances where it is detrimental to long-term (and short-term) family wealth preservation, such as when the deceased has unused portions of their lifetime capital gains exemption (LCGE).

Where there is an unused portion of the LCGE, the taxpayer's representative may elect to have some or all of their shares transfer to their surviving spouse at FMV, while other shares may be transferred at ACB pursuant to the 73(1) rollover.

That is to say that one can pick and choose those shares which will not have 73(1) apply in order to max-out the deceased taxpayer's LCGE.
This in turn leaves the surviving taxpayer with two sets of shares: those acquired from the deceased taxpayer at ACB, pursuant to the 73(1) rollover, and those acquired at the FMV at death with FMV being the ACB of those shares.

EXAMPLE 2 – ROLLOVER WITH BOOT:

Deceased has $500,000 LCGE remaining
Surviving Spouse has $0 LCGE remaining
Deceased had 1,000,000 shares
These shares were acquired for 50cents each = $500,000 total
The share has a fair market value at death of $1 each = $1,000,000

Scenario A: If the spouse receives all the shares with an automatic spousal rollover and then sells them all for fair market value the next day

- Spouse receives 1,000,000 shares
- The "ACB" of the shares in the surviving spouse's hands is the same as it was in the deceased spouse's hands (i.e.: $500,000).
- When the spouse sells the shares for $1,000,000, there is a capital gain of (sale price – ACB), which is ($1,000,000 - $500,000) = $500,000
- Spouse pays a capital gain on the $500,000, which is about $125,000
- The surviving spouse is left with $875,000 in cash.

Scenario B: If the spouse elects not to have the automatic spousal rollover apply and then sells them all for fair market value the next day

- Spouse receives 1,000,000 shares
- Spouse elects for the automatic rollover NOT to occur
- Spouse elects to receive the shares at fair market value
- Absent the automatic rollover, the deceased spouse is deemed to have sold the shares to the surviving spouse at fair market value.

- Since the deceased spouse is deemed to have sold the shares to the surviving spouse for $1,000,000, the deceased has a capital gain of (sale price – ACB), which is ($1,000,000 - $500,000) = $500,000
- Since the deceased spouse has $500,000 room remaining in their LCGE, they essentially don't pay any tax on the capital gain.
- The "ACB" of the shares in the surviving spouse's hands is fair market value ($1,000,000) – Remember they were deemed to have acquired the shares from the deceased spouse at fair market value.
- When the spouse sells the shares for $1,000,000 cash, they have a capital gain of (sale price – ACB), which is ($1,000,000 - $1,000,000) = 0. So, they pocket the entire $1,000,000.

For further information visit:

https://www.canada.ca/en/revenue-agency/services/tax/individuals/topics/about-your-tax-return/tax-return/completing-a-tax-return/personal-income/line-127-capital-gains/transfers-capital-property/transfers-property-a-spouse-common-law-partner-a-trust-a-spouse-common-law-partner.html

Draft a Secondary Will to Segregate Assets Not Subject to Probate

While people have historically had multiple wills to deal with assets on multiple jurisdictions (an Ontario will and a US will and a Quebec will for example for a person who has property in Ontario, the US and Quebec), depending on your province of residence it may be advantageous to have multiple wills to segregate assets which are all located in the same province. This strategy is typically used by people who own share of a private business.

For example, in Ontario where probate fees are 1.5% of the value of one's assets it is important to segregate assets into two wills – one will which will be subject to probate and another which contains those assets which are not necessary to probate. If an Ontario resident were to put the shares of their private corporation (worth $1 million dollars) into a separate will, they can avoid probate on those shares and save $15,000. In Alberta this strategy is less important since the probate fees are only several hundred dollars. The legal fees for the second will in Alberta may be more than one would save in probate.

EXAMPLE

For on Ontario Resident with a house, investments and shares of a private corporation.

Note: Ontario probate fees are 0% for the first $50,000 and 1.5% of the remainder of the estate.

Single Will

House	$1,000,000
Shares of a Private corporation	$800,000
Investments	$500,000
Total Value of Estate	$2,300,000
Probate Fees	$5,300
Probate Fees 0% of the first $50,000 1.5% of the remainder Total Probate Fees	 $0 $33,750 $33,750

Two Wills

Asset	Primary Will	Secondary Will
House	$1,000,000	
Shares of Private Corp		$800,000
Investments	$500,000	
Total Value of Estate	$1,5000,000	$800,000
Probate Fees 0% of the first $50,000 1.5% of the remainder Total Probate Fees	 $0 $21,750 $21,750	 $0

For this individual, the segregation of their corporation shares into a secondary will saves $12,000 in probate fees.

Probate Fees by Province

British Columbia

Where the gross value of personal properly located in BC exceeds $25,000, probate fees are:

Portion over $25,000 - $50,000	$6 per $1000 (.6%)
Portion over $50,000	$14 per $1000 (1.4%)

Alberta

$10,000 or less	$35
$10,001 - $25,000	$135
$25,001-$125,000	$275
$125,001 - $250,000	$400
Over $250,000	$525

Saskatchewan

$7 for every $1,000 (0.7%)
Note: For real estate, fees are due on the equity (not market value of property)

Manitoba

Probate fees eliminated in 2020

Ontario

First $50,000	0%
After $50,000	$15 per $1000 (1.5%)

Quebec

No probate fees. $202 court filing fee for will verification

New Brunswick	$5,000 or less	$25
	$5,001 - $10,000	$50
	$10,001 - $15,000	$75
	$15,001 - $20,000	$100
	Over $20,000	$5 per $1000 (.5%)

Nova Scotia	$10,000 or less	$85.60
	$10,001 - $25,000	$215.20
	$25,001 - $50,000	$358.15
	$50,001 - $100,000	$1002.65
	First $100,000	$1002.65
	Amounts over $100,000	$16.95 per $1000 (1.695%)

Prince Edward Island	$10,000 or less	$50
	$10,001 - $25,000	$100
	$25,001 - $50,000	$200
	$50,001 - $100,000	$400
	First $100,000	$400
	Amounts over $100,000	$4 per $1000 (.4%)

Newfoundland & Labrador	$1000 or less	$60
	First $1000	$60
	Over $1000	$6 per $1000 (.6%)

Yukon — For estates over $25,000 $140 filing fee

Nunavut	$10,000 or less	$25
	$10,001 - $25,000	$100
	$25,000 - $125,000	$200
	$125,001 - $250,000	$300
	Over $250,000	$400

Northwest Territories	$10,000 or less	$30
	$10,001 - $25,000	$110
	$25,000 - $125,000	$215
	$125,001 - $250,000	$325
	Over $250,000	$435

Invest Chid Tax Benefit in Your Children's Name

The Canada Child Benefit, a non-taxable amount available to Canadian parents, beyond supporting families and covering expenses, creates opportunities to invest in a child's future with significantly reduced tax consequences.

The CCB is a monthly sum of non-taxable money that Canadians with children are entitled to. It is to assist with the cost of raising children under 18 years of age. The amount of CCB varies depending on the amount of their children, the age of their children, and the adjusted net income of the family. An Ontarian may be eligible of up to $119.50 per month per child. A family eligible for this amount with two children would gain an additional $2,868 annually, tax free. Due to COVID-19 and general increases in the CCB, beginning July 2020, the maximum annual the CCB will increase, meaning that having only one child under the age of 6 entitles Canadian parents to up to $6,756 per year; and, for a child between 6 and 17, $5,708.

For investing purposes, the most important feature of the CCB income is that it is exempt from attribution rules of the Income Tax Act. This means that if children earn interest and dividend income, or capital gains, from CCB invested, then the parent's will not be required to pay income tax (at their marginal tax rate) on those amounts. Normally, and pursuant to ss. 74.1(2) of the ITA, when parent's give money or property to their kids to invest or watch grow, any dividends and interest earned on that money or property is "attributed" back to the grantor/parent.

With the CCB, a parent can open an in-trust bank account and leverage CCB payments to invest in stock or bond markets on their child's behalf, notwithstanding that money otherwise used to invest in this account would be taxed in the hands of the parent were it not from the CCB. In spite of the fact that children cannot make these investments from the shelter of a Tax-Free Savings Account because they are not 18, they will likely be taxed at the lowest marginal rate of income tax.

When they turn 18, they can transfer the investment accumulated into a TFSA and open their own investment account. They will not pay income tax before money is entered into that account, given that income tax has been paid at their low marginal rate throughout the years. From the TFSA, they can shelter future interest, dividends and capital gains against income tax.

Otherwise, investing amounts in a Registered Education Savings Plan (RESP) for the later benefit of a child. With an RESP, post-tax funds are deposited into an account. Interest and dividends are earned in the account without income taxes from property income applying annually, and the money can be withdrawn for the benefit of a student enrolled in a higher education program, such as a university, college, or trade school. The money is withdrawn at their tax rate.

There are two major benefits for investing the CCB in an RRSP. One, income tax is not payable before the CCB enters the RESP, the amounts will grow within that account without income tax applying to property income, and the child can withdraw the money at their more favourable tax rate when they are in a higher education program. Two, by using an RESP, the child can benefit from grants which are added to that account by the government. As money is added to an RESP, the government adds grants at a maximum of $500 per year that do not have to be paid back, with a cap of $7,200. Children in middle and low-income families may be eligible for an extra 10% to 20% on the first $500 contributed each year in an RESP.

14 EMIGRATION

There are two ways that one may proceed to alert the CRA that they are becoming a non-resident. One would be to file a departure return, which would include all of one's Canadian source income up to the point they left Canada. The second option would be to submit a NR73 application to have the CRA determine their residency as a form of an advanced ruling.

The departure return is simplest and quickest option, as you would only need to really file their tax return and indicate that they have become a non-resident the day they left Canada. There is a possible drawback: if enough ties are maintained with Canada, the CRA may still consider one to be a resident for tax purposes.

The second option is to file an NR73 form (see below) which provides the advantage that if accepted by the CRA, the CRA will have already acknowledged you as being a non-resident, which means that you will not have to worry about them investigating this later on unless the CRA found evidence of fraud. The only issue with the NR73 is that the applications can take a long time to process, and this was even before COVID 19 slowed down the CRA even further. I would currently estimate it to take at least 6-12 months to receive a determination.

Ultimately there are pros and cons to each of the two methods to be determined a non-resident, but which ever option you choose, there are important tax saving measures to consider once you are deemed to be a non-resident.

Factors Considered by the CRA when Determining Residency

A rather succinct and abbreviated summary of these factors is found in this passage from the decision of the Federal Court of Canada in The Queen v. Reeder :

- Past and present habits of life;
- Regularity and length of visits in the jurisdiction asserting residence;
- Ties within that jurisdiction;
- Ties elsewhere;
- Permanence or otherwise of purposes of stay abroad.

The Tax Court of Canada Decision in Wassick v. M.N.R lists the following 33 indicia that could be considered:

1. past and present habits of life;
2. regularity and length of visits in the jurisdiction asserting residence;
3. ties within the jurisdiction;
4. ties elsewhere;
5. permanence or otherwise of purposes of stay;
6. ownership of a dwelling in Canada or rental of a dwelling on a long-term basis (for example, a lease for one or more years);
7. residence of spouse, children and other dependent family members in a dwelling maintained by the individual in Canada;
8. memberships with Canadian churches or synagogues, recreational and social clubs, unions and professional organizations;
9. registration and maintenance of automobiles, boats and airplanes in Canada;
10. holding credit cards issued by Canadian financial institutions and other commercial entities including stores, car rental agencies, etc.;
11. local newspaper subscriptions sent to a Canadian address;
12. rental of Canadian safe deposit box or post office box;
13. subscriptions for life or general insurance including health insurance through a Canadian insurance company;
14. mailing address in Canada;
15. telephone listing in Canada;
16. stationery including business cards showing a Canadian address;
17. magazine and other periodical subscriptions sent to a Canadian address;
18. Canadian bank accounts other than a non-resident bank account;
19. active securities accounts with Canadian brokers;
20. Canadian driver's licence;
21. membership in a Canadian pension plan;
22. holding directorships of Canadian corporations;
23. membership in Canadian partnerships;
24. frequent visits to Canada for social or business purposes;
25. burial plot in Canada;
26. will prepared in Canada;
27. legal documentation indicating Canadian residence;
28. filing a Canadian income tax return as a Canadian resident;
29. ownership of a Canadian vacation property;
30. active involvement in business activities in Canada;
31. employment in Canada;
32. maintenance or storage in Canada of personal belongings including clothing, furniture, family pets, etc.;

33. obtaining landed immigrant status or appropriate work permits in Canada

The CRA also has restated these same positions in their own information circulars stating the following with respect to significant residential ties:

Significant residential ties

The residential ties of an individual that will almost always be significant residential ties for the purpose of determining residence status are the individual's:

- dwelling place (or places);
- spouse or common-law partner; and
- dependents.

Where an individual who leaves Canada keeps a dwelling place in Canada (whether owned or leased), available for his or his occupation, that dwelling place will be considered to be a significant residential tie with Canada during the individual's stay abroad.

However, if an individual leases a dwelling place located in Canada to a third party on arm's-length terms and conditions, the CRA will take into account all of the circumstances of the situation (including the relationship between the individual and the third party, the real estate market at the time of the individual's departure from Canada, and the purpose of the stay abroad), and may consider the dwelling place not to be a significant residential tie with Canada except when taken together with other residential ties.

If an individual who is married or cohabiting with a common-law partner leaves Canada, but his or his spouse or common-law partner remains in Canada, then that spouse or common-law partner will usually be a significant residential tie with Canada during the individual's absence from Canada. Similarly, if an individual with dependents leaves Canada, but his or his dependents remain behind, then those dependents will usually be considered to be a significant residential tie with Canada while the individual is abroad. Where an individual was living separate and apart from his or his spouse or common-law partner prior to leaving Canada, by reason of a breakdown of their marriage or common-law partnership, that spouse or common-law partner will not be considered to be a significant tie with Canada.

Secondary residential ties

Generally, secondary residential ties must be looked at collectively in order to evaluate the significance of any one such tie. For this reason, it would be unusual for a single secondary residential tie with Canada to be sufficient on its own to lead to a determination that an individual is factually resident in Canada while abroad. Secondary residential ties that will be taken into account in determining the residence status of an individual while outside Canada are:

- personal property in Canada (such as furniture, clothing, automobiles, and recreational vehicles);
- social ties with Canada (such as memberships in Canadian recreational or religious organizations);
- economic ties with Canada (such as employment with a Canadian employer and active involvement in a Canadian business, and Canadian bank accounts, retirement savings plans, credit cards, and securities accounts);
- landed immigrant status or appropriate work permits in Canada;
- hospitalization and medical insurance coverage from a province or territory of Canada;
- a driver's license from a province or territory of Canada;
- a vehicle registered in a province or territory of Canada;
- a seasonal dwelling place in Canada or a leased dwelling place;
- a Canadian passport; and
- memberships in Canadian unions or professional organizations.

In analyzing the above noted factors, the Courts have noted:

"The question of residency is one of fact and depends on the specific facts of each case.... It should be noted that no one or any group of two or three items will in themselves establish that the individual is resident in Canada. However, a number of factors considered together could establish that the individual is a resident of Canada for Canadian income tax purposes"

Deemed Disposition Upon Emigration

When a taxpayer ceases to be a resident of Canada for tax purposes, they must pay a departure tax. When your clients leave, they are considered to have sold some types of properties and reacquired them for the same price (fair market value). Note that this applies even if you didn't actually sell their property to another party - wherein lies the deemed disposition.

The difference between the adjusted cost base, and the fair market value (FMV) sales price is used to calculate the taxable capital gain that you will have to pay taxes upon when emigrating. You cannot avoid this tax by simply saying that the value of the property is nil, or equal to the acquisition cost. If the CRA were to find out that the FMV of the property disposed of was higher than what was stated, they can reassess you for the difference with added penalties. Your accountant can also be penalized.

The form that an emigrating taxpayer needs to fill out upon departure is the Form T1243, Deemed Disposition of Property by an Emigrant of Canada. An NR73 form (see a sample form below) should be completed at the same time. This form lets the CRA know that a taxpayer is leaving and wishes to be considered as a non-resident for tax purposes. While the NR73 is not required, it is nevertheless recommended.

File an Election Under 220(4.5) of The Income Tax Act to Avoid a Deemed Disposition Upon Emigration

If you intend to return to Canada at a future date, and do not wish to dispose of the property, or have it seen as a deemed disposition, the CRA offers a way to defer the taxes payable by way of an election under Subsection 220(4.5) of the *Income Tax Act.*

T1243 Form

Canada Revenue Agency / Agence du revenu du Canada

Protected B
when completed

Deemed Disposition of Property by an Emigrant of Canada

Last name (print)	First name (print)	Social insurance number
Mailing address (print)	Date of emigration from Canada	Year Month Day

Fill out this form if you ceased to be a resident of Canada in the year and you were deemed to have disposed of property when you left Canada, **excluding** properties such as:

1) Canadian real or immovable property, Canadian resource property, and timber resource property

2) Canadian business property (including inventory) if the business is carried on through a permanent establishment in Canada

3) pension plans, annuities, registered retirement savings plans, pooled registered pension plans, registered retirement income funds, registered education savings plans, registered disability savings plans, tax-free savings accounts, deferred profit-sharing plans, employee profit-sharing plans, employee benefit plans, salary deferral arrangements, retirement compensation arrangements, employee life and health trusts, rights or interests in certain other trusts, employee security options subject to Canadian tax, interests in certain personal trusts resident in Canada, and interests in life insurance policies in Canada (other than segregated fund policies). For a complete list, refer to the definition of "excluded right or interest" in Subsection 128.1(10) of the Income Tax Act

4) property you owned when you last became a resident of Canada, or property you inherited after you last became a resident of Canada, if you were a resident of Canada for 60 months or less during the 10-year period before you emigrated

Note
If you ceased to be a resident of Canada and you elected to declare the deemed disposition of properties listed in items 1 or 2 above, include those properties when calculating your deemed dispositions and fill out Form T2061A, Election by an Emigrant to Report Deemed Dispositions of Property and Any Resulting Capital Gain or Loss.

Use the table on the next page to calculate your capital gains (or losses) for the properties you were deemed to have disposed of. Indicate either (C) for Canadian properties or (F) for foreign properties (outside of Canada). If some or all of your investments are in a portfolio, please provide a complete breakdown. Make sure you include those capital gains (or losses) on your Schedule 3, Capital Gains (or Losses). If applicable, also fill out Form T1161, List of Properties by an Emigrant of Canada.

Note
You can elect to defer the payment of tax on income relating to the deemed disposition of property by completing Form T1244, Election, Under Subsection 220(4.5) of the Income Tax Act, to Defer the Payment of Tax on Income Relating to the Deemed Disposition of Property.

Attach your Form T1243 and Schedule 3 to your tax return.

Protected B
when completed

(1) Number of shares (if applicable)	(2) Description of property (such as name of corporation and class of shares including its stock symbol or the address or location for buildings or land)	(3) Canadian (C) or foreign (F)	(4) Year of acquisition	(5) Fair market value on the date you emigrated	(6) Adjusted cost base	(7) Gain (or loss) (column 5 minus column 6)

See the privacy notice on your return.

File an NR73 Form Upon Emigration

If you plan on leaving the country and stopping to pay Canadian taxes altogether, this is important.

Sometimes a taxpayer inadvertently leaves the country and leaves behind enough connections which can cause the CRA to still consider them a resident notwithstanding the fact that they have factually left the country.

This causes the taxpayer's worldwide income to be subject to Canadian taxation, notwithstanding the fact that they have emigrated and consider themselves to be a non-resident.

In such a case, if the taxpayer would have completed the NR73 form and the CRA was not satisfied that enough ties had been severed for residency to have been terminated, the taxpayer would have received an early warning to sever further ties or risk being taxed by the CRA on their worldwide income.

EXAMPLE

Scenario A: You leave the country and complete the NR73 form

- You leave the country, but leave your furniture in storage, you rent your house, you keep your Ontario driver's license, keep some credit cards and bank accounts
- You complete the NR73 form and provide the CRA with a forwarding address
- The CRA advises you that based on the information provided you would still be considered a Canadian resident for tax purposes
- You sell your house, cancel your driver's license, sell your furniture and get rid of most of your bank accounts and credit cards
- You live in another country and pay taxes there for 8 years. You do not file Canadian returns for that time
- You decide to move back to Canada
- After a year in Canada, you file Canadian tax returns
- No problem. Smooth sailing.

Scenario B: You leave the country and don't complete the NR73 form

- You leave the country, but leave your furniture in storage, you rent your house, you keep your Ontario driver's license, keep some credit cards and bank accounts
- You live in another country and pay taxes there for 8 years. You do not file Canadian returns for that time
- You decide to move back to Canada
- After a year in Canada, you file Canadian tax returns
- The next year you are audited and the CRA asks you about the tax returns for the previous 8 years
- The CRA declares you to have been a resident of Canada (for tax purposes) the whole time
- You have to file the 8 years of tax returns and pay Canadian income tax on your worldwide income for the 8 years you were away

NR73 Form

Canada Revenue Agency / Agence du revenu du Canada

DETERMINATION OF RESIDENCY STATUS (LEAVING CANADA)

Protected B when completed

- Complete all areas of this form if you plan to leave or have left Canada, either permanently or temporarily. Give all the facts about your residency status while living inside and outside Canada.
- Mail only one completed copy of this form for the tax years in question (an additional form is not necessary for each tax year unless your situation changes, or directed otherwise) to the International tax and non-resident enquiries office, Post Office Box 20000, Station A, Sudbury ON P3A 5C1, CANADA. If you prefer, you can send the form by fax to **705-671-0794**.
- If you need help completing this form, see Income Tax Folio S5-F1-C1: *Determining an Individual's Residence Status*, or call the International tax and non-resident enquiries line at:
  - Calls from anywhere in Canada and the United States **1-800-959-8281**
  - Calls from outside Canada and the United States (we accept collect calls) **613-940-8495**
- You can find most of our forms and publications, as well as information on taxes, programs and credits, on our website at **canada.ca/taxes**.

Attach any necessary additional information to this form.

Identification

Last name	Usual first name and initial	Social insurance number (SIN)	Tax Year
Address while outside Canada			Telephone number
Do you want us to change our records to show this as your mailing address for all future correspondence? ☐ Yes ☐ No			
Mailing address ONLY (if different from above)	Citizenship	In what province did you reside?	In what country will you live?
Date of departure: Year Month Day	Marital status: ☐ Married ☐ Divorced ☐ Separated ☐ Widowed ☐ Living common-law ☐ Single		Date of birth: Year Month Day

Outside Canada

How long do you expect to live outside Canada?

Number of days: ____ Number of months: ____ Number of years: ____ ☐ Leaving or left Canada permanently and no plan to return to Canada.

General Information

Indicate which one of the following situations apply to you by ticking (✓) the appropriate box:

- ☐ You usually live in another country and you were temporarily living in Canada for ____ days in the year, but will leave, or have left Canada during the year (we will calculate the number of days if you give us the dates you were, or will be, in Canada).
- ☐ You usually live in another country, but enter and leave Canada on the same day to work, shop, or study.
- ☐ You usually live in Canada, but you leave Canada during the day to work, shop, or study in another country, and return to Canada the same day.
- ☐ You are vacationing outside Canada and will return to Canada after your vacation.
- ☐ None of the above — explain: ____________________

Leaving Canada

Indicate why you are leaving Canada by ticking (✓) the appropriate box:

- ☐ Employment
- ☐ Retirement
- ☐ Studying or doing research
- ☐ Self-employment
- ☐ Professional or improvement leave
- ☐ Spouse (or common-law partner) of an individual leaving Canada
- ☐ Dependant of an individual leaving Canada
- ☐ None of the above—specify: ____________________

Relationship

If you are a spouse (or common-law partner), child, or other dependant of an individual who has left Canada, or will be leaving, indicate whether your spouse (or common-law partner), parent, or individual you are dependent on after the person has left Canada, has been determined to be a:

☐ Factual resident of Canada ☐ Deemed resident of Canada ☐ Non-resident of Canada ☐ Residency status not determined

Give the name, SIN, and address of this individual: ____________________

If you do not know the residency status of your spouse (or common-law partner), parent, or the individual you are dependent on, have the individual complete Form NR73, *Determination of Residency Status (Leaving Canada)*, and file it with this request.

If you are the spouse (or common-law partner) of a person leaving Canada:

- Are you, or were you, a resident of Canada in the current year, before leaving Canada? ☐ Yes ☐ No
- Were you a resident of Canada in a previous year? ☐ Yes ☐ No
- Will you live with your spouse (or common-law partner) at any time in the year? ☐ Yes ☐ No
- Will you be exempt from tax in the foreign country because of your relationship to your spouse (or common-law partner)? ☐ Yes ☐ No

Protected B when completed

Are you the spouse (or common-law partner) of an individual employed by the Canadian Forces who has been posted abroad? ☐ Yes ☐ No

If *yes*, what is the length of the posting? ______________ and,

Will you be returning to Canada at the end of the posting? ☐ Yes ☐ No

If you are a child or dependant of a person leaving Canada, tick (✓) the appropriate box:

☐ you are under 18 years old at any time during the year.

☐ you are 18 or older and you are dependent because of a mental or physical disability.

Enter your net world income for the current year: ______________

Employment

If you will be employed while you live abroad, tick (✓) the boxes that apply to you:

☐ You are a member of the Canadian Forces.

☐ You are a member of the overseas Canadian Forces school staff.

Will you choose to file a Canadian income tax return each year to report your world income? ☐ Yes ☐ No

Were you living in the province of Quebec immediately prior to your departure? ☐ Yes ☐ No

☐ You are a locally engaged employee (you lived outside of Canada after severing ties and were then hired locally) of a Canadian embassy or mission abroad.

☐ You are an ambassador, a high commissioner, an agent general of a province or territory of Canada, or an officer or servant (employee) of Canada or of a province or territory of Canada.

☐ Will you receive a representation allowance for the year? ☐ Yes ☐ No

☐ Were you a Canadian resident (including factual or deemed) just before your appointment or employment by Canada, the province, the territory, or the Crown corporation? ☐ Yes ☐ No

☐ You are an employee or officer of a Canadian Crown corporation, either federal or provincial, where:

☐ the corporation is designated as an agent of Canada;

☐ the employees of the corporation have been given the status of servants of Canada; or

☐ none of the above apply—explain: ______________

☐ Will you receive a representation allowance for the year? ☐ Yes ☐ No

☐ Were you a Canadian resident (including factual or deemed) just before your appointment or employment by Canada, the province, the territory, or the Crown corporation? ☐ Yes ☐ No

☐ You are performing services as an employee, co-operant, advisor, contractor, or subcontractor under a prescribed international development assistance program of the Government of Canada that is financed with Canadian funds.

Specify: ______________

Were you a resident (including factual or deemed) at any time during the three months before the day you started your service abroad? ☐ Yes ☐ No

☐ You are a missionary.

Will you file a Canadian income tax return for each year you are living outside Canada to report your world income? ☐ Yes ☐ No

Are you a Canadian citizen or landed immigrant? ☐ Yes ☐ No

Will you be employed by a Canadian religious organization while you are outside Canada? ☐ Yes ☐ No

How many years will you be outside Canada? ______________

☐ You are an employee of an employer or an organization other than those described above.

Give your employer's name and address: ______________

Is this a Canadian employer? ☐ Yes ☐ No

Do you expect to return to reside in Canada because of a contract with your employer, or because you have a specific date to report back to work in Canada? ☐ Yes ☐ No

If you have a contract with your employer, attach a copy of the contract.

If you do not have a contract with your employer or a return date to Canada specified by your employer, will your job in Canada be kept available for you on your return to Canada? ☐ Yes ☐ No

STATEMENT OF RESIDENCY

Are you, under a tax treaty with another country, considered resident in the other country and not resident in Canada? ☐ Yes ☐ No

Are you subject to income tax in that country on your world income? (total income from inside and outside Canada) ☐ Yes ☐ No

Are you considered resident of a country that does not have a tax treaty with Canada? ☐ Yes ☐ No

We may ask you for confirmation from that government that you are considered resident and are subject to tax as a resident for the year in question.
We may also ask you to give us proof that your income is subject to tax in that country. (e.g. Copy of the foreign tax return, notice of tax assessment, a statement from the foreign authorities with the equivalent information as the tax return, Form 6166)

Ties in Canada

Which of the following ties will you have in Canada while living in another country? Tick (✓) the boxes that apply to you.

☐ Your spouse or common-law partner will stay in Canada. Give the name, SIN, citizenship, and current address of your spouse or common-law partner. If you are legally separated, this item does not apply to you. List any reason for your spouse or common-law partner to stay in Canada:

____

☐ You will leave children or dependants in Canada. Give their names, ages, citizenship, and current address, as well as the name and address of the school they attend and the grade in which they are enrolled. List any reasons why they are staying in Canada:

____

Protected B when completed

Which of the following ties will you have in Canada while living in another country? Tick (✓) the boxes that apply to you. (continued)

- ☐ You will continue to support a person in Canada who lives in a dwelling (e.g., a house, apartment, trailer, room, suite) that you occupied before your departure.
- ☐ You did not own but you rented a dwelling in Canada. You will sublet it for the period of your absence from Canada, and you intend to renew the lease when it expires.

You will continue to own a dwelling in Canada that is suitable for year-round occupancy and:

a) ☐ keep the dwelling vacant;
b) ☐ rent the dwelling to a related person;
c) ☐ rent the dwelling on non-arm's length terms, (for example, under fair market value);
d) ☐ rent the dwelling without a written lease; or
e) ☐ rent the dwelling at arms length, at fair market value, and with a written lease. Explain: ____________

- ☐ You will keep the majority (or a significant part) of such things as your furniture, furnishings, appliances, and utensils) in Canada.
- ☐ You will have personal possessions in Canada such as your clothing or personal items or pets.
- ☐ You will keep vehicles in Canada that are registered in a province or territory of Canada.
- ☐ You will keep your driver's licence from a province or territory of Canada.
- ☐ You will have a valid Canadian passport.
- ☐ You will have a guaranteed job available on your return to Canada.
- ☐ You will be employed by a Canadian employer while outside Canada.
- ☐ You will stay eligible for medical coverage from a province or territory of Canada for more than three months after you leave Canada. To find out whether or not you will be eligible for provincial or territorial medical coverage while living outside Canada, contact the provincial or territorial health authorities where you live.
- ☐ You will keep memberships in Canadian social, recreational, or religious organizations. List these memberships: ____________
- ☐ You will keep professional or union memberships in Canada that depend on Canadian residency. List these memberships: ____________
- ☐ You will keep bank accounts in Canada. Explain why you keep these accounts: ____________
- ☐ You will keep and use credit cards or debit cards issued by Canadian financial institutions.
- ☐ You will have investments (RRSPs, securities accounts, etc.) in Canada. Describe these investments: ____________
- ☐ You will keep a seasonal residence in Canada (e.g., a cottage or chalet).
- ☐ You will have a telephone listing or service in Canada. Even if it is not listed, give the address for any telephone service and indicate if it is a personal or business service: ____________
- ☐ You will use personal stationery or business cards with a Canadian address. Give the address you will use: ____________
- ☐ You will keep a mailing address, a post office box, or a safety deposit box in Canada. Give the address for these items: ____________
- ☐ You will have newspaper or magazine subscriptions sent to a Canadian address.
- ☐ You will have subscriptions for life or general insurance, including health insurance, through a Canadian insurance company.
- ☐ You will be involved with and have responsibilities in partnerships, corporate or business relationships, or endorsement contracts in Canada.
  Specify: ____________
- ☐ You will keep landed immigrant status (if you are a landed immigrant) or a temporary work permit in Canada. Give the date of application for landed immigrant status or list the type of visa you have and the expiry date. ____________
- ☐ You will have other ties with Canada. Describe them: ____________
- ☐ None of the items in this section apply to you.

Intention

Do you intend to return to Canada to live? ☐ Yes ☐ No

Please state your long-term career goals:

Note – If it is determined that you are a non-resident of Canada you are expected to pay or post acceptable security for departure tax and advise Canadian financial institutions making payments to you that you may be subject to non-resident withholding taxes on certain income, i.e. dividends. For more information see Form T1161 and Guide T4061.

Visiting Canada

You will make return visits to Canada. ☐ Yes ☐ No

If yes, select which of the following best describes your visits to Canada.

- ☐ Lengthy
- ☐ Regular
- ☐ Frequent
- ☐ None of the above

Please provide details ____________

Ties in another country **Protected B** when completed

a) If your spouse (or common-law partner) will not stay in Canada, give: Social Insurance Number ______
Spouse's (or common-law partner's) name ______ Citizenship ______
Spouse's (or common-law partner's) current address ______
Spouse's (or common-law partner's) date of departure (year/month/day) ______
Number of months your spouse (or common-law partner) expects to live outside of Canada ______

b) If you have children or dependants not staying in Canada, give their name, age, citizenship, and current address, as well as the name and address of the school they attend and the grade in which they are enrolled:

c) If you have children and dependants who will follow you at a later date, give:
Their date of departure (year/month/day) ______
Number of months they expect to live outside of Canada ______

d) If you support individuals, other than through a charitable organization, give the name and current address of these people and financial details of your support:

e) Describe the dwelling in which you live in the other country. Include details such as address, type, size, and whether you rent or own the dwelling. If you rent the dwelling, give the length of time you have agreed to be a tenant:

f) Describe the personal possessions (e.g., clothing, furniture, personal items, pets) you will have in the other country:

g) If you have a driver's licence issued in a country other than Canada, state for which country it is issued, the expiry date, and whether you will renew it:

h) If you have a foreign passport, give details as to which country it is for and if you will renew it when it expires:

i) If applicable, give the name of the insurer of your medical and hospitalization coverage while living outside Canada and the length of the coverage:

j) List the professional, social, or recreational organizations in which you will be a member in countries other than Canada:

k) Describe the investments you will have in countries other than Canada. Include details of chequing and savings accounts, pension and retirement plans, property, and shares in companies you will have in these countries. Explain why these investments are kept outside Canada:

l) Give details of other consumer relationships, such as lines of credit and credit cards, you will have in other countries:

m) Give the address for your telephone service in other countries, even if it is not listed, and indicate if it is a personal or business service:

n) Give the address you use for any personal stationery and business cards in other countries:

o) Give the address for any post office boxes and safety deposit boxes you use in other countries:

p) Give details of your involvement and responsibilities in any partnerships, corporate or business relationships, and endorsement contracts you have in other countries:

q) List the countries, other than Canada, you have visited in this calendar year, the length of time spent in each country, and the reason for visiting these countries. Include the dates of entry and departure for each country visited:

Certification

We use this form as a starting point to get the facts we need in order to give an opinion on your residency status. Contact us if your situation changes since your residency status could also change.

I, ______ (print) certify that the information given on this form is to the best of my knowledge, correct and complete.

Date ______ Signature ______

More information

If there is more information that we have not asked for and that you feel will help us determine your residency status, give this information here:

Privacy Act, personal information bank number CRA PPU 005

Elect to Defer Taxes Payable upon Emigration

When you emigrate from Canada, if you do not actually sell your property, the CRA imputes a "deemed disposition", which means that they will tax you as though you have sold the property to a third party at fair market value.

If you file a form "T2144, Election, Under Subsection 220(4.5) of the Income Tax Act, to Defer the Payment of Tax on Income Relating to the Deemed Disposition of Property" , you can avoid the deemed disposition rules, and simply report any gains when you eventually dispose of the property.

While this may seem like the obvious option for most emigrating taxpayers, there is a catch in that if the deemed disposition results in federal taxes of $16,500, you will need to post adequate security in order to avoid paying the departure taxes on your deemed disposition.

Security is established by calling the CRA and making an arrangement prior to filing the election. There is no set standard for the amount of security that is needed to cover the federal taxes owing, although they generally equal the departure taxes owing. Likewise, there is no set standard for what qualifies as security, although the CRA does list common types that would include bank letters of guarantee, bank letters of credit, shares in a private of publicly traded company, charge or mortgage on real or immovable property certificates in precious metals, or bonds from the Government of Canada, or a Province of Canada.

It is important to note that you the CRA will not act on these securities unless the property in question is sold. If the property is sold, you can simply file a return and pay the applicable taxes owing from the transaction. Once this done the CRA will release their hold on the security.

https://www.canada.ca/content/dam/cra-arc/formspubs/pbg/t1244/t1244-19e.pdf

If Emigrating, Don't Collapse RRSPs Until You Become a Non-Resident

If one collapses their RRSP before leaving Canada, the entire amount is added to the individual's taxable income for the year. This results in a significant tax – especially if the individual is in a high tax bracket or if the withdrawal pushes the individual into a higher bracket.

However, if left intact, the RRSP can continue to exist even once an individual becomes a non-resident. Withdrawals after becoming a non-resident are only subject to a 25% withholding tax which may be reduced to as low as 15% if the individual emigrates to a country which has a tax treaty with Canada.

15 ELECTIONS

Take Advantage of Elections

Many taxpayers make the mistake of not taking advantage of elections available to them – and there are many, a few of which are described below.

The best way to think of elections is like special cards in a game. One card may allow you to get out of jail free. Another one may allow you to get double rent. And another one may allow you to steal something from an opponent. Just like in a game, if you don't use your elections, they are of no help to you.

Common Elections

One of the ways that you might find yourself interfacing with the CRA is through the filing (or late filing) of common elections. In the following pages I provide a brief taste of a few of the more common elections and some tips about how to use these elections to reduce your tax bill.

Principal Residence Elections

In 2016, the CRA changed its administrative policy relating to the reporting of the principal residence exemption. This has made reporting the disposition or deemed disposition of a principal residence more important in recent years.

For 2016 and later tax years, the CRA will only allow the principal residence exemption if the sale is reported and a designation of a principal residence is made in the taxpayer's return for the relevant taxation year. If the disposition is not reported or the taxpayer forgets to make the designation with the T2091IND, the full amount of the capital gain will be taxable.

A principal residence is defined as a housing unit (house, apartment, cottage, trailer, etc.); a leasehold interest in a housing unit; or a share of the capital stock of a co-operative housing corporation.

The taxpayer must own the property in the year or years for which it is designated as a principal residence. Further, the CRA has the "ordinarily inhabited" rule which means the housing unit must be inhabited in the year or part of the year by the taxpayer, spouse, or child. The status of whether a housing unit is ordinarily inhabited in the year or part of the year is dealt with on a case-by-case basis for each taxpayer.

It is also possible for a property to be considered a taxpayer's principal residence for the year if not ordinarily inhabited by filing an appropriate election.

Disposition of Taxpayer's Principal Residence

In the year the principal residence is disposed, two forms must be completed and filed with the CRA. These forms are "T2091(IND), Designation of a Property as a Principal Residence by an Individual" and "Schedule 3, Capital Gains or (Losses)". On the Schedule 3 Form, the taxpayer would declare the capital gains earned from the disposition, but the taxpayer would be exempt from paying taxes on the disposition by completing the T2091 which would designate the residence as the principal residence in that tax year.

T2019IND

Canada Revenue Agency | Agence du revenu du Canada

Protected B when completed

Designation of a Property as a Principal Residence by an Individual (Other than a Personal Trust)

Tax year

Use this form to designate a property as a principal residence. You must also complete the "Principal residence designation" section of Schedule 3 for the year you are in one of the following situations:

- you disposed of, or were considered to have disposed of, your principal residence, or any part of it
- you granted someone an option to buy your principal residence, or any part of it

Note
If you were not a resident of Canada for the entire time you owned the designated property, call **1-800-959-8281**. Your period of non-residence may reduce or eliminate the availability of the principal residence exemption.

For more information about designating a principal residence and what qualifies as a principal residence, see Income Tax Folio S1-F3-C2, Principal Residence, or the "Principal residence" chapter in Guide T4037, Capital Gains.

You can only designate one property as your principal residence for any specific year. However, where you sell a principal residence and buy another (or move to another property that you own) in the same year, the "plus one" rule in calculating the principal residence exemption amount will allow you to claim the principal residence exemption for both properties for that year even though you can only designate one property as your principal residence.

For dispositions that occurred after October 2, 2016, if you were a non-resident throughout the taxation year in which the property was purchased or acquired, the "plus 1" rule does **not** apply.

If you ticked box 1 at line 17900 of Schedule 3, you only need to complete the first page of this form. You do not need to report any gain amount on Schedule 3 for this property.

If you are filing electronically, keep this form in case we ask to see it later. If you are filing a paper return, you **must** complete, **sign**, and attach this form to your return.

Description of property

Provide the information requested below for the property you disposed of in the tax year. Complete a separate form for each property you sold.

Address				Year of acquisition	Proceeds of disposition
Street number, street name, and unit number if applicable				9955	9954
Prov./Terr	Postal code	City	Country		

Designation

I, ______________________ (print your name), hereby designate the property described above to have been my principal residence for the following **number of tax years ending after the acquisition date**:

• After 1981		______	1
• After 1971 and before 1982		+ ______	2
Total number of years designated (line 1 **plus** line 2)	9956	= ______	3

For those years after 1981, I also confirm that neither I, nor my spouse or common-law partner (who was not separated and living apart from me throughout the year under a judicial separation or written separation agreement), nor any of my children (who were under 18 and unmarried or not in a common-law partnership throughout the year) designated any other property as a principal residence. For any tax year after 1981 for which I am designating the property and throughout which I was under 18 and unmarried or not in a common-law partnership, I also confirm that neither my mother, father, nor any of my brothers and sisters (who were under 18 and unmarried or not in a common-law partnership throughout the year) designated any other property as a principal residence.

For those years before 1982, I confirm that I have not designated any other property as my principal residence.

Note
If the property was designated as a principal residence for the purpose of filing Form T664 or T664(Seniors), you have to include those previously designated tax years as part of this principal residence designation.

Signature	Social insurance number	Date

T2091 (IND) E (19)

(Ce formulaire est disponible en français.)

Canada

Schedule 3, Capital Gains or Losses

Protected B when completed

T1-2019 **Capital Gains (or Losses) in 2019** **Schedule 3**

Complete this schedule and **attach** it to your return to report your capital gains (or losses) on line 12700 of your return.
For more information, see Guide T4037, Capital Gains. If you need more space, attach a separate sheet.

Note: If you have a business investment loss, see Guide T4037.	(1) Year of acquisition	(2) Proceeds of disposition	(3) Adjusted cost base	(4) Outlays and expenses (from dispositions)	(5) Gain (or loss) (column 2 minus columns 3 and 4)

1. Qualified small business corporation shares (If you realized a gain on a disposition, you may be able to claim a capital gains deduction on line 25400 of your return.)

(Report, in section 3 below, publicly traded shares, mutual fund units, deferral of eligible small business corporation shares, and other shares.)

Number | Name of corp. and class of shares

Total 10699 Gain (or loss) 10700

2. Qualified farm or fishing property (If you realized a gain on a disposition, you may be able to claim a capital gains deduction on line 25400 of your return.)

Address or legal description | Prov./Terr.

Total 10999 Gain (or loss) 11000 +

Mortgage foreclosures and conditional sales repossessions – address or legal description | Prov./Terr.

Total 12399 Gain (or loss) 12400 +

3. Publicly traded shares, mutual fund units, deferral of eligible small business corporation shares, and other shares

(Note: If you have capital gains (or losses) on your T5, T5013, T4PS, and T3 information slips, report them on line 17400 or line 17600.)

Number | Name of fund/corp. and class of shares

Total 13199 Gain (or loss) 13200 +

4. Real estate, depreciable property, and other properties (see the next page for a **principal residence**)

Address or legal description | Prov./Terr.

Total 13599 Gain (or loss) 13800 +

5. Bonds, debentures, promissory notes, and other similar properties

Face value | Maturity date | Name of issuer

Total 15199 Gain (or loss) 15300 +

6. Other mortgage foreclosures and conditional sales repossessions

Address or legal description | Prov./Terr.

Total 15499 Gain (or loss) 15500 +

7. Personal-use property (provide a full description) (see the next page for a **principal residence**)

Gain only 15800 +

8. Listed personal property (LPP) (provide a full description)

Note: You can apply LPP losses only against LPP gains.

Subtract: unapplied LPP losses from other years –

Net gain only 15900 +

Add lines 10700, 11000, 12400, 13200, 13800, 15300, 15500, 15800, and 15900. Enter this amount on line B on the next page. **Total of gains (or losses) of qualified properties and other properties** = A

5000-S3 **Continue on the next page.**

Protected **B** when completed

Enter the amount from line A on the previous page.				B
Capital gains deferral from qualifying dispositions of eligible small business corporation shares (included on line 13200 in item **3** on the previous page)	16100	–		C
Line B minus line C		=		D
T5, T5013, and T4PS information slips – Capital gains (or losses)	17400	+		E
T3 information slips – Capital gains (or losses)	17600	+		F
Add lines D, E, and F		=		G
Capital loss from a reduction in your business investment loss	17800	–		H
Total of all gains (or losses) before reserves: line G minus line H	19100	=		I
Reserves from line 67060 of Form T2017 (if negative, show it in brackets and subtract it)	19200	+		J
Total capital gains (or losses): line I plus line J	19700	=		K
Multiply the amount on line 19700 by 50%. If the result is positive, enter it on line 12700 of your return. If negative (loss), read the instructions below. **Taxable capital gains (or net capital loss) in 2019**	19900	=		

If the result is negative (loss) do not report the amount on line 12700 of your return (the loss will show on your latest notice of assessment or reassessment). This helps you keep track of your net capital losses, which you may be able to use to reduce your taxable capital gains of other years.

If you have a net capital loss in 2019 and would like to apply it against taxable capital gains you reported on your 2016, 2017, or 2018 return, get and complete Form T1A, Request for Loss Carryback.

You can carry forward your net capital losses indefinitely and apply them against your taxable capital gains in the future.

Principal residence

Complete this section if you disposed of a property (or properties) in 2019 that you are claiming a principal residence exemption for.

In all cases, you have to get and **complete** Form T2091(IND), Designation of a property as a principal residence by an individual, **or** Form T1255, Designation of a Property as a Principal Residence by the Legal Representative of a Deceased Individual, whichever applies.

Even if you do not sell your property, you may have a **deemed disposition** you must report. A deemed disposition occurs when you are considered to have disposed of property, even though you did not actually sell it. For example, a deemed disposition may occur when you change how you use your principal residence, such as:

- you change all or part of your principal residence to a rental or business operation
- you change all or part of your rental or business operation to a principal residence

If you were **not** a resident of Canada for the entire time you owned the designated property, your period of non-residence may reduce the amount of the principal residence exemption or eliminate it. For more information, call the CRA at **1-800-959-8281**.

Principal residence designation

Tick the box that applies to your designation.

17900

1 ☐ I designate the property described on Form T2091(IND) or Form T1255 to have been my principal residence for **all years owned** or for all years owned except one year in which I replaced my principal residence.

2 ☐ I designate the property described on Form T2091(IND) or Form T1255 to have been my principal residence for **some but not all years owned**.

3 ☐ I designate the **properties** described on Form T2091(IND) or Form T1255 to have been my principal residences for **some or all of the years owned**.

See the privacy notice on your return.

5000-S3

Disposition of Deceased Taxpayer's Principal Residence

If a taxpayer is deceased, the legal representative will use form "T1255, Designation of a Property as a Principal Residence by the Legal Representative of a Deceased Individual" in conjunction with Schedule 3 if the property was not the deceased individual's principal residence every year it was owned. Further, the legal representative must also complete the "Principal residence designation" section of Schedule 3 of the deceased person for the year if one of the following applies to the deceased person:

- they disposed of, or was considered to have disposed of, their principal residence, or any part of it
- they granted someone an option to buy their principal residence, or any part of it

T1255 Form

Canada Revenue Agency / Agence du revenu du Canada

Protected B when completed

Designation of a Property as a Principal Residence by the Legal Representative of a Deceased Individual

Tax year

Use this form to designate a property as a principal residence. You must also complete the "Principal residence designation" section of Schedule 3 of the deceased person for the year if one of the following applies to the deceased person:

- they disposed of, or was considered to have disposed of, their principal residence, or any part of it
- they granted someone an option to buy their principal residence, or any part of it

Note
If the deceased person was not a resident of Canada for the entire time they owned the designated property, call **1-800-959-8281**. The period of non-residence may reduce or eliminate the availability of the principal residence exemption.

For more information about designating a principal residence and what qualifies as a principal residence, see Income Tax Folio S1-F3-C2, Principal Residence, or the "Principal residence" chapter in Guide T4037, Capital Gains.

You can only designate one property as the deceased's principal residence for any specific year. However, where the principal residence is sold and another one bought (or where the deceased moved to another of their properties) in the same year, the "plus one" rule in calculating the principal residence exemption amount will allow you to claim the principal residence exemption for both properties for that year even though you can only designate one property as the deceased's principal residence.
For dispositions that occurred after October 2, 2016, if the deceased was a non-resident throughout the taxation year in which the property was purchased or acquired, the "plus 1" rule does **not** apply.

If you ticked box 1 at line 17900 of Schedule 3, you only need to complete the first page of this form. You do not need to report any gain amount on Schedule 3 for this property.

If you are filing electronically, keep this form in case we ask to see it later. If you are filing a paper return, you **must** complete, **sign**, and attach this form to your return.

Description of property

Provide the information requested below for the property disposed of in the tax year. Complete a separate form for each disposition.

Address				Year of acquisition	Proceeds of disposition
Street number, Street name, and unit number if applicable				9955	9954
Prov./Terr	Postal code	City	Country		

Designation

I, __________ (print your name), the legal representative for the Estate of the Late __________ (Deceased's name), hereby designate the property described above to have been the principal residence of the deceased person for the following **tax years ending after the acquisition date**:

- After 1981 ____ 1
- After 1971 and before 1982 + ____ 2

Total number of years designated (line 1 **plus** line 2) 9956 = ____ 3

For those years after 1981, I also confirm that neither the deceased person, nor their spouse or common-law partner (who was not separated and living apart from the deceased person throughout the year under a judicial separation or written separation agreement), nor any of the deceased person's children (who were under 18 and unmarried or not in a common-law partnership throughout the year) designated any other property as a principal residence. For any tax year after 1981 for which the deceased person designated the property and throughout which they were under 18 and unmarried or not in a common-law partnership, I also confirm that neither the deceased person's mother, father, nor any of their brothers and sisters (who were under 18 and unmarried or not in a common-law partnership throughout the year) designated any other property as a principal residence.

For those years before 1982, I confirm that the deceased person has not designated any other property as their principal residence.

Note
If the property was designated as a principal residence for the purpose of filing Form T664 or T664(Seniors), the legal representative has to include those previously designated tax years as part of the deceased person's principal residence designation.

Signature	Deceased's social insurance number	Date (YYYYMMDD)

T1255 E (19)

(Ce formulaire est disponible en français.)

Canada

Disposition of Trust's Property

If the property was the trust's principal residence for all or part of the years it was owned then "Form T1079, Designation of a Property as a Principal Residence by a Personal Trust" should be used. Use this form to calculate the capital gain for the year if either of the following situations apply:

- the trust disposed of, or the CRA considers the trust to have disposed of, its principal residence or any part of it; or
- the trust gave someone an option to buy the trust's principal residence or any part of it.

T1079 Form

Designation by a personal trust

For the purpose of this form, the acquisition date is the date on which the trust acquired or last reacquired the property or December 31, 1971, whichever is later. However, if the trust filed Form 94-115, Election to Report a Capital Gain on Property Owned by a Personal Trust at the End of February 22, 1994, the CRA does not consider the trust to have disposed of and at once reacquired the property as a result of the election.

Note: If the trust designated the property as its principal residence for the purpose of the election, the trust has to include those previously designated tax years as part of its principal residence designation.

Description of designated property: ______________________________

I, ______________________________ (Print name), hereby designate the property described above to have been the trust's principal residence for the following **number of tax years ending after the acquisition date**:

After 2016 (see discussion of eligible trust under General Information on page 2)		1
After 1981 and before 2017	+	2
After 1971 and before 1982	+	3
Total number of years designated (add line 1 to line 3)	=	4

I confirm that the trust did not designate any other property as its principal residence. I also confirm that none of the following designated any other property in the above tax years as a principal residence: a specified beneficiary of the trust; a person who throughout those years was the spouse or common-law partner of a specified beneficiary (who was not separated and living apart from the specified beneficiary throughout the year under a judicial separation or written separation agreement); any child of a specified beneficiary who was throughout those years under 18, unmarried, and not in a common-law relationship; the mother, father, or any of the brothers or sisters who were under 18, unmarried, and not in a common-law relationship of a specified beneficiary who was under 18, unmarried, and not in a common-law relationship throughout the years the trust designated the property as a principal residence.

Also, I confirm that no partnership or corporation (other than a registered charity) held a beneficial interest in the trust at any time in the years the trust designated the property as its principal residence.

Name of trust	Address		
Date of designation	Signature	Position or title	Account number T | | – | | | | – |

Specified beneficiaries

Name, address, and social insurance number of the specified beneficiary and other persons affected by the designation (spouse or common-law partner, child, parent, brother, or sister)			Years affected by the designation
Name	Address	Social insurance number	
Name	Address	Social insurance number	
Name	Address	Social insurance number	

Attach a separate sheet if necessary.

T1079 E (19) (Ce formulaire est disponible en français.) Page 1 of 6 Canada

Use a 45(2) Election to Defer a Capital Gain upon the Change in Use from Principal Residence to Income Producing Property

When there is a change in use of residential property from personal to income producing, the Income Tax Act deems a taxpayer to have disposed of and reacquired the property at fair market value ("FMV").

The result of the change in use is that the property ceases to be subject to the principal residence exemption following the change. As a result, when a taxpayer disposes of the residence for FMV in the future, any gain from the change in use until the sale date would be considered a taxable capital gain.

This taxable gain can be minimized or avoided altogether if you file an election under subsection 45(2).

So, for example if you begin using your principal residence as a rental property and either do not acquire a new principal residence, or if you do acquire a new principal residence, but think that the old one will increase in value faster than the new one, subsection 45(2) allows you to elect out of being deemed to have disposed of the property at FMV and reacquire it immediately thereafter at the same amount.

The way it works is that by filing a subsection 45(2) election, a taxpayer would be deemed to not have begun using the property as a rental property (i.e., there will be no change in use) until the taxpayer disposes of the property or rescinds the subsection 45(2) election.

This election can help you extend principal residence status by up to 4 years while the property is rented out.

In order to make the election, simply attach a letter to your T1 return for the year in which the change of use occurs. Simply describe the property and ask that 45(2) of the Income Tax be applied.

A late election may be accepted at the CRA's discretion as long as CCA has not been claimed.

File a 45(3) Election to Defer the Capital Gain upon the Change in Use of a Property from Income-Producing to Principal Residence

If a taxpayer has changed the use of a residence from a rental property to a principal residence, subsection 45(3) provides an election to avoid the deemed disposition on the change in use. This permits you to defer the tax payable on the capital gains accrued while the property was income-producing – only having to be paid upon disposition.

A subsection 45(3) election is only applicable where capital cost allowance has not been claimed on the property in question.

This election must be filed by the due date for the tax return for the year of disposition.

File a T2054 Election for a Capital Dividend under Subsection 83(2)

Capital dividends paid by private corporations are generally non-taxable, if a Form T2054 is property filed with the Canada Revenue Agency (CRA) and certain other contingencies are met. Subsection 83(2) of the Income Tax Act allows a private corporation to elect for a dividend paid out to Canadian shareholders to be a capital dividend, and therefore, for that amount not to be included when the shareholders compute their income.

The dividend is deemed to be the extent of the corporation's capital dividend account (CDA) immediately before the particular time, pursuant to ss. 83(2)(a). A CDA tracks certain tax-free amounts that have been accumulated by the corporation. A capital dividend cannot exceed a corporation's CDA. Paying a capital dividend is a form of tax-free return of capital because it is based on tax-free surpluses that have been accumulated by the corporation. The CDA balance includes the following: non-taxable portion of capital gains; capital dividends received by the corporation; eligible capital amounts; life insurance policy proceeds; and trust distributions.

When a corporation pays a capital dividend, it must file an election in respect of the dividend when the dividend is paid or becomes payable. An election to pay a capital dividend should be filed with a Form T2054 by the earlier of the day on which the dividend becomes payable, and the first day on which any part of the dividend is paid. Only in certain circumstances is a late-filed election acceptable.

Do not pay a capital dividend which exceeds the balance of the capital dividend account, or else there will be tax consequences. Specifically, the corporation will be subject to additional tax that is 60% of the excess amount plus interest until the date of payment.

Save Tax with the Quick Method of Accounting for GST/HST

The GST/HST quick method of accounting can save business time and money.

When using the quick method, instead of claiming the GST/HST paid on purchases as an input tax credit, a taxpayer needs to only remit a portion of the tax they collect to the CRA. This may be a good option for some of you.

Do the calculation both ways and see what works best for you. The Quick Method could potentially save you a bundle if it makes sense.

A business that uses the quick method still has the ability to claim the input tax credits for capital purchases.

The form "Election and Revocation of an Election to Use the Quick Method of Accounting" can be completed and filed with the CRA to begin using the quick method of accounting. A taxpayer can also elect this method by using the CRA online services.

The same form or online service can be used to revoke the election to use the quick method. The form outlines some important details regarding the quick method of accounting including the revenue limit to use quick method and when a taxpayer can choose the quick method during their reporting period. You can revoke the election after the quick method election has been in effect for at least a year, and generally it must be revoked by the due date of the GST/HST return for the last reporting period prior to revoking the quick method.

GST74E Election Form

Canada Revenue Agency / Agence du revenu du Canada

Protected B
when completed

Election and Revocation of an Election to Use the Quick Method of Accounting

Use this form to either elect to start using the quick method of accounting, or to stop using the method. You can also make or revoke this election by using our online services at **canada.ca/my-cra-business-account** or at **canada.ca/taxes-representatives.** If you use our online services, do not send this form.

Generally, you can use the quick method if the total annual revenue (including the GST/HST) from your worldwide taxable supplies (including zero-rated supplies) and those of your associates is no more than $400,000 in either the first four or the last four consecutive fiscal quarters out of the last five fiscal quarters. If you previously elected to use the quick method and have revoked that election, you have to wait at least one year from the date the revocation became effective before you can elect to use the quick method again.

Certain businesses **cannot** use the quick method. For more information, see Guide RC4058, Quick Method of Accounting for GST/HST or call **1-800-959-5525.** To get our forms and publications, go to **canada.ca/gst-hst-pub**.

To elect to use the quick method, fill out parts A, B and D. To revoke the election, fill out parts A, C and D. Send this form to your tax services office. You can find the address at **canada.ca/cra-offices.**

Part A – Identification

Name and trading name (if different from name)

Business number RT

Part B – Election

Select this box to elect to use the quick method of accounting to calculate your net tax. ☐

I want to start using the quick method of accounting on the first day of my reporting period beginning: Year Month Day

Notes
If you file annual GST/HST returns, you have to make the election by the first day of your second fiscal quarter.
If you file monthly or quarterly GST/HST returns, you have to make your election by the due date of the return in which you start using the quick method.

How long does the election stay in effect?
Generally, the election stays in effect unless **either**:

- the total annual revenue (including the GST/HST) from your worldwide taxable supplies (including zero-rated supplies), and those of your associates, is more than $400,000
- you become a person that cannot use the quick method because of the type of business you carry on

If your election ceases to be in effect, you have to start using the regular method to calculate your net tax. For more information, see Guide RC4058.

Part C – Revocation of election

Select this box to revoke the election that you made to use the quick method of accounting to calculate your net tax. ☐

Enter the date of revocation of election (you have to revoke the election by the due date of the GST/HST return for the last reporting period in which you want to use the quick method): Year Month Day

Note
The effective date of revocation has to be at least one year after the date of the election.

Part D – Certification

I, ______________________ (print name), certify that the information given on this form is correct and complete.

I understand that this election to use the quick method of accounting is binding for a minimum of one year, unless the business no longer meets the eligibility criteria. I also understand that once this election is revoked, I must wait at least one year before I can elect to use the quick method again.

______________________ Signature of the authorized person

Year Month Day

Personal information is collected under the Excise Tax Act to administer tax, rebates, and elections. It may also be used for any purpose related to the enforcement of the Act such as audit, compliance and collection activities. It may be shared or verified with other federal, provincial, territorial or foreign government institutions to the extent authorized by law. Failure to provide this information may result in interest payable, penalties or other actions. Under the Privacy Act, individuals have the right to access, or request corrections of, their personal information, or to file a complaint with the Privacy Commissioner of Canada regarding the handling of their personal information. Refer to Personal Information Bank CRA PPU 241 at **canada.ca/cra-info-source**.

GST74 E (19) (Ce formulaire est disponible en français.) Canada

Take Advantage of the Replacement Property Rules

The replacement property rules under the Income Tax Act allow a taxpayer to elect to defer reporting a capital gain, or recapture of capital cost allowances when they dispose of a business property voluntarily, or involuntarily, such as in cases of a fire destroying the property.

The replacement property rules do not allow you to avoid paying any taxes related to the disposition of a business property, but it does allow you to defer it until the subsequently acquired (replacement) property is eventually disposed of.

It should be noted that under no circumstances, could a rental property qualify a business property for the purpose of this election.

Criteria

The Canada Revenue Agency has set out some basic requirements for what would constitute a replacement property. Depending on the type of property disposed of there may be additional requirements.

The first requirement is that the newly acquired business property had to have been purchased to replace the previously disposed property.

Next, the new business property must have been acquired for the same, or a similar use .

What this means is that the newly acquired property should have the same rough physical description to describe it as the previously disposed property. You would need to replace a building with a building, or land with land. A junkyard owner would not be able to dispose of the land being used as a junkyard, and then buy a small hotel using the replacement property rules since the rough description would be entirely different.
The final requirement is that the new business property must be acquired to produce income from the same, or a similar business.

Now this does not mean that the new property has to produce income in an identical way to the previous property (such as a pizza shop being required to open a new pizza shop), but rather it has to produce income from the same general category of similar business. The CRA provides a list of the following types of categories for businesses:

- merchandising - retailing and wholesaling.

- farming;
- fishing;
- forestry and forest products;
- extractive industries, including refining;
- financial services;
- communications;
- transportation;
- construction, including subcontracting; and
- manufacturing and processing.

For example, this would mean that potato farmer would be able to dispose of his farm in order to buy a cattle ranch and use the replacement property rules as they are both similar businesses as they both deal with farming.

Timing

The CRA requires that replacement properties be acquired shortly after disposing of the previous property, or while in the process of disposing of the property. The CRA is generally more lenient in timing providing twice as long to use the replacement property rules for involuntarily disposed of business properties as oppose to voluntarily disposed of business properties. Falling outside of the set time periods will result in the taxpayer being unable to exercise the replacement property election.

The CRA states that "(f)or involuntary dispositions, the replacement property must be acquired before the later of:

- the end of the second tax year following the initial year; and
- 24 months after the end of the initial year.

And that for voluntary dispositions of a former business property, the replacement property must be acquired before the later of:

- the end of the first tax year following the initial year; and
- 12 months after the end of the initial year.

According to the CRA the 44(1) election should be made as follows:

- If the disposition and replacement take place in the same year, your calculation (in the income tax return for that year) of the recaptured CCA or the capital gain by virtue of subsection 44(1) will be considered to constitute an election.
- If the property is not replaced until a subsequent year, the election should take the form of a letter attached to the income tax return for the year the replacement property is acquired. The letter should include

a description of the replacement property and the former property, a request for an adjustment to the recapture of capital cost or the taxable capital gain reported, and a calculation of the revised recapture or taxable capital gain.

- If the replacement property is acquired prior to the year of disposition of the property, the election should take the form of a letter attached to the income tax return for the year in which the replacement property is acquired. The letter should include descriptions of the replacement property and the property that is to be replaced. If the taxpayer late-files such an election, it will be accepted if it is filed in the income tax return for the year in which the former property is disposed of, provided it is evident that the new property qualifies as a replacement property.

For further information, visit https://www.canada.ca/en/revenue-agency/services/tax/technical-information/income-tax/income-tax-folios-index/series-3-property-investments-savings-plans/folio-3-capital-transactions/income-tax-folio-s3-f3-c1-replacement-property.html#toc6

Make Appropriate Elections when Selling Property after Marital Breakdown

Taxpayers may not consider the tax implications of dividing property during a separation or divorce, but they or their advisor should. If you and your spouse are living apart because of a breakdown in your relationship and one of you sells a property, the two of you can avoid reporting the capital gain at the time of sale by filing an election with your tax return.

This gives you additional time to report the gain and to sort out your affairs.

The election must be filed within a year of disposition of the property. The election is a simple letter, signed by the taxpayer and the spouse stating that they do not want section 74.2 of the Income Tax Act to apply.

For more information, visit: https://www.canada.ca/en/revenue-agency/services/tax/individuals/topics/about-your-tax-return/tax-return/completing-a-tax-return/personal-income/line-127-capital-gains/transfers-capital-property/election-report-capital-gain-loss.html

Transfer Property to Your Corporation on a Tax-Free Basis with a Section 85 Rollover

In a nutshell, a Section 85 rollover is a technique which allows a taxpayer to transfer a property to their corporation without having to incur taxes.

Instead of transferring the property to the corporation at fair market value (and thus triggering a capital gain), the parties elect to transfer the property at another value – usually the adjusted cost base.

After the eligible property has been transferred by you to a corporation, you or your accountant needs to file a T2057 Election on Disposition of Property by a Taxpayer to a Taxable Canadian Corporation. The election cannot be electronically filed and must be mailed to the Tax Centre of the Transferor.

The election must be filed on the earliest date on which you or the corporation must file an income tax return. Elections can still be filed up to three years after the transfer took place, but they will be subject to a late filing penalty. A late filing penalty ranges in severity, but the max that can be fined is $8,000. The calculation for the penalty is ¼ of the agreed upon amount, multiplied by 1% for each month that the election is past due.
If you file the election after 3 years, you must include a detailed explanation regarding why the election was not filed on time. If the CRA accepts it then you will only need to worry about paying the maximum fine indicated earlier, however, if they reject it, the rollover will be considered null and void and taxes will need to be paid on the disposition.

T2057 Election Form

Canada Revenue Agency / Agence du revenu du Canada

Protected B when completed

Election on Disposition of Property by a Taxpayer to a Taxable Canadian Corporation

Do not use this area

- This form is used by a taxpayer and a taxable Canadian corporation to jointly elect under subsection 85(1) where the taxpayer has disposed of **eligible property** under subsection 85(1.1) to the corporation and the taxpayer receives as consideration shares of capital stock of the corporation.
- Unless otherwise indicated, all legislative references are to the *Income Tax Act*.
- Mail one copy of this election and related schedules (as specified), completed by the transferor, as follows:
  - to the tax centre of the transferor;
  - on or before the earliest date on which any party to the election has to file an income tax return for the tax year in which the transaction occurred (due date). This due date must consider any election under subsection 25(1) or 99(2); and
  - separately from any other return.

When many transferors elect to transfer the same property (co-ownership) or many members of the same partnership elect to transfer their partnership interests, the elections will be processed together and should be filed:

- at the tax centre of the transferee;
- on or before the due date; and
- by a designated transferor to file all of the completed forms for each transferor, together with a list of all of the electing transferors. This list should contain the name, address and social insurance number, trust account number or business number of each transferor.

Find the address of the transferor's and transferee's tax centre at **canada.ca/tax-centres**.

Taxpayer's name (transferor)	Social insurance, trust account or business number
Address	Postal code
Tax year of the taxpayer — Start: Year Month Day — End: Year Month Day	Tax services office

Name of co-owner(s), if any (if more than one, attach schedule giving similar details)		Social insurance number
Address	Postal code	Tax services office

Corporation's name (transferee)	Business number
Address	Postal code
Tax year of the corporation — Start: Year Month Day — End: Year Month Day	Tax services office
Name of the contact person	Telephone number

Penalty for late-filed and amended elections

An election that is filed after its due date is subject to a late-filing penalty. You can file Form T2057 within three years after its due date if you pay an estimate of the penalty at the time of filing. You can also amend or file Form T2057 after the three-year period, but, in addition to the payment of an estimated penalty amount, you must attach a written explanation justifying the changes or reasons for the delay for consideration by the minister.

Calculation of late-filing penalty:

Do not use this area

Fair market value (FMV) of property transferred ________

Agreed amount ________

Subtotal (FMV **minus** agreed amount) ________ A

Amount A ________ × ¼ × 1% × N * ____ = ________ B

$100 × N * ____ = ________ C

Amount C cannot exceed $8,000.

Late-filing penalty (amount B or amount C, whichever is less) ________

Amount enclosed ________

Make your cheque or money order payable to the Receiver General. On the back, write T2057, the transferor's name, and their social insurance, trust account or business number.

Unpaid amounts including late-filing penalties are subject to daily compound interest at a prescribed rate.

* N is the sum of each month or each part of a month in the period from the filing due date to the actual date filed.

Protected B when completed

Information required

On the following page, list, describe, and state the fair market value (FMV) of transferred properties. The description and FMV of the consideration received has to be shown opposite of the related property transferred. Where the transferred property is a partnership interest, attach a schedule of the calculation of the adjusted cost base. If there is not enough space on the form, attach schedules giving similar details. You have to designate the order of disposition of each depreciable property. The following material may be prepared in order to complete the form: a summary of the method of evaluating the FMV of each property transferred; schedules supporting this election; and documentation relating to the responses to the questions below. This material does not need to be filed with the election but must be kept in case we ask to see them at a later date.

1. Is there a written agreement relating to this transfer? .... Yes ☐ No ☐
2. Does a price adjustment clause apply to any of the properties? (See Income Tax Folio S4-F3-C1 for details.) .... Yes ☐ No ☐
3. Do any persons other than the taxpayer own or control directly or indirectly any shares of any class of the transferee? .... Yes ☐ No ☐
4. Does a non-arm's length rollover exist between 2 or more corporations? .... Yes ☐ No ☐

   If **yes** to question 4, have all or substantially all (90% or more) of all the properties of the corporation(s) been transferred to the transferee corporation? .... Yes ☐ No ☐
5. Is the taxpayer a non-resident of Canada? .... Yes ☐ No ☐
6. Are any of the properties transferred capital properties? .... Yes ☐ No ☐

   If **yes**, a) have they been owned continuously since Valuation Day (V-Day is defined in section 24 of the *Income Tax Applications Rules*)? .... Yes ☐ No ☐

   b) have they been acquired after V-Day in a transaction considered not to be at arm's length? .... Yes ☐ No ☐

   c) since V-Day, has the taxpayer or any person from whom shares were acquired in a non-arm's length transaction received any subsection 83(1) dividends for transferred shares? (If **yes**, attach a schedule, provide details of amounts and dates received.) .... Yes ☐ No ☐
7. Is the agreed amount of any of the transferred properties based on an estimate of FMV on V-Day? .... Yes ☐ No ☐

   If **yes** to question 7, does a formal documented V-Day value report exist? .... Yes ☐ No ☐
8. Has an election under subsection 26(7) of the *Income Tax Application Rules* (Form T2076) been filed by or on behalf of the taxpayer? .... Yes ☐ No ☐

Where shares of the capital stock of a private corporation are included in the property disposed of, provide the following:

Corporation's name

Business number	Paid-up capital of shares transferred
_ _ _ _ _ _ _ _ _ R C _ _ _ _	

Description of shares received

Number of shares transferor received	Class of shares	Redemption value per share	Paid-up capital	Voting or non-voting	Are shares redeemable at the holder's option?
					Yes ☐ No ☐
					Yes ☐ No ☐
					Yes ☐ No ☐
					Yes ☐ No ☐
					Yes ☐ No ☐

Informative notes

- The rules for section 85 elections are complex. Essential information is contained in Information Circular IC76-19, Interpretation Bulletins IT-291 and IT-378 and Income Tax Folio S4-F3-C1.
- Complete all the information areas and answer all questions. If this form is incomplete, we may consider the election invalid and a late-filing penalty may apply to future submissions.
- If the agreed amount is more than the adjusted cost base of the property in the election, you must report the difference as a capital gain, as income or a combination of both, whichever applies.

Election and certification

The taxpayer **and** the corporation jointly elect under subsection 85(1) in respect of the property specified, and certify that the information given in this election and in any attached documents is correct and complete.

Signature of Transferor, Authorized Officer or Authorized Person* **and** Signature of Authorized Officer of Transferee

* Attach a copy of the authorizing agreement.

Date (yyyy-mm-dd)

Information on the eligible property disposed of and consideration received — **Protected B** when completed

	Date of sale or transfer of all properties listed below:	Year Month Day		Note: For properties sold or transferred on different dates, use a separate Form T2057.				
	Property disposed of			B Agreed amount (cannot be zero)	Amount to be reported B – A (if greater than 0, see note 5)	Consideration received		
	Description	Elected amount limits (see note 1)				Non-share	Share	Fair market value of total consideration
		Fair market value	A			Description	Number and class	
Capital property excluding depreciable property	(brief legal)		(see note 2)					
Depreciable property	(description and prescribed class)		(see note 3)					
Eligible capital property	(kind)		(see note 4)					
Inventory excluding real property	(kind)		(cost amount)					
Resource property	(brief legal)		nil nil nil					
Security or debt obligation property	(description)		(cost amount)					
Specified Debt Obligation (for financial institutions only)			(cost amount)					
Capital property that is real property owned by a non-resident person	(description)							
AgriInvest fund no. 2 (see note 6)			(cost amount)					

Reduce Tax Payable by Electing Out of Withholding Tax

Certain sources of income such as dividends and rent are taxable in Canada even for non-residents of Canada. This tax is commonly referred to as withholding tax and has a rate that is 25% of the gross amount of the payments received from the Canadian source.

The Canadian resident who pays the rent to the non-resident is required to withhold the tax from the payment and remit it to the Canada Revenue Agency. The non-resident is not required to file an income tax return. If an international tax treaty in place between Canada and the country of the non-resident, then the rate of withholding tax may be reduced or eliminated under certain circumstances.

For rental income, non-residents of Canada can elect to be taxed on the net rent they receive instead of the gross amount. This can significantly reduce the amount of tax withheld from the non-resident once the costs and expenses are factored in.

In order to pay tax on the Net and avoid the withholding tax you must file a section 216 Election for Withholding Tax. Non-residents who choose this election must also file T1-NR tax returns annually in order to qualify.

You must use Form T1159 Income Tax Return for Electing Under Section 216. See copy reproduced below.

For more information on withholding tax, visit: https://www.canada.ca/content/dam/cra-arc/formspubs/pub/t4061/t4061-19e.pdf

T2057 Election Form

Protected B when completed

Canada Revenue Agency / Agence du revenu du Canada **2019**

Income Tax Return for Electing Under Section 216 11

Identification

Print your name and address below.

First name and initial

Last name

Mailing address: Apt No. – Street No. Street name

PO Box | RR

City | Prov./Terr. | Postal code

Country

Information about you

Enter your social insurance number (SIN), temporary tax number (TTN), or individual tax number (ITN):

Enter your date of birth: Year Month Day

Your language of correspondence: / Votre langue de correspondance : English ☐ Français ☐

Email address

By providing an email address, you are **registering** to receive email notifications from the CRA and **agree** to the **Terms of use** on page 7 of the Income Tax Guide for Electing Under Section 216.

Enter an email address:

Is this return for a deceased person?

If this **return** is for a **deceased person**, enter the date of death: Year Month Day

Do not use this area.

Income

Rental income and timber royalties Gross **12599** Net **12600**

Total income 15000

Deductions

RRSP/pooled registered pension plan (PRPP) deduction (attach receipts) **20800**

Support payments made Total **21999** Allowable deduction **22000** +

Other deductions (see line 23200 in the guide) Specify: **23200** +

Add lines 20800, 22000, and 23200. **23300** = ▶ –

Line 15000 minus line 23300 (if negative, enter "0") This is your **taxable income. 26000** = 1

Federal tax

Part 1 – Federal tax on taxable income

Complete the appropriate column depending on the amount on line 1.	Line 1 is **$47,630** or less	Line 1 is more than **$47,630** but not more than **$95,259**	Line 1 is more than **$95,259** but not more than **$147,667**	Line 1 is more than **$147,667** but not more than **$210,371**	Line 1 is more than **$210,371**	
Enter the amount from line 1.						2
	– 0 00	– 47,630 00	– 95,259 00	– 147,667 00	– 210,371 00	3
Line 2 minus line 3 (cannot be negative)	=	=	=	=	=	4
	× 15%	× 20.5%	× 26%	× 29%	× 33%	5
Multiply line 4 by line 5.	=	=	=	=	=	6
	+ 0 00	+ 7,145 00	+ 16,908 00	+ 30,535 00	+ 48,719 00	7
Add lines 6 and 7. Enter this amount on line 9.	=	=	=	=	=	8

Continue on the next page.

Do not use this area. 17100 17200 55240

T1159 E (19) (Ce formulaire est disponible en français.)

Protected **B** when completed

Part 2 – Federal tax

Enter the amount from line 8.			9
Minimum tax carryover (see line 40427 in the guide)	40427	–	• 10
Line 9 minus line 10		=	11
Surtax for non-residents of Canada: Enter the amount from line 11.	× 48% =	+	12
Add lines 11 and 12.	**Federal tax**	=	13

Refund or balance owing

Enter the amount from line 13. This is your **total payable**.	43500			•
Total non-resident tax withheld (from your NR4 slips; see line 43700 in the guide)	43700	•		
Total tax remitted for the recapture of capital cost allowance (from Form T2064 or Form T2068)	47600	+ •		
Add lines 43700 and 47600.	48200	= ▶	–	
Line 43500 minus line 48200 This is your **refund** or **balance owing**.			=	

If the result is negative, you have a **refund**. If the result is positive, you have a **balance owing**.

Enter the amount below on whichever line applies.

Generally, we do not charge or refund a difference of $2 or less.

Refund 48400 _______ •

Balance owing 48500 _______ •

Do not use this area.	48600 _______ •

For more information on how to receive your refund by direct deposit, see line 48400 in the guide or go to **canada.ca/cra-direct-deposit**.

For more information on how to make your payment, see line 48500 in the guide or go to **canada.ca/payments**.

Your payment is due no later than **April 30, 2020**.

I certify that the information given on this return and in any documents attached is correct and complete and fully discloses all my income from rents and timber royalties on which I am electing under section 216 of the Income Tax Act.

Sign here ____________________

It is a serious offence to make a false return.

Telephone ____________ Date ____________

49000

If a fee was charged for preparing this return, complete the following:

Name of preparer: ____________

Telephone: ____________

Reduce the Amount of Withholding Tax by Filing a Non-Resident 217 Election, Emigration

Canadians who emigrate but still draw income from certain Canadian sources have filing options. Canadian payers have to withhold non-resident tax on certain types of money that they paid to a non-resident of Canada (such as CPP, RSP, and EI payments).
Under section 217, a non-resident can choose to file a Canadian return. This results in the non-resident paying tax on this income using an alternative taxing method and may receive a refund of some of the non-resident tax withheld.

If the non-resident has already filed a Form NR5 ("Application by a Non-Resident of Canada for a Reduction in the Amount of Non-Resident Tax Required to be Withheld") which has been approved by the CRA, then a Section 217 return must be filed.
Section 217 is also available to non-residents if they have not filed Form NR5 but received certain types of Canadian-sourced income.

Please see the following CRA publication for more information:
https://www.canada.ca/en/revenue-agency/services/tax/international-non-residents/individuals-leaving-entering-canada-non-residents/electing-under-section-217.html

File an Election Under 220(4.5) of the Income Tax Act to Avoid a Deemed Disposition Upon Emigration

If you intend to return to Canada at a future date, and do not wish to dispose of the property, or have it seen as a deemed disposition, the CRA offers a way to defer the taxes payable by way of an election under Subsection 220(4.5) of the Income Tax Act.

For more information see Part 13 "Emigration".

Elect to Split Pension Income Between Spouses

The Canadian Pension Plan (CPP) income can be split between spouses. As long as certain criteria are met spouses may split their CPP income by completing the joint election on Form T1032.

By filing Form T1032, spouses may jointly elect to split pension income. This form does not affect payments under the Canadian Pension Plan (CPP) or from old age security. Jointly electing using this form simply can cause the following annuity income to be split: from a superannuation, from a pension fund or plan, form an annuity and registered retirement income fund, from a registered retirement savings plan, and form a retirement compensation arrangement. A spouse under this rule includes married and common law spouses.

16 TAXPAYER RELIEF PROVISIONS

The taxpayer relief provisions of the Income Tax Act were designed to provide a little bit of softness to the CRA and provide relief where warranted.

They provide relief to taxpayers by allowing them to apply for:

1. Interest and Penalty relief due to financial hardship or extraordinary circumstances;
2. Interest and Penalty relief through the Voluntary Disclosures Program (VDP);
3. The acceptance of late filed elections;
4. Refunds outside the normal refund period.

In order for you to successfully receive relief, you must draft an application which is clear, thorough, and well-written. I have seen the CRA use virtually every excuse possible to deny taxpayer relief – even though it is one of the rights listed in the Taxpayer Bill of Rights.

File a Request for Taxpayer Relief if You Owe Interest & Penalties

The Taxpayer Relief program, formerly known as the "Fairness Program" empowers the CRA by law to waive interest and penalties at its discretion. Perhaps because the system is not always fair, or because the CRA did not want to be thought of as being fair, this program was renamed.

You must remember that the principal tax amount cannot be altered through this program, and it is only interest and penalty amounts which can be forgiven.

If you are burdened with a debt to the CRA, which includes interest and/ or penalties, in order to potentially receive a reduction of interest and penalties, you can complete and submit the Request for Taxpayer Relief (form RC4288).

Item 12 in the Taxpayer Bill of Rights indicates that under legislation a taxpayer has the "right to interest and penalty relief because of extraordinary circumstances," and despite this legislated right, if taxpayers simply complete the three-page form on their own, unless they have a bulletproof case, I would not expect any sort of fairness.

Here is a bulletproof case:

Imagine somebody who always filed his taxes on time, yet one year he became injured in an automobile accident and fell into a coma, and was kept on life-support for eight years, shortly after waking up (with tax return still clutched in his hand), he runs to the mail room at the hospital and sends the returns off at the earliest opportunity.

I can guarantee that a relief application for this taxpayer would succeed. It would be unfair to deny relief to this taxpayer.

However, if a taxpayer's case is not bulletproof, and the person has not been on life-support for the better part of a decade, you must ensure that they qualify for the program by meeting the relevant criteria, and you must prepare a case that is as strong as possible.

A taxpayer can qualify for interest and penalty relief in three basic ways:

1. Extraordinary circumstances

If the interest and /or penalties arose as a result of circumstances beyond the reasonable control of the taxpayer, such as accidents, severe illnesses, mental distress, fires, floods, or other disasters.

2. Financial Hardship

If a debt to the CRA, with its interest and penalties, is causing financial hardship, or if a taxpayer has a demonstrated in ability to pay the debt.

3.Actions of the CRA

If actions of the CRA, such as processing delays or errors, have caused or contributed to the interest and penalties.

Before you can file a request for taxpayer relief, you must ensure that you have filed all your returns to date.

The CRA will not provide relief to delinquent taxpayers. In order to be granted relief, a taxpayer must have a payment plan in place with the CRA for outstanding debt.

To learn more about Interest and Penalty Relief, please consult the CRA's Information Circular IC07-1 "Taxpayer Relief Provisions."

Sometimes it is not enough that you have been in a coma and were unable to file.

Sometimes the CRA will look at your past history before considering a grant for relief. A number of factors are considered by the CRA when it decides whether or not to grant relief. These factors do not come from legislation but come from the CRA itself.

Remember, the CRA does not write the law--it only administers it. So, when the CRA uses a list of factors that it has created in order to prevent a taxpayer from gaining relief under a law written by parliament it may not be applying the law as it was intended. In such cases, it is possible for the taxpayer to have the matter examined by a judge of the Federal Court in order to judicially review whether the CRA's denial of his or her application based on such a factor was reasonable. Such factors include a taxpayer's compliance history, whether the taxpayer knowingly allowed a balance to exist, and whether the taxpayer has not been negligent or careless in his or her filings.

Extraordinary Circumstances

There are many circumstances beyond a taxpayer's control which could lead to the application of interest and penalties. For example, if the taxpayer is the victim of a man-made disaster such as a fire which destroyed an office and all records, or a natural disaster such as a storm flooding the taxpayer's house and washing away all the ink on all receipts. When such circumstances have occurred, the Taxpayer Bill of Rights says that a taxpayer has the right to relief, "You have the right to relief from penalties and interest under tax legislation because of extraordinary circumstances."

Besides the case of natural and man-made disasters, the CRA may also waive or decrease interest and penalties in cases where the taxpayer has been the victim of crime, when he or she has suffered a substance abuse problem, when he or she has been depressed, or addicted to gambling. In addition, the CRA will consider cancelling penalties and interest when a taxpayer has suffered a serious illness or accident or when the taxpayer is under serious emotional or mental distress.

However, don't expect the CRA to offer relief simply because you have a sob story (no matter how compelling the story). The CRA usually requires that the sob story to coincide with the taxpayer's failure to file or pay when required.

For example: if the person was to use the hospitalization for a terrible accident as the grounds for relief, if he or she was in hospital from September 2011 to December 2015, and missed the 2011, '12, '13 and' 14 filings, the person could likely expect to be able to get relief from the late filing penalties for those particular years. But not for 2010 and 2009 and 2008 which could have easily been filed prior to the accident.

The CRA may even grant interest relief for all debts during the time of the hospitalization if the taxpayer was not able to make his or her payments during that period. But, if the next few years were also filed late (for no good reason), the taxpayer would likely not receive relief for any of those years.

Financial Hardship

I speak to taxpayers every day who have debts to the CRA which are so high that they cannot even afford to pay the interest charges, even though they keep paying what they can every month, their debts keep on growing. It would appear for these taxpayers, as though they could never pay off the debt without selling everything they own. Many choose bankruptcy as an alternative. The good news is that in many cases, when they consider the true amount of tax principal without the interest and penalties, with the same monthly payment, these taxpayers would be able to pay down their tax debts within a few short years. The bad news is that most taxpayers do not know about the taxpayer relief program, and many others have not adequately made the case to the CRA that they are deserving of relief. The key is to demonstrate to the CRA that with the reduction of interest and penalties they would be able to retire the debt in a reasonable time frame, and that without such relief, financial ruin is a real possibility.

If a taxpayer can demonstrate that payment of the debt with interest and penalties would result in his or her inability to meet basic necessities of life such as shelter, food, medical needs, heat, and transportation, they may receive relief on the grounds of financial hardship.

What is important is that in order for you to receive relief, you must document your case. You must provide financial records and details including assets and liabilities as well as income and monthly expenses.

Actions of the CRA

Sometimes an error or failure on the part of the CRA is the cause of a taxpayer's interest and penalties, and when this is the case, a taxpayer may make a case for relief. When it can be shown that the CRA was the cause, or even part of the cause of your interest and / or penalties, it should be documented on the request for taxpayer relief form.

In Information Circular IC07-1, the CRA cites six different types of occasions where taxpayers' interest and penalties may be waived. These are when the interest or penalties were as a result of:

- processing delays that result in the taxpayer not being informed of his or her debt, within a reasonable time;
- errors in CRA publications;
- incorrect information provided to a taxpayer by the CRA;
- processing errors;
- delays in providing information to a taxpayer; or
- undue delays in completing an audit or resolving an objection or appeal.

File an Application for a Late-Filed Election

As hinted to earlier on, the relief provisions allow the CRA to accept certain late-filed elections.

A list of these Deemed Prescribed Elections is available on the CRA's web site at:
https://www.canada.ca/en/revenue-agency/services/forms-publications/publications/ic07-1/taxpayer-relief-provisions-1r1.html#s55

And a list of Prescribed Elections (Appendix A to Information Circular IC07-1R1, Taxpayer Relief Provisions) is available at the following link:

https://www.canada.ca/en/revenue-agency/services/forms-publications/publications/ic07-1/taxpayer-relief-provisions-1r1.html#aa

File an Application for Refunds Outside the Normal Refund Period

For individual taxpayers, under the Income Tax Act there is a three-year limitation period from the end of the tax year to file an income tax return to claim a refund. Similarly, there is a three-year limitation period from the date of an original notice of income tax assessments to request an adjustment to an assessment issued for a previous tax year.

Upon request the Minister (the CRA) may provide a refund outside of the ordinary refund period and it may allow an adjustment to an assessment outside of the normal period. It just depends on being able to successfully justify your position in the application.

File an Application Under the Voluntary Disclosures Program for Undeclared income / Overclaimed Expenses

The Voluntary Disclosures Program falls under taxpayer relief provisions. A Voluntary Disclosures Program ("VDP") application is an application whereby a taxpayer can file returns or elections that are past due or amend returns already filed and receive more preferential treatment if program's conditions are met, than they would if filed through the normal channels.

Currently there are two separate programs within the VDP process, which depending on which stream the taxpayer is accepted into, and each stream offers a different set of benefits.

The General Program is by far the most advantageous of these programs offering partial interest and penalty relief for any applicable tax arrears. The Limited Program only provides relief from criminal prosecution, and gross negligence penalties, and is normally reserved for applications where the original omission was clearly intentional to defraud the government. Both of these programs are discussed in more detail below.

The General Program

The General Program is designed for most taxpayers who did not use intentional measures to shelter their income, either domestically, or internationally, and whose omission does not include huge amounts of underreported income. Unfortunately, the CRA does not provide a dollar threshold for what constitutes a huge amount, however, in my experience it would involve amounts greater than $10,000,000.

If accepted into the general program, the information submitted through the program will ensure that the taxpayer will not be criminally charged for the omission and it will cancel all penalties for the preceding 10 years. However, returns outside of this 10-year period would still be subject to full penalties, and the taxpayer will only receive partial interest relief.

The Limited Program

The Limited Program is for taxpayers who do not qualify for the General Program for some of the reasons mentioned earlier. Unfortunately, if the taxpayer is accepted through the limited program the only benefit the taxpayer receives is that they will not be criminally charged for the omission. It is therefore important that every effort is made to show that your omission was not intentional in an effort to qualify under the General Program.

Acceptance Criteria

The CRA lists 5 criteria for an application to qualify for relief under either the General or Limited Program:

- The disclosure must be voluntary;
- The disclosure must be complete;
- The disclosure must involve the application of potential application of a penalty;
- The disclosure must include information that is at least one year past due; and
- The disclosure must include payment of the estimated tax owing.

1. Voluntary

In order for an application to be considered voluntary, it needs to be just that, voluntary. A taxpayer cannot be aware of any enforcement action against them, or a related party. Enforcement action is pretty broad but can include things like letters demanding that returns be filed, audits or investigations, or calls from the CRA.

It should be noted that enforcement action does not include letters inviting someone to participate in the program, or a recent audit for an unrelated account. In order for a recent audit to not preclude an individual's application from being considered voluntary, the taxpayer must establish that there was no correlation between the audit, and the information being disclosed.

The notion of a "related party" is pretty broad, but for the most part includes individuals or corporations who the taxpayer would have a direct connection with and can be easily shown that the enforcement action against that party led to the taxpayer coming forward. Usually this would be people that are related to the taxpayer, or a corporation for which they are connected. A taxpayer that owned shares in a publicly traded corporation who has been audited would not preclude their application from being considered voluntary since it hard to show that the taxpayer was connected to that corporation (unless they had vast holdings in it).

2. Complete

The next condition for an application to be accepted is that it must be complete. This means that all years that were previously not filed, or inaccurate are filed with your client's application. Unfortunately, this does mean that if they have been not reporting all their income for a long time you may have to report for more than the last 10 years, even though the CRA cannot grant penalty and interest relief for more than the last 10 years. If there are certain years for which the taxpayer cannot accurately determine their omission, the CRA requests that they estimate their underreported income for the years in question.

The CRA will not deny a VDP application due to minor errors or omissions related to years in which the taxpayer cannot accurately determine the amounts and needs to provide estimates; however, they must be satisfied that all reasonable efforts were made to either locate the documents or make an educated estimated.

3. Application of a Penalty

An application must involve a penalty, or potential penalty in order to be accepted into the program. The usual applicable penalty are late filing penalties; however, instalment penalties also qualify.

4. One-Year Past Due

A VDP application must contain information that is at least one year past due. A VDP application will meet this criterion if an application contains information that is at least 1 year past due, as well as information that is less than 1 year past due.

5. Payment of Estimated Taxes Owing

If there are taxes owing as a result of filings submitted through a VDP application, the taxpayer must include a cheque, or other proof of payment to cover the estimated taxes owing. The amount does not need to perfectly match the actual amounts owing that will be shown in notices of reassessment but must be an educated guess. When calculating the estimated taxes owing you will need to also estimate the interest you owe, but you do not need to estimate or pay any penalties.

If you are unable to pay the full amount owing, you can request that the CRA's collection department reaches out to you in order to set up a payment plan. In order to qualify for a payment plan, a taxpayer must show that they do not have the financial means to pay the estimated taxes owing all at once. A collection officer will then work with you in order to determine the maximum amount that you can pay towards your estimated taxes owing each month. Once this is approved, the VDP application should be processed as if the payment had of estimated taxes owing had been made in full.

The Application

After determining that an application meets the five criteria mentioned above, it is time to actually prepare the application. In order to do so the taxpayer needs to prepare an RC199, Voluntary Disclosure Program (VDP)

Application. In this application the taxpayer must fill out all of the sections that are relevant to their disclosure. The form contains sections for offshore and domestic income, GST/HST returns, and information returns; however, the taxpayer only needs to fill in the sections for the information that they are disclosing.

Some taxpayers will find the form is quite limited, and that they wish to express more than what is being requested, especially when it pertains to the reasons behind the omission. Therefore, we often recommend including a covering letter that details all of the reasons that led to the omission, as well as what brought you to make this disclosure.

Once all of the information is ready including the RC199, the income tax returns or adjustments themselves, and the payment the application is ready to be sent. If you choose to submit a voluntary disclosure on your own without the help of a lawyer (which is not advised for amounts which are significant or involve offshore components, or where there is the possibility of criminal prosecution). An application can be made either online through the taxpayer's My Account / My Business Account, or by mailing it to the CRA.

After the application has been sent, you should expect to receive a letter from the CRA indicating that your application has met the preliminary requirements to be accepted into the program. This letter does not mean that the application has been accepted, but rather that they have acknowledged receiving it. The CRA will also provide an effective date of disclosure (EDD), which means that any enforcement action taken by the CRA between the EDD and the time that your application is accepted or denied will not disqualify you from the program.

After receiving this letter there is not much that can be done besides wait. You should continue to file all other returns on time, and with complete information even before your application is accepted. Unfortunately, estimated wait times for the CRA to process a VDP application can easily exceed 18 months.

Once an application is accepted then you will receive a letter indicating that the application has been accepted and indicating which program that it was accepted into. After being accepted into the program the returns are sent to the processing centre to be processed, and you will receive reassessments.

If a VDP application is denied, then a similar letter will be sent to you informing that you application was denied, and the reasons why it was denied. The letter will indicate that the returns will be sent to the processing centre to be processed as normal, and you will not receive any of the benefits of the program – including the protection against prosecution.

If you do not agree with the decision, a second administrative review can be requested by submitting a letter to the assistant director of the VDP program explaining why they were wrong in their decision and requesting that they review the application and render a new decision. If you didn't seek professional advice in the preparation of your initial application, it is probably a good idea to do so at this stage. If the assistant director agrees with your second submission, then another letter will be sent indicating that the application upon reconsideration has been allowed into the program. If assessments had been issued during this time due to the application being originally denied, new reassessments will be issued reflecting the change to the interest and penalties where applicable.

If the VDP application is still denied upon second review, then you do have the option of filing an application to the Federal Court for a Judicial review of the CRA's decision. Any taxpayer looking to pursue this option should immediately consult with a tax lawyer, as there is a 30-day deadline to file the application after the decision is received.

If All Else Fails (Or is Too Late) File for Tax Remission

If you are in the unfortunate position where it is either too late to pursue traditional remedies such as objections, administrative reviews, and appeals to the court, or where all the other remedies have failed, you have one last-ditch attempt to obtain relief, and this involves having the federal government grant a remission order to cancel your tax owing.

A remission order may be granted in extreme cases where it would be seriously unfair to make somebody pay his or her amount owing which could not be cancelled or reduced other than by a remission order.

Since a remission order has to be approved by many levels of the CRA before even reaching the government, the process can take years, and taxpayers should not count on receiving one. Only a few are granted each year and they are for particularly exceptional cases.

If you do want to pursue tax remission, it would be wise to contact a tax lawyer.

17 OTHER MISCELLANEOUS TAX-FRIENDLY TIPS

Use Insurance to Pass Cottage on to Kids

While most cottage owners want their families to be able to enjoy the cottage long after their deaths, what many don't realize is that at the time of their passing there is going to be a large capital gains tax burden.

At the time of one's death there is a deemed disposition on all one's property – for tax purposes it is treated as if one sells their property back to their estate at fair market value.

The problem is that if a cottage has gone up by $500,000 for example, there could be a capital gains tax of $125,000. This means that in order for the kids to keep the cottage they have to be able to shell out $125,000 in cash in order to pay the taxes. This means that oftentimes the cottage must actually be sold in order to pay the taxes on the capital gain.

A helpful strategy is to have a life insurance policy which is earmarked specifically to pay the capital gains tax. This way your heirs don't have to be forced to sell the property in order to pay taxes.

Deduct the Cost of Life Insurance Under Certain Circumstances

Paragraph 20(1)(e.2) of the Income Tax Act allows one to deduct the cost of life insurance under certain circumstances.

A company or one of its business units may have one or more key persons — perhaps executives or company rainmakers. A key person may be a technical person like a researcher or a chief technology officer.

What is common about these people is that their death would prove to be detrimental to the business. As such, it is commonplace for a company to buy insurance against the loss of a person who is integral to its business or who is perhaps difficult or impossible to replace. This insurance comes in the form of a life insurance policy, commonly referred to as "key person insurance."

Key person insurance is meant to mitigate the losses that would take place by a business should a key person die. It allows the business to use the payout to try to find a replacement or to give the business an opportunity to get back on track.

Aside from their direct value to the company, many key employees have a value to financial institutions which often agree to finance a company on the basis of their faith in that person and their value to the business. As part of a financial arrangement based in part on an individual's merit, credentials or experience, the lending institution may require collateral to compensate in the event something happens to that person.

Key person insurance may then be taken out by the company and used as collateral in the loan agreement, or an already existing life insurance policy may be assigned. This will protect the lending institution against something happening to the individual whose merit ensures continued loan repayment.

In such a case, paragraph 20(1)(e.2) becomes a valuable tool for the borrower. The way that it works is that this provision allows the borrower to deduct from their income, reasonable costs of a life insurance policy which in turn facilitated the financing with the lending institution.

From a tax perspective, a life insurance policy assigned to a financial institution to earn income or one which is specifically taken out to facilitate a business loan is different from a policy purchased specifically to mitigate the loss of a key person.

Since the borrowed funds are used to earn income and an interest in the life insurance has been assigned, the expense of owning life insurance has changed. Similar to any other reasonable expense used to earn income, it is deductible when reporting at the end of each tax year, but only by virtue of paragraph 20(1)(e.2) of the ITA.

Before deducting the cost of insurance you should speak to your tax advisor.

Know the Benefit of an Accountant and the Limitations of Tax Software.

Many people opt to do their own taxes and prepare and file their own returns and there is certainly nothing wrong with this. But software has its limitations – especially if your situation is complicated.

For those who are more complicated than the average taxpayer you should be aware that a good accountant can be worth their weight in gold. And while this book may help you identify many strategies to help you pay way less tax, so too can an accountant. Just something to consider.

Turn Income from a Property Sale into Capital Gains

Since a capital gains results in half the tax of business income it is preferable to have one's profit from selling a property considered to be a capital gain rather than business income.

That being said, if you improve and flip a property the CRA's default position is that the profit made on the sale is business income and entirely subject to tax.

However, if the property was rented out for a period of time (the longer the better), then you may be able to convince the CRA that the profit made on the sale is a capital gain and only pay half the tax. But remember to rent the property out for as long as possible.

And also, you should take note that a primary way in which the CRA makes the determination as to whether it is a capital gain vs. business income is based on one's intention when they purchased the property. If the CRA determines that one's intention wasn't to acquire the property for the purpose of renting it, but rather to acquire the property for the purpose of flipping it – regardless of how long the property was rented out for you may be stuck paying tax on the entire gain.

Max out your RESP contribution

While many Canadians are aware that the government provides annual grants on contribution to RESPs, many people are simply unaware of the small but important nuances in maximizing those grants.

The Canada Education Savings Grant ("CESG") is essentially free money handed out by the Federal government for RESP contributions. The CESG is currently limited to 20% of annual RESP contributions, up to a maximum annual amount of $500 per child. Make the most of this grant money and maximize the grant amounts early on by maxing out your RESP contributions. While there is a lifetime maximum grant amount of $7,200 per child, the sooner funds are contributed or maximized, the sooner they begin earning tax-deferred interest.

Not to mention, if the annual amount is not maxed out, there may be a limit on your ability to carry forward these grants. While the carry forward deadline is technically once the child reaches 17, it can be very difficult to catch up on utilizing any unused grants. This is because one may only go back one year at a time to make up for missed contributions; the accumulated carry forward cannot be utilized simultaneously. If you begin making up the contributions too late, you may miss out on unused carry forwards.

If there is unused grant room from a prior year, which may be the case if there is an eligible carry forward or if you were unable to contribute enough to receive the CESG, then the basic grant limit is increased from $500 to $1,000 per child on a yearly basis ($500 for the year and $500 in unused carry forward).

If you miss a year of contributing, you may only catch up one year at a time to receive unclaimed entitlements up to the $500 basic CESG annual limit. If you begin catching up when your child is young, it may still be possible to play catch up. If, however you wait until your child is much older, it may be impossible to maximize the annual grant amounts of $500 per child and lifetime grant amount of $7,200 per child. Not to mention, the sooner your child has funds accumulating in the RESP, the greater the opportunity for the investment to grow on a tax-deferred basis.

If possible, you should ensure you contribute enough annually to maximize the grant.

While there is no annual contribution limit, there is a lifetime contribution limit currently set at $50,000 per child. Of this $50,000, only $36,000 qualifies for the 20% CESG grant to reach the lifetime $7,200 grant limit.

In order to obtain the annual maximum basic CESG, ideally $2,500 should be contributed annually to the RESP by the December 31st deadline, or $5,000 if to have a carry forward.

Based on adjusted income, additional CESG may be available for those who qualify, earning an extra 10 or 20% on the first $500 of contributions up to an additional $100 annually. Unlike basic CESG, additional CESG may not be carried forward. Additional CESG can be shown in the following chart:

Canada education savings grant summary chart

Adjusted income for 2019	$47,630 or less	more than $47,630 but less than $95,259	More than $95,259
CESG on the first $500 of annual RESP contribution	20% = $100	10% = $50	Beneficiary is not eligible
Basic CESG on the first $2,500 of annual RESP contribution	20% = $500	20% = $500	20% = $500
Maximum yearly CESG depending on income and contributions	$600	$550	$500
Lifetime maximum CESG for which you may qualify	$7,200	$7,200	$7,200

EXAMPLE – WHY THE RESP CONTRIBUTION SHOULD BE MAXIMIZED

If you maximized your RESP contributions annually and contributed $2,500 annually, you would have put in $42,500 by the time your child reaches the age of 17. The 20% CESG would be provided at a rate of $500 annually, to a limit of $7,200. With the RESP contribution and grants, $49,700 has been deposited in the RESP. This does not factor in compound growth and inflation. A larger contribution early on also provides for a greater return on the investment.

When compared with annual contributions of $1,000 to the child's RESPs, by the time your child is 17, only $17,000 would have been deposited. The 20% CESG would be provided at a rate of $200 annually, totalling only $3,400, which means you are losing half of the possible grant money by way of failure to maximum RESP contributions. With the RESP contribution of $17,000 and $3,40 of grants, $20,400 has been deposited in the RESP by the time you child has reached 18.

It's best to max out your yearly CESG and to begin RESP contributions when your child is born. Take some time to check in on your RESP contribution amounts and ensure that any missed annual contributions are dealt with prior to December 31st in order to maximize contributions amounts, CESG grants, and unused carry forwards. To maximize the tax-deferred investment growth and what is essentially free government money, one should consider contributing $2,500 annually to your child's RESP and to play catch up for any past years that were not maximized.

Careful of Unintended Shareholder Benefits

While certain transfers of value or wealth from a corporation to the shareholder, or rather shareholder benefits, are generally known to be included as taxable income, many unintended shareholder benefits can incidentally increase your tax bill. Shareholders who use corporate assets for personal use may find themselves in just this predicament. What's worse is that these unintended shareholder benefits become taxable not just in the hands of the shareholder but are also not deductible from taxation for the corporation, effectively being taxed twice.

Loans from companies for personal use can easily be imputed as taxable income and are by default classified by the CRA as taxable shareholder benefits. To avoid this from occurring, precautions should be made to ensure that an exception, such as one of the following, applies:

1. the loan should not be cyclical or as part of a series of loans, and should be repaid within the year the loan was made;
2. the loan is provided to the shareholder in their capacity as an employee, rather than as a shareholder, and the employee is not a "specified employee";
3. the loan is provided to the shareholder in their capacity as an employee, rather than as a shareholder, with bona fide repayment terms. The funds must be used to purchase a home, a vehicle for purposes of employment, or for shares of certain corporations; or
4. The corporation is in the business of lending money.

Shareholders often run into issues with the CRA when there has been an exchange of property between the corporation and shareholder for less than fair market value. If the shareholder has benefited from the exchange, an appropriation of property has occurred, whereby under subsection 15(1) of the Income Tax Act, the shareholder must include the amount as income. The amount to be taxed "is the amount by which the fair market value, at the time of the exchange, of all the property transferred by the corporation exceeds the fair market value, at that same time, of all property received by the corporation, to the extent that the excess is not deemed to be a dividend by virtue of subsection 84(1)."

By example, if a shareholder uses corporate assets for personal use, such as a corporate vehicle, and does not pay the corporation fair market value for use of those assets, then the shareholder is required to count as taxable income the amount appropriated. Similarly, should the corporation provide a discount to a shareholder that is not provided to all employees, but rather as special preference to the shareholder, then the value between the discounted amount and fair market value is considered a taxable benefit to the shareholder.

As a general tip, shareholders should ensure that adequate consideration has been provided for receipt of something of value from the corporation or ensure that the benefit falls under an exception prior to assuming that the benefit is tax-free.

Careful of Unintended Employee Benefits

Often times jobs come with certain perks, such as goods or services, or allowances or reimbursements of personal expenses, like health benefits, which can be very attractive to the employee. It is important to know that while attractive, these are generally not "free" to the employee and in fact often count as taxable benefits, which must be included on one's income tax return. While some benefits are obvious as such, others are not so much.

One must be careful about unintended employee benefits that will increase your tax bill. Some examples of unintended employee benefits often include business trips, professional development, rent-free or subsidized housing, gym memberships, cellular phones, transit passes, lodging, and use of company vehicles for purposes unrelated to employment.

A good tip to know whether a taxable benefit exists is to first ask whether it was you or your employer that primarily benefited. If you received "an economic advantage that can be measured in money" and are the primary beneficiary of a benefit, then it is generally taxable.

Take a business trip as an example. While on the trip, were you directly engaged in employment duties for the substantial part of each day? If so, the employer is most likely the primary beneficiary whereby the trip would not be considered a benefit. If however, the trip was an incentive, then the employee has benefited from the award or incentive and the trip becomes taxable to the employee to the extent of the personal benefit.

A good tip prior to receiving any benefit is to consider whether there is business purpose involved. If the CRA considers there to be a combination of both business and personal use, then only the personal use should be taxable.

Careful with Non-Arm's Length Transactions (avoid them with Tax Debtors)

An arm's length transaction is a transaction between certain parties which the CRA deems to be related. Some of these non-arm's length parties are actually related, such as individual family members. Other times these non-arm's length parties are not actually related but are treated as being related to one another. An example is a corporation and a related corporation or a corporation and a person who controls the corporation.

For more information about which parties are deemed by the CRA to be related, refer to Income Tax Folio S1-F5-C1, Related Persons and Dealing at Arm's Length.

(https://www.canada.ca/en/revenue-agency/services/tax/technical-information/income-tax/income-tax-folios-index/series-1-individuals/series-1-individuals/income-tax-folio-s1-f5-c1-related-persons-dealing-arms-length.html#N1044D)

Paragraph 251(1)(a) ITA deems that related persons do not deal with each other at arm's length. This is the case regardless of how they actually deal with one another. So, if you decide to sell your $1,000,000 business to your child for $1, the CRA will treat the transaction for tax purposes as if you sold the business for its Fair Market Value ("FMV"). This means that if you bought the shares for $100 when you first established the business, in this case you would have a capital gain of $999,900 – regardless of the fact that you received $1 as the purchase price from your kid.

Subsection 251(2) defines related persons for the purposes of the Act. Subsections 251(3) to 251(6) clarify and expand on the definitions.

Paragraphs 251(2)(b) and (c) set out the statutory rules for determining when a corporation and another person will be considered to be related persons for purposes of the Act.

It is very important to get proper legal advice prior to making transfers between non-arm's length parties when the transferor has a tax debt, or where the consideration paid is less than FMV.

When the collections agent has determined that there is nothing left to be collected from a tax debtor, besides going after directors (which is only available for corporate tax debtors), the CRA can also go after any non-arm's length recipients of assets.

The ITA says that if person or a corporation owes a tax debt, and while they owe a tax debt they transfer assets to a non-arm's length (related) person for less than fair market consideration, the recipient of the assets can be assessed for the lesser of the tax debt and the benefit received by the transfer.

EXAMPLE

Scenario A: A benefit greater than the tax owing

If a tax debtor owes $100,000 of tax to the CRA and transfers a $20,000 vehicle to their spouse (a non-arm's length party) for $1, that transferee (the spouse) would have received a benefit of $19,999.

And having taken a $19,999 benefit from the taxpayer to the detriment of their ability to pay the CRA, that transferee can be assessed to pay up to $19,999 of the transferor's taxes.

Scenario B: A benefit less than the tax owing

If a tax debtor owes $6,000 of tax to the CRA and transfers a $20,000 vehicle to their spouse (a non-arm's length party) for $1, that transferee (the spouse) would have received a benefit of $19,999.

And having taken a $19,999 benefit from the taxpayer to the detriment of their ability to pay the CRA, that transferee can be assessed to pay up to $19,999 of the transferor's taxes.

But since the transferor only owed $6,000 at the time of transfer the CRA could assess the transferee only for up to the $6,000 owed.

This rule prevents a taxpayer from artificially impoverishing themselves to the detriment of their ability to pay the CRA.

So, if a corporation pays dividends to a shareholder, or if a sole proprietor deposits their pay cheques into their spouse's bank account, they can trigger a non-arm's length assessment of the related party. Sometimes these transfers are intentional ways to try to avoid paying taxes, or ways to try to protect assets. Other times these transfers are no more than depositing money into a spouse's account to help pay for the monthly bills. And of course, when the amount is no more than a contribution for bill payments the cases are generally found in favour of the taxpayer when the amounts are reasonable. But in other cases, the results can be disastrous. Below is an article which explains why.

IMPORTANT TIP: Avoid non-arm's length transactions where you receive property for less than fair market value from somebody who owes tax to the CRA. The CRA can force you to pay some or all of their tax debt in such a circumstance.

And remember that the CRA may reassess a taxpayer for a previous year. So even though somebody may not owe tax to the CRA today, next week the CRA could audit them and reassess them for taxes owed in the past. And even though at the time of transfer (today) the person didn't owe any taxes, if they are reassessed for past taxes, they would be deemed by the CRA to owe taxes today, and thus you would have received property from somebody who owed taxes to the CRA. And this may put you in the position where the CRA will force you to pay some or all of that person's tax debt – up to the benefit you received (i.e. The fair market value of the asset you received less the purchase price).

The Peril of Family Asset Transfers

Originally Published on the Lawyer's Daily

Most people don't think twice before transferring assets between family members. Why would they? People deposit money into each other's accounts. They put each other's names on their properties in order to get mortgages. They sell assets to one another for one dollar. They move closely held company shares back and forth. And they inadvertently create massive tax problems for themselves, some of which are impossible to fix.

Sometimes as a result of such transfers and transactions, people create capital gains tax debts which otherwise would not have existed, and other times people are forced to pay a related party's tax debt, which normally would not have been collectible against them.

What most people are not aware of is that there exist provisions in Canadian tax legislation which act to prevent non-arm's length parties (spouses, siblings, parents and their children) from contracting with one another freely by deeming non-arm's length transactions to occur at fair market value, and other provisions which penalize people for the transfer of property to one another under certain conditions.

Subsection 160(1) of the Income Tax Act and ss. 325(1) of the Excise Tax Act are powerful collections tools used by the CRA to ensure that tax debtors do not artificially impoverish themselves to the detriment of their ability to pay taxes owed to the CRA. These provisions accomplish their goal by punishing the recipient when assets are transferred by tax debtors to related persons (including corporations) or when assets are sold by tax debtors to related persons for less than fair market value.

These provisions provide that the transferor and the transferee are jointly and severally liable for the payment of the tax of the transfer or up to the amount of the benefit received by the transferee. For example, if a car worth $20,000 is transferred from one spouse to another for consideration of one dollar, then the transferee received a benefit of $19,999 in this transaction, and thus can be held liable to pay $19,999 towards the tax debt of the transferor.

There was a case of an elderly retired woman who gave her son a bank card (from a disused account) to use because his accounts were frozen and thus he didn't have anywhere to deposit his pay cheque. Over three years he deposited $150,000 of his pay into his mother's bank account. He in turn withdrew all the money and used it for his living expenses.

It was argued in court that the mother didn't receive any benefit from the money deposited into her account because $150,000 went in, and $150,000 went back out to her son.

The judge disagreed. At the moment the funds were deposited, a non-arm's length transfer had taken place. And while the son received all his money back (in the absence of an agreement to return the money or a trust agreement), the money he received in return for the deposits was seen by the court as a gratuitous gift, rather than as consideration. Had it been seen as consideration, then the mother would have paid $150,000 consideration for the transfer of $150,000, which would have left her with no "benefit" and no liability for his tax.

Instead, since the court viewed this case as a non-arm's length transfer for no consideration followed by a gift, the ss. 160(1) assessment against the mother was upheld. Sadly, she ended up having to pay $150,000 towards her son's tax debt which depleted her retirement account.

The scarier, hidden danger is when one receives a non-arm's length transfer of property from an individual who at the time of transfer is not a tax debtor. In such a case, even if the transferee verified that the transferor had no tax debt at the date of transfer, at some point in time after the transfer is concluded the CRA could possibly reassess the transferor for a tax year prior to the transfer.

The resulting tax liability from this reassessment is deemed to have occurred retroactively and would thus pre-date the transfer. This means that at the date of transfer, the transferor actually would been retroactively considered to be a tax debtor. And if the transferor does not pay the tax debt the CRA can go after the transferee even though they had done their due diligence at the time of the transfer.

Besides the collection tools at the CRA's disposal there are other provisions dealing with non-arm's length transactions which accomplish different objectives.

Subsections 69(1) and (2) of the Income Tax Act deem that if the price paid by a recipient for an asset transferred to them by a non-arm's length transferor exceeds the asset's fair market value, the recipient is deemed to have acquired the asset at fair market value, and conversely, if the transferor receives less than fair market consideration for said asset, they are deemed to have received proceeds of disposition equal to fair market value.

There are a number of reasons for the existence of these provisions. One such reason is that they prevent parents from selling the cottage to their kids at the price they paid (thus avoiding capital gains tax), and prevents the kids in turn 50 years later from selling that same cottage to their kids. In essence it ensures that capital gains tax will eventually be paid when a property (except a principal residence) passes from generation to generation. Without the provision, the CRA could be indefinitely deprived of capital gains tax where a property keeps being sold from generation to generation for the original purchase price.

One of the big issues with these provisions is the collateral damage: sometimes they inadvertently catch unintended taxpayers. For example, when children cannot qualify for a condo mortgage on their own, they routinely put their parents on title with them, even though the parent never contributes towards the down payment or the mortgage payments, and even though the parent is on title as a convenience and not because of actual ownership. In such cases, when it comes time later on to remove the parent from title, a couple of different issues arise.

On one hand, if the parent owes a tax debt to the CRA, the child is often assessed under ss. 160(1) ITA or ss. 325(1) ETA as a result of having received a transfer of half a condo for no consideration. On the other hand, the CRA sometimes likes to assess capital gains tax against the parent for having sold a 50 per cent share in a condo — even though the share of the condo was sold for one dollar or gifted back to the child for $0 consideration.

When such a condo was worth $200,000 at purchase and $500,000 at time of transfer, even though there was no (or minimal) consideration provided for the transfer, the CRA deems that the sale of the share of the condo was made at fair market value (or $250,000 — half of the $500,000 fair market value), and a capital gain of $150,000 is triggered against the parent.

So, if you are contemplating the transfer of an asset to a family member or another related party as defined by tax legislation, it is important to seek legal advice and to consider all the unintended tax consequences which may result.

Careful of Attribution Rules (and TOSI)

There is a principle in Canada's income tax system that taxes are paid by the person who has a nexus to the income source. Income splitting is an attempt by taxpayers to subvert that rule by transferring income from one person to another — the transferee being subject to a lower marginal rate. Provisions in the Income Tax Act including 74.1-74.5 and 75.1 stop individuals from redistributing their income to their spouses or kids who are subject to lower tax rates. These rules empower the Canada Revenue Agency ("CRA") to assess amounts transferred to non-arm's length parties, as being income attributable to the transferor's income tax.

Attribution rules generally apply to property income, including interest, dividends, rent and royalties, as well as capital gains. If income or the proceeds of sale from the types of property is transferred to a spouse or common law partner, or children under the age of 18 who do not deal at arm's length with the transferor, then the attribution rules apply.

This means that if a person transfers shares in a corporation to their spouse and that spouse sells the shares, then the capital gain will be attributed to the transferor spouse. With a minor, there is an automatic deemed disposition at fair market value. This means that the parent in the year they transferred the property, regardless of whether the property was actually sold, will be required to pay capital gains tax. One can avoid the application of attribution rules with a spouse or minor by electing to sell the property at its fair market value.

As of January 1, 2018, a new set of rules referred to as Tax on Split Income ("TOSI") came into effect, supplementing the attribution rules. These new complex rules are contained in s. 120.4(1) of the Act. The purpose of the TOSI rules are to further discourage sprinkling income to minor children or young adults. The rules should be fully explained and applied by a lawyer with expertise in tax law. However, here is very brief overview.

The rules are divided into three parts depending on the children's age, and if TOSI applies to income, then it is taxed at the highest federal marginal rate. The TOSI rules generally apply to children under the age of 18 when they receive income from a business in which a related person has shares or is actively engaged that business. A related person is someone connected by blood, marriage, common law partnership, or adoption according to s. 251(2)(a)) of the ITA. This rule circumvents the possibility of a minor child being actively engaged in the family business and earning income at their tax rate from their efforts.

However, for 18 to 24-year-olds, the rules differ in that sense. If an 18 to 24-year-old is actively engaged in a related business, meaning they work 20 hours per week, then that person can earn a "reasonable" salary.

For 25-year-olds and above, in certain cases, shares from a related business are "excluded shares," and that person can benefit from capital gains of selling those shares without TOSI. This is in addition to the potential for earning a reasonable salary without TOSI applying. Excluded shares include shares owned in a related business where they represent 10% or more of the votes and value of the corporation, less than 90% of the corporation's business income was from the provision of services and is not a Professional Corporation, and all or substantially all of the income of that business is not derived from another Related Business.

Reasonableness according to TOSI, is based on the work performed in support of the related business, the risks assumed for the related business, whether property was contributed in support of the related business, the total amounts payable to the worker or for their benefit, and "such other factors as may be relevant." This is different than s. 67 which simply looks at comparably competitive salaries paid to the employee (family member or not), and the "reasonableness" from a business expense standpoint.

Active engagement is established by the taxpayer. An amount of time spent working per week, sufficient to equal "active engagement," is 20 hours. For young adults that work less than 20 hours, it is a question of fact whether the work was on a regular, continuous and substantial basis. For businesses that operate seasonally, such as with a farm or fishing property, the engagement requirement only applies to the time of the year during which the business operates.

The key point is that attribution rules, especially the TOSI rules are very complicated. Before engaging in a transaction between related parties it is important to get good advice.

Beware of Personal Services Businesses

What is a Personal Service Business?

The Personal Services Business ("PSB") is defined by the CRA as "a business that a corporation carried on providing services to another entity (such as a person or a partnership) that an officer or employee of that entity would usually perform. Instead, an individual performs the services on behalf of the corporation. That individual is called an incorporated employee."

The way I describe a PSB to somebody is as follows. Phil has an incorporation. It is called PhilCo. PhilCo is hired by a factory. PhilCo sends Phil every day to do work at the factory. Phil stands on the assembly line and does the same work as Mike (an employee) and Jimbo (an employee) and Chloé and Claire (also employees). In fact, Phil, Mike, Jimbo, Chloé and Claire all do the exact same job. They have done so for years. But Jimbo, Chloé and Claire all receive a pay cheque with the usual deductions, and Phil sends the factory an invoice once a month, plus he includes HST on top of the work done. As a business, PhilCo can write off expenses such as a phone, home office, vehicle, etc. Life is great for Phil.

CRA's conclusion: Phil is an employee masquerading as a business PhilCo. PhilCo is a PSB. So: The income from PhilCo is not eligible for the Small Business Deduction and the deductions which are allowed in order to compute income of PhilCo are severely restricted. It is almost as if PhilCo never existed in the first place.

A lot of corporations ask their workers to become incorporated. This happens in the trucking industry and in many others. You should consider whether you are actually operating a PSB and beware of the pitfalls.

Take Advantage of the Quick Method for GST/HST

What is the Quick Method of Accounting for GST/HST?

The Quick Method allows certain qualified taxpayers to only remit a portion of the tax they collect instead of claiming the GST/HST paid on purchases as an input tax credit.

Not only is the simple method less costly in terms of time spent to prepare returns, it is possible that by using this method you will end up saving some HST which you would have otherwise paid to the CRA.

The answer is in the numbers. You can run the calculation both ways and see which is more advantageous. If you qualify it may be a great way to save a few thousand dollars a year.

While most ITCs are not available when using the Quick Method, a taxpayer still has the ability to claim the input tax credits for capital purchases.

The form "Election and Revocation of an Election to Use the Quick Method of Accounting" can be completed and filed with the CRA to begin using the quick method of accounting. A taxpayer can also elect this method by using the CRA online services.
The same form or online service can be used to revoke the election to use the quick method. The form outlines some important details regarding the quick method of accounting including the revenue limit to use quick method and when a taxpayer can choose the quick method during their reporting period. You can revoke the election for after the quick method election has been in effect for at least a year, and generally it must be revoked by the due date of the GST/HST return for the last reporting period prior to revoking the quick method.

For more information see: https://www.canada.ca/en/revenue-agency/services/forms-publications/publications/rc4058/quick-method-accounting-gst-hst.html#P100_5211

GST74E Election Form

Canada Revenue Agency / Agence du revenu du Canada

Protected B
when completed

Election and Revocation of an Election to Use the Quick Method of Accounting

Use this form to either elect to start using the quick method of accounting, or to stop using the method. You can also make or revoke this election by using our online services at **canada.ca/my-cra-business-account** or at **canada.ca/taxes-representatives**. If you use our online services, do not send this form.

Generally, you can use the quick method if the total annual revenue (including the GST/HST) from your worldwide taxable supplies (including zero-rated supplies) and those of your associates is no more than $400,000 in either the first four or the last four consecutive fiscal quarters out of the last five fiscal quarters. If you previously elected to use the quick method and have revoked that election, you have to wait at least one year from the date the revocation became effective before you can elect to use the quick method again.

Certain businesses **cannot** use the quick method. For more information, see Guide RC4058, Quick Method of Accounting for GST/HST or call **1-800-959-5525**. To get our forms and publications, go to **canada.ca/gst-hst-pub**.

To elect to use the quick method, fill out parts A, B and D. To revoke the election, fill out parts A, C and D. Send this form to your tax services office. You can find the address at **canada.ca/cra-offices**.

Part A – Identification

Name and trading name (if different from name)

Business number | | | | | | | | | R | T | | | |

Part B – Election

Select this box to elect to use the quick method of accounting to calculate your net tax. ☐

I want to start using the quick method of accounting on the first day of my reporting period beginning: Year Month Day

Notes
If you file annual GST/HST returns, you have to make the election by the first day of your second fiscal quarter.
If you file monthly or quarterly GST/HST returns, you have to make your election by the due date of the return in which you start using the quick method.

How long does the election stay in effect?

Generally, the election stays in effect unless **either**:

- the total annual revenue (including the GST/HST) from your worldwide taxable supplies (including zero-rated supplies), and those of your associates, is more than $400,000
- you become a person that cannot use the quick method because of the type of business you carry on

If your election ceases to be in effect, you have to start using the regular method to calculate your net tax. For more information, see Guide RC4058.

Part C – Revocation of election

Select this box to revoke the election that you made to use the quick method of accounting to calculate your net tax. ☐

Enter the date of revocation of election (you have to revoke the election by the due date of the GST/HST return for the last reporting period in which you want to use the quick method): Year Month Day

Note
The effective date of revocation has to be at least one year after the date of the election.

Part D – Certification

I, ______________________ (print name), certify that the information given on this form is correct and complete.

I understand that this election to use the quick method of accounting is binding for a minimum of one year, unless the business no longer meets the eligibility criteria. I also understand that once this election is revoked, I must wait at least one year before I can elect to use the quick method again.

______________________ Year Month Day
Signature of the authorized person

Personal information is collected under the Excise Tax Act to administer tax, rebates, and elections. It may also be used for any purpose related to the enforcement of the Act such as audit, compliance and collection activities. It may be shared or verified with other federal, provincial, territorial or foreign government institutions to the extent authorized by law. Failure to provide this information may result in interest payable, penalties or other actions. Under the Privacy Act, individuals have the right to: access, or request corrections of, their personal information, or to file a complaint with the Privacy Commissioner of Canada regarding the handling of their personal information. Refer to Personal Information Bank CRA PPU 241 at **canada.ca/cra-info-source**.

GST74 E (19) (Ce formulaire est disponible en français.) Canada

Turn Passive Income into Active Income

As a business, earning active income instead passive investment income or income from a personal service business, allows the business to be taxed in a more favourable manner.

Passive investment income includes income from investments or property. Income from a personal service business generally results where a taxpayer is an employee who is being paid through a corporation – I like to call this a situation where an employee is masquerading as a corporation. They do all the same work that the employee at the next desk does, but they bill their employer from their corporation.

A Canadian Controlled Private Corporation (CCPC) can claim an annual tax credit of 18% on up to $500,000 of its "active business income" (ABI) that it earns in Canada. Thus, earning ABI will save a business-taxpayer on their annual return. Conversely, passive income may decrease the tax benefits associated with ABI. If a CCPC earns more than $150,000 of passive investment income, then their small business deduction disappears. When the business begins earning more than $50,000 of passive income, the amount that qualifies for the small business deduction (SBD) decreases with each extra dollar earned, until reaching $150,000. It is worth noting that the term "passive income" is used broadly here however, in practice, corporations from passive income will determine an amount called their Adjusted Aggregate Investment Income, which is essentially passive income (including life insurance and capital gains) minus the corporation's total losses for the year from property.

For the reasons above, corporations seeking to benefit from the SBD should be earning ABI instead of passive investment income, or at least not passive income in an excess of $50,000. For the grey areas, to determine whether income is active or passive, consider the following factors (which courts and the CRA will apply): the activity associated with the generation of the income; the number and value of transactions; the relationship between the income in question and total income; and the relationship between the value of the assets producing the income in question and total assets.

Hence, in order to turn passive income into ABI, income must be part of the income earning process of the business. For example, selling one property will result in a capital gain (passive, property income); however, selling five in a year is "active" in the sense that a business doing so may have that as part of their operations. If the income from five properties is that businesses total income, then the conclusion of it being "active" is nearly confirmed.

Consider Offshore Structures

A strategy employed by many in order to decrease their taxes is to operate a business offshore. There are many legal strategies which can be put in place to take advantage of low tax offshore jurisdictions. There are many interesting jurisdiction where you can set up business in order to save on taxes. Included in these are Estonia, British Virgin Islands, Cayman Islands, Singapore and others.

If you are considering having an offshore structure, you should always make sure that you consult a tax advisor. There are many complicated rules which you must be aware of so that you are not offside.

Consider Whether You Want to Leave Canada Altogether

While Canada is a great place to live for many reasons, often the best way to save on taxes is to leave Canada altogether.

There are many people, most of whom are high income earners, who simply cannot justify paying upwards of 50% of their income to the CRA. And many of these high-income earners simply opt to leave the country and move to a jurisdiction which is far more tax-friendly. This is always an option.

I have had clients who used to pay millions of dollars each year to the CRA. For them, the universal health care was not enough to make this tax payment worthwhile. So they left.

Remember though, if you leave the country and still maintain a business here, you will still be subject (as a non-resident) to Canadian taxation.

Probably the wisest thing you can do before you leave the country and head for the islands is to have a consultation with a tax lawyer.

Stop Earning Income

Probably the easiest way to avoid paying tax to the CRA or to anybody else is to quit your job. Just stop working. The problem is that most people cannot afford to do this, and those who can afford to do this will likely end up paying tax anyway if they end up earning interest on the amounts they have in the bank.

Go Work for the United Nations

Many people have no idea that United Nations employees do not pay tax – to anybody, including the CRA. So, if you want to avoid tax altogether without breaking the law or quitting your job you may want to consider a job with the UN.

Earn Income from Gambling (but not too much)

In Canada lottery and gambling winnings as well as winnings from horse racing, betting and other games of chance are tax free. However, there is an exception.

In Canada we have the "source concept of income". That is to say that all "sources" of income are taxed. These sources are office, employment, business, and property. A lottery win, or an occasional win at a casino is seen as a "windfall," not a "source" of income, so it is not taxed.

But if one earns their income primarily from gambling the CRA adopts a very different position – those people are considered to be professional gamblers. Gambling is how they earn their income. It is not a windfall. And professional gamblers must declare their winnings to the CRA and pay tax on them.

So, while you can earn some tax-free "income" from gambling, ensure that it is not too much or too often. And in order to determine what is too much, consider whether the gambling represents a substantial proportion of your income. If it does, then you may be a professional gambler and may have to pay tax on your winnings.

Use Tax Treaties to Your Advantage

Use Tax Treaties to Your Advantage

The Canadian government taxes resident Canadians on sources of income inside and outside of Canada. Additionally, non-residents are taxed on income they earn in Canada.

Without domestic rules and tax treaties between Canadian and foreign governments, double taxation would occur in many circumstances.

Domestically, for business and non-business income, section 126 of the Income Tax Act allows resident Canadian taxpayers to claim a credit for taxes paid in another jurisdiction.

Consider for example a Canadian earning income in the US. If they were still a tax resident of Canada, they would end up paying tax to the IRS and the CRA on the very same income. But we have rules which prevent such double taxation - so when a Canadian resident pays tax to the IRS, they get a tax credit locally.

The rules established in s. 126 differ depending on whether the taxpayer is earning business or non-business income. For non-business income, such as income from property or employment, tax paid in another jurisdiction can be counted against a Canadian's tax payable. The credit cannot exceed the tax otherwise payable in Canada. In other words, it cannot offset other sources of income.

For property that is not real or immovable, according to s. 20(11), 85% is counted against income from that source, and the remaining 15% becomes a tax credit. Regarding business income, the rules apply to a similar effect of those for non-business income with the important exception that credits above Canadian tax payable can be carried back three years and forward ten years.

Keeping s. 126 in mind, what is the benefit of an international tax treaty, namely, if a Canadian taxpayer can claim tax credits for tax payable in other jurisdictions? There are two main benefits. The first is that bilateral agreements further integrate tax systems to prevent double taxation. As mentioned, section 126 only applies to resident Canadians and would be no avail to Canadians working and living abroad. They would be required to file a tax return for amounts earned in Canada while also complying with the tax system of a foreign jurisdiction. Another example, specifically in the context of our relations with the United States, is for students learning or training abroad and being paid from their country of citizenship. The United States – Canada Income Tax Convention provides that those amounts are not taxed by the country of residence. In other words, a Canadian who qualifies as a student can be living in the United States being paid by an employer in Canada, and not be required to pay U.S. income tax on those amounts.

The second important benefit is to prevent or reduce the size of withholding tax. An example of this benefit, since the Canadian and U.S. tax systems are integrated by bilateral agreement, is that a taxpayer who earns income in the United States can file a form W-8BEN. This form indicates to U.S. tax authorities that they will not be subject to tax in the U.S. and will report their U.S. income in Canada.

Assert Your Taxpayer Rights

Whenever you deal with the CRA, remember that you have various rights which are outlined in the Taxpayer Bill of Rights. And remember to assert them. Don't be pushed around arbitrarily. If you feel that the CRA is violating one or more of your rights don't be scared to push back and insist that they (the auditor / the collector / etc.) respect your rights. If necessary, get in touch with a tax lawyer or the Taxpayer's Ombudsman (see below).

Use the Ombudsman to Protect your Rights

The Taxpayer's Ombudsman is an independent official, who advocates for taxpayers and assists with complaints.

The Ombudsman's office will not be able to help with incorrect assessments or substantive matters. What they can help with, however, is finding a solution when a taxpayer's rights have been infringed. In such cases the Ombudsman will investigate the taxpayer complaint and they will bring the matter up with the CRA. If a taxpayer complained to the Ombudsman's office of an auditor who was being prejudicial because they were racist / sexist / homophobic / anti-Semitic / etc., then a complaint to the Ombudsman's office would generally have the effect of very quickly having the auditor changed.

Being independent of the CRA, the Ombudsman has no actual power to make changes at the CRA or force them to take any particular action. The office does, however, produce an annual report and offers recommendations to the CRA, which are within the exclusive domain of the CRA to act on or not.

Specifically, the Ombudsman's primary goal is to help uphold taxpayers' rights under the Taxpayer's Bill of Rights by getting involved when the rights numbers 5, 6, 9, 10, 11, 13, 14, and 15 are infringed. And in terms of protecting these rights, the Ombudsman does a fine job. But it is important before seeking help, to understand what can and cannot be achieved.

In order to file a complaint, one can visit the Ombudsman's website at www.oto-boc.gc.ca. According to the web site, the Ombudsman can assist with misunderstandings, omissions or oversights, undue delays, poor or misleading CRA information, unfair taxpayer treatment and poor staff behaviour.

Once a complaint is filed, it will be acknowledged by the Ombudsman, it will be screened to see if the complaint falls under their mandate, they will then examine the matter and conduct a fair and impartial investigation, and then they will provide the CRA with recommendations and the taxpayer with details as to the outcome.

A complaint form and relevant information can be found on the ombudsman's website: www.oto-boc.gc.ca. Services that the ombudsman provides (according to their website) include aid for me: mistakes that refer to misunderstandings, omissions, or oversights. Undue delays. Poor or misleading information. Unfair treatment and poor staff behaviour.

There are four steps after the complaint is filed:

a. Acknowledgement: After the complaint is submitted, one will have to wait for the ombudsman to formally acknowledge it
b. Screening: The ombudsman will have to determine whether the complaint falls under their purview and has merit. Also, if the taxpayer has exhausted all other avenues in attempting to solve the matter before approaching them
c. Review Process: An examination officer takes the matter under consideration and attempts to take in part a fair and impartial investigation
d. Conclusion: After the investigation the office of the ombudsman will provide an outcome to the query of the taxpayer based on their complaint as well as giving recommendations, they believe are just to the CRA

Get an Advance Tax Ruling if you are Not Sure

What is an Advance Ruling?

An advanced ruling is a mechanism whereby a Taxpayer or their representative can request an interpretation of how a certain transaction would comply with a provision of Canadian Income Tax Law. It can be made under any act that relates to Federal taxation, but is most commonly used for Income Tax Act, and Excise Tax Act provisions.

An advanced ruling is an interpretation of how the CRA interprets how a transaction would be treated, similar to if the Taxpayer had been subjected to an audit. The whole process is designed to encourage voluntary compliance by providing a clear answer on a proposed accounting question.

Advanced rulings are designed to give assurance to a Taxpayer before they file their returns as these rulings are binding on the CRA, provided that the transaction occurred exactly as it was laid out in the ruling request. The only things that can change a ruling's validity would be changes brought forward by the Legislature, or Court cases.

How to Request an Advance Income Tax Ruling

Once you know that you want to request an advanced ruling you will need to draft a letter to CRA outlining the transaction in detail, as well as the purpose of the proposed transaction (both tax and non-tax reasons). Finally, you need to confirm which provision of the Canadian Income Tax Act (or Excise Tax Act) you are concerned your transaction will violate. The CRA provides a good template of how the request can be formulated at:

https://www.canada.ca/en/revenue-agency/services/forms-publications/publications/ic70-6/ic70-6-advance-income-tax-rulings-and-technical-interpretations.html#toc0

Once the request has been drafted you will need to include some additional paperwork. The first of these is a letter authorizing the CRA to release your Ruling to commercial publishers. This is done so that others might be able to benefit from the same ruling, but all confidential information is redacted.

Next is that either the Taxpayer or their representative must provide an undertaking to pay the fees, as advanced rulings are not free, and can range from $100 an hour to $155 an hour. The first 10 hours that the CRA spends considering the request costs $100 an hour, with any subsequent hour spent on request costing $155 an hour. For this reason, a $2,500 deposit is required to be made with any request. This amount is held in trust, much like a law firm with any amounts not used being refunded.

Once all of this is prepared advanced ruling requests can be sent by mail to the following address:

Income Tax Rulings Directorate
Canada Revenue Agency
9th floor, Tower A
Place de Ville, 320 Queen Street
Ottawa ON K1A 0L5

Or by fax: 613-957-2088

Or by email: itrulingsdirectorate@cra-arc.gc.ca

It is important to note that the CRA will not consider all ruling requests. The CRA provides a non-exhaustive list of types of transactions that will likely not be considered for an advanced ruling. These include:

1. proposed transactions or issues that are the same as or substantially similar to transactions or issues that are:
   a. in a previously filed tax return of the taxpayer or a related person and:
      i. being considered by the CRA in connection with such return;
      ii. under objection by the taxpayer or a related person; or
      iii. the subject of a current or completed court process involving the taxpayer or a related person; or
   b. the subject of a Ruling request previously considered by the Directorate;
2. proposed transactions that are not being seriously contemplated or are to be completed at some indefinite future time;
3. alternative courses of action;
4. the determination of the fair market value of a property;
5. the confirmation of tax-related calculations;
6. the interpretation of a provision of the tax legislation that has either not been enacted or would require a regulation and the particular regulation is not yet enacted. However, a non-binding interpretation of a provision that has not been enacted may be provided;
7. proposed transactions in respect of which a provision can only result in one outcome and there is no reasonable alternative interpretation. That includes circumstances where the request is to confirm that a provision does not apply, where the information provided in support of a Ruling request on a provision does not support any reasonable ambiguity that would suggest that the provision might apply. An example of the latter would be a request to rule on subsections 15(1) and 246(1) where no potential benefit was identified in the Ruling request. Another example would be a request to rule that subsection 107(2) will apply to deem that there is no gain or loss on a proposed distribution of capital from a personal trust to a beneficiary, where the requirements of that provision are met, and no ambiguity was identified in the Ruling request. However, a Ruling might still be provided on such provisions to confirm that their application will not be denied under subsection 245(2);
8. primarily a factual or legal determination. This may include issues involving residence, the income or capital nature of a transaction, carrying on a business or the existence of a partnership;

9. issues and/or types of transactions in respect of which the Directorate has publicly announced that it will not issue a ruling;
10. transactions that pertain to provisions of tax legislation or positions that are under review;
11. issues that would require interpretation of a law not administered by the CRA, including foreign law;
12. an opinion on accounting or commercial principles, practices, or guidelines;
13. a request in respect of which the requestor (generally the taxpayer's representative) has not undertaken to pay the fees; or
14. a request in respect of which the taxpayer has not consented to release the Ruling in a severed form to the public.

It is therefore important to make sure that your request will not be denied due to one of the factors mentioned in the list above.

Carry Forward Your Losses

When capital is sold, there is generally a capital gain or capital loss. To determine if there is a capital gain or capital loss, one should subtract the property's Adjusted Cost Base ("ACB"), as well as any outlay and expenses incurred from the disposition, from the proceeds of disposition.

If there is a capital loss, it may only be used against capital gains and not other types of income. This may be done by applying for inclusion rate (which for 2019 is ½) of the capital loss against any taxable capital gains. The capital loss may be carried backward 3 years and forward indefinitely, subject to the certain loss application rules and annual deduction limits but may only be used to offset taxable capital gains. If however, there are remaining losses by the time of the taxpayer's death, the capital losses may be used against any type of taxable income for the year of death and prior year.

Carrying forward a net capital loss from a prior year to reduce will effectively reduce the taxable income for the current year, however, the "net income, which is used to calculate certain credit and benefits, will not change."

To carry forward a capital loss, a deduction must be claimed on line 25300 (or for years prior to 2019, line 253) of your income tax return. The deduction amount will be based off the inclusion rate and when the loss was incurred. The inclusion rate should be referred to prior to claiming the loss and determining the taxable capital gain. For 2019, the inclusion rate was ½ of the capital loss.

There are rules in place when claiming a net capital loss for earlier years, including that losses from earlier years must be applied prior to those of later years. When claiming a loss from earlier years, special consideration should be taken to account for the applicable inclusion rate for that year.

If claiming a loss incurred prior to May 23, 1985, special rules apply whereby the loss may be applied to other taxable income (not just capital income). "This also includes losses you incurred after May 22, 1985, on any disposition of capital property made under an agreement of sale you entered into before May 23, 1985."
Non-capital losses are generally losses that are non-capital, such as from employment, property, or business. Unlike capital losses, non-capital losses may be used towards taxable income. This is helpful in that it can be applied towards income from other sources, such as from employment, interest amounts or RRSP income, effectively reducing or eliminating taxable income.

Non-capital losses may be carried back 3 years or generally if incurred after 2005, carried forward 20 years. Other rules apply for non-capital losses incurred prior to 2005. For non-capital losses arising from allowable business investment losses ("ABIL"), however, the carry forward must be used within 10 years, or will become a net capital loss in the 11th year. Farming or fishing losses must also be used within 10 years and are subject to certain restrictions that are beyond the scope of this discussion. Regular non-capital losses, unlike ABILs, if unused within the carry forward period do not convert to capital losses, but rather expire and are lost forever.

To carry forward non-capital losses, one must claim the amount of allowable non-capital losses of prior years on line 25200 (or for years prior to 2019, line 252) on your income tax return.

Max Out Your TFSA contribution

If you are not concerned about saving for your retirement, and you are more concerned with saving for the short term or earning investment income tax-free, a good vehicle is the Tax-Free Savings Account (the "TFSA").

Think of the TFSA as your piggy bank which grows tax free. You can dip into it at any time and you can replace the amount you took at any time. Your contribution limit does not disappear. The money can be used for anything you like from home renovations to a trip.

And the money invested in a TFSA account can be used and invested in so many different ways from mutual funds to GICs, stocks, bonds, ETFs and more.

Avoid Penalties

There are many different consequences that can result from not filing tax returns. These consequences range from a small penalty to jail time. And when the CRA decides to pursue criminal prosecution, they have a success rate of close to 100%.
And where they see fit, the CRA recommends that the prosecutors take on cases for tax evasion or failure to file, both of which result a permanent criminal record (unless a pardon is granted) but also fines of up to $25,000 for every count of failure to file an information return. Of course, the most serious of all the consequences could be imprisonment and having a permanent public record on the CRA's website.
Some mistakenly believe that if they cannot afford to pay the tax bill then they should not file. This couldn't be further from the truth.

There is absolutely no excuse for not filing.

Remember, it is illegal not to file. It is NOT illegal not to pay.

But First, the Reminders

Taxpayers don't just wake up one morning to find that they have been criminally charged for not filing. The CRA is very careful to follow the correct procedure, and that procedure involves plenty of warning.

Typically, taxpayers will start to receive letter mail and phone calls from the CRA, requesting that they file certain tax returns within a certain time period. Over time these letters may either become sterner and then the requests become demands, or these letters may cease altogether and the CRA may go ahead and file arbitrary assessments (more about that below). In those cases where the requests become demands, those demands culminate (in every case I have ever seen) with a personal visit by the CRA to the taxpayer during which the CRA advises the taxpayer that they will be subject to prosecution if they do not comply and provide returns by a certain date. Only then does the CRA proceed with the prosecution, and this process takes months in most cases.

In those cases where the CRA does not pursue prosecution they often process arbitrary (or notional) assessments against the taxpayer. What this means is that the CRA creates notices of assessment based on certain information that they have. In the case of a business the CRA will make a guess about the taxable income (usually based on previous returns) and they will process this without the benefit of any deductions. The idea is that the taxpayer is supposed to be taken by surprise when they see the assessments, and thus coaxed into providing the CRA with the actual numbers in the form of a properly filed tax return. Once the return is filed, subject to the CRA's right to audit, the new numbers override the old ones, and a notice of reassessment is issued.

Interest & Penalties

In all cases, where tax returns are filed after the due date, interest will be applied from the date the amount was initially due. And it is important to remember that the interest accrues on a daily basis – even on penalty amounts.

The interest rate fluctuates on a regular basis, and after a short number of years taxpayers find that the interest on top of the tax and the penalties, becomes impossible to manage. Filing on time will help avoid the penalties but paying as much as possible as soon as possible after the payment deadline will help avoid the interest.

In the case of late filing, there will always be a penalty applied. The penalty will depend on whether the late filing is because of an audit, or if it was just a case of late filing, or it was a case of a voluntary disclosure.

Late Filing Penalties

Late filing penalties depend on whether a taxpayer has had previous offenses before in regard to late filing. If it is the first-time offense the penalty for income tax is 5% of the balance plus 1% of the balance they owe for every month it is late up to a maximum of one year. This brings the total to 17%. However, if a taxpayer has repeat offences, the penalty can double to 10% plus 2% per month for up to 20 months.

GST/HST Penalties

Late filing penalties also apply to GST/HST and source deductions

GST/ HST, penalties for late filing are calculated according to the following formula A + (B x C). A is 1 percent of the amount owing; B is 25 percent of A, and C is the number of months overdue to a maximum of 12.

EXAMPLE

A taxpayer who is late in filing their GST or HST return by 12 months, owes $10,000, the CRA's formula looks like this:

$100 + (25 x 12) = $400, a 4 percent penalty.

Source Deductions Penalties

For source deductions, the CRA assesses penalties for late remittances (payments) of 3 percent if the amount is one to three days late, 5 percent if it is four to five days late, 7 percent if it is six to seven days late, and 10 percent if it is more than seven days late or if no amount was remitted. In cases where the taxpayer has been penalized once in a calendar year, all subsequent late filings may be assessed a penalty of 20 percent if such filings were made knowingly or negligently.

If a taxpayer owes $10,000 and is 30 days late, they would be subject to a penalty of 10 percent or $1,000, which would increase to $2,000 on a subsequent failure.

In Quebec, a penalty of 15 percent or $1,500 would apply.

For further information on penalty amounts for GST or HST returns when the CRA has issued a demand to file, and where a taxpayer was required to file electronically but did not, or where the taxpayer failed to accurately report information, please refer to the CRA's web page entitled "Penalties and Interest" in the business section.

Gross Negligence Penalties

The most severe penalties assessed by the CRA are the gross negligence penalty under subsection 163(2) of the Act. This penalty may be assessed when the taxpayer "knowingly or under circumstances amounting to gross negligence, has made or has participated in, assented to or acquiesced in the making of a false statement or omission in a tax return."

The penalty of 50% of the underreported tax (or 25% in the case of HST) is designed to ensure that taxpayers complete their returns correctly and resist the temptation to play games.

One of the big problems is that these penalties are often applied by auditors when they are not justified. And whether justified or not, a taxpayer is best served by always challenge the gross negligence penalty. Like a speeding ticket, if there is a defect in the "penalty recommendation report," or of the report is absent, the penalty can be dismissed. Always ask to see the penalty recommendation report when you challenge a gross negligence penalty.

According to Canadian courts, gross negligence penalties should be applied cautiously and only where truly warranted. They have been seen as akin to a criminal type of penalty because of their severity. That is why the burden of proof is reversed in court with respect to the penalties: The CRA must prove that the penalty was justified. In all other matters the burden of proof rests upon the taxpayer.

---

[38] CRA, "ARCHIVED - Property Transfers After Separation, Divorce and Annulment," June 22, 2017, https://www.canada.ca/en/revenue-agency/services/forms-publications/publications/it325r2/archived-property-transfers-after-separation-divorce-annulment.html#:~:text=This%20bulletin%20discusses%20transfers%20of,a%20former%20common%2Dlaw%20spouse.

[39] Income Tax Act, subsection 73(3): When subsection (3.1) applies, November 27, 2020, https://laws-lois.justice.gc.ca/eng/acts/I-3.3/section-73.html?wbdisable=true

[40] CRA Publication: "Eligible small business corporation shares," January 21, 2020, https://www.canada.ca/en/revenue-agency/services/tax/individuals/topics/about-your-tax-return/tax-return/completing-a-tax-return/personal-income/line-127-capital-gains/capital-losses-deductions/capital-gains-deferral-investment-small-business/eligible-small-business-corporation-shares.html

[41] The Queen v. Reeder, 75 DTC 5160

[42] Wassick (R.) v. Canada, [1994] 2 C.T.C. 2235, 95 D.T.C. 19 (Tax Court of Canada)

[43] Wassick supra, at para. 11

[44] https://www.canada.ca/content/dam/cra-arc/formspubs/pbg/t1244/t1244-19e.pdf

[45] https://www.canada.ca/en/revenue-agency/services/tax/international-non-residents/individuals-leaving-entering-canada-non-residents/dispositions-property.html

[46] http://support.drtax.ca/dtmax/eng/kb/dtmax/eng/t4056-13e.pdf

[47] https://www.canada.ca/en/revenue-agency/services/tax/technical-information/income-tax/income-tax-folios-index/series-3-property-investments-savings-plans/folio-3-capital-transactions/income-tax-folio-s3-f3-c1-replacement-property.html#toc10

[48] Ibid at para 1.36

[49] Ibid at para 1.37

[50] Ibid at para 1.41

[51] Ibid

[52] Ibid a para 1.6-1.7

[53] https://www.canada.ca/en/revenue-agency/services/forms-publications/publications/ic00-1/ic00-1r6-voluntary-disclosures-program.html at para 28

[54] CRA, Canada Education Savings Grant (CESG), November 8, 2019, https://www.canada.ca/en/revenue-agency/services/tax/individuals/topics/registered-education-savings-plans-resps/canada-education-savings-programs-cesp/canada-education-savings-grant-cesg.html

[55] IT-432R2, February 10, 1995, https://www.canada.ca/content/dam/cra-arc/formspubs/pub/it432r2/it432r2-e.pdf

[56] T4130(E) Rev. 19, Employers' Guide – Taxble Benefits and Allowances, https://www.canada.ca/en/revenue-agency/services/forms-publications/publications/t4130/employers-guide-taxable-benefits-allowances.html#benefit_taxable

[57] https://www.canada.ca/en/revenue-agency/services/forms-publications/publications/ic70-6/ic70-6-advance-income-tax-rulings-and-technical-interpretations.html#toc0 at para 19

[58] CRA: "Capital losses and deductions; How do you use a capital loss?" January 21, 2020, https://www.canada.ca/en/revenue-agency/services/tax/individuals/topics/about-your-tax-return/tax-return/completing-a-tax-return/personal-income/line-127-capital-gains/capital-losses-deductions/you-use-a-capital-loss.html

[59] CRA: "Definitions for capital gains," January 21, 2020, https://www.canada.ca/en/revenue-agency/services/tax/individuals/topics/about-your-tax-return/tax-return/completing-a-tax-return/personal-income/line-127-capital-gains/definitions-capital-gains.html#InclusionrateIR

[60] CRA: "Losses incurred before May 23, 1985," January 21, 2020, https://www.canada.ca/en/revenue-agency/services/tax/individuals/topics/about-your-tax-return/tax-return/completing-a-tax-return/personal-income/line-127-capital-gains/capital-losses-deductions/other-year-losses-carried-forward/losses-incurred-before-may-23-1985.html

[61] CRA: "Deductions Credits and Expenses; Line 25200 - Non-capital losses of other years," January 21, 2020, https://www.canada.ca/en/revenue-agency/services/tax/individuals/topics/about-your-tax-return/tax-return/completing-a-tax-return/deductions-credits-expenses/line-25200-non-capital-losses-other-years.html

[62] Supra 7.

ABOUT THE AUTHOR

Dale Barrett is a leading Canadian tax lawyer, founder and managing partner of Barrett Tax Law, founder of Lawyers & Lattes Legal Café, #1 Best selling author of Tax Survival for Canadians, #1 Best selling author of A Quick and Dirty Business Start-Up Guide From the Perspective of a Tax Lawyer and Serial Entrepreneur, #1 Best selling author of Victory Over the CRA – An Accountant's Guide to Representing a Client, editor of Lexis Nexis' Family Law and Tax Handbook, tax columnist at The Lawyer's Daily and frequent tax lecturer, primarily for accountants, lawyers and other financial professionals. But Dale's favourite job is being a husband to his amazing wife Nicole (who is the best mother in the world), and father to his three beautiful children, Chloé, Claire and Joshua.

Manufactured by Amazon.ca
Bolton, ON

32466574R00138